はじめに

　近年、国際的なビジネスや研究の場、あるいは外国人との付き合いやパーティなどの場で、自分自身の意見や考えを論理的に述べる機会が増えています。

　さまざまなコミュニケーションの機会において、「英語で自分の意見や考えをしっかり伝えたい」という人たちが増えてきましたが、その要望にきちんと応えた本が少ないのではないかと思います。本書は、本物の英語力を身につけるという基本的理念の下、この現状に応えるために書きました。

　本書は、多彩なテーマを設定し、いろいろな有益な情報、注目すべき意見、面白い考えなどを満載した「英語で論理的に意見や考えを伝える」ための英文表現集です。

　「面白く、ためになり、分かりやすい」ということを常に念頭に置き、論理的な例文を提供しています。読んで面白くないと読み進められません。また、ただ面白いだけではなく、実際に役に立つ例文でなければなりません。さらに、たとえ役に立っても、全体が分かりにくければ価値が半減します。だから、「面白く、ためになり、分かりやすい」（私は「オタワ」の法則と呼んでいます）ことを目指しているわけです。

　本書の中核部分である「表現集」の章は、大きく３部に分かれています。第１部では論理的なトークのための基礎表現を扱っています。第２部では、さまざまな具体的テーマに関していろいろな角度から意見を述べるのに必要な表現を載せています。第３部では、内容的にやや難しいテーマをはじめ、ユニークで役に立つ考え方や言葉遊びなども組み込んだ応用表現を豊富に紹介しています。

　第１部は「分かりやすい」、第２部は「ためになる」、第３部は「面白い」がメインテーマといえるでしょう。第２部が本書の中心的な部分で、さまざまな機会で利用可能な極めて重要な具体的例文が織り込まれています。そのため第２部の全表現がCDに収録されています。何度も聴いて、実際のトークで活用してください。

　さらに、本書は、一歩進んだ応用例文も巻末に付録としてつけています。時間に余裕がある方は活用していただければと思います。

　また、本書は扱っているテーマが豊富なので、英検１級２次試験にも大いに役立つと確信しております。

　本書を通じて、さまざまな意見発表の場や、ビジネスにおける自己主張の場、知的な会話の場面などで、自由で楽しい、しかも、奥の深い会話ができる能力を少しでも身につけることができれば、著者としてこれに勝る喜びはありません。

****

本書を書くにあたり、さまざまな人にお世話になりました。私が言語学研究主任を務める清光総研の横尾清志氏には、有益な助言と暖かい励ましの言葉をいただきました。また、私が顧問を務める実用英語研究所所長である山口修氏には、有意義なコメントと激励の言葉をいただきました。私が代表を務めるオフィスエングライトの田中貴子氏には、第1章から第3章において有益な資料をいただきました。M-English代表の村上直之氏には、第4章から第12章までの一部において執筆協力いただきました。TAC言語文化研究所の主任研究員である田村清子氏には、本書のテーマに関して資料提供をいただき、同研究所編集主任である岩本康隆氏には、資料の整理および校正を担当していただきました。英文校閲は、私の大学での同僚、Thomas Koch氏にお世話になりました。最後に、ベレ出版の安達正氏には、編集面において大変お世話になりました。本書の成立に関わった全てのかたがたに、心からの謝意を表明したいと思います。

著者　石井　隆之

石井隆之 [著]
Ishii Takayuki

意見・考えを論理的に述べる英語表現集

Hints on How to Communicate well
in Various Talks

CD BOOK
[CD2枚付]

ペレ出版

意見・考えを論理的に述べる英語表現集●目次

はじめに
　本書の使い方と記号の意味……………………………………………………9

第1部　基礎編

第1章　論理的に話すための基礎表現
　1．情報提供の表現………………………………………………………12
　2．意見表明の表現………………………………………………………15
　3．順接と逆接……………………………………………………………18
　4．論理的展開の5つの手法……………………………………………21
　　　1．定義に関する表現　21
　　　2．具体例に関わる表現　22
　　　3．証拠と論拠に関する表現　23
　　　4．推論に関わる表現　24
　　　5．一歩進んだ論理展開の表現　25

第2部　実践編

第2章　自分について伝えるための表現
　1．印象的自己紹介の手法………………………………………………28
　2．趣味や興味に関する表現……………………………………………31
　3．自分を売り込むトーク………………………………………………33
　4．身近なテーマの好き嫌い……………………………………………35
　　　1．動物・植物の好き嫌い　35
　　　2．数字の好き嫌い　35
　　　3．色の好き嫌い　36
　　　4．食べ物の好き嫌い　36
　　　5．歴史上の人物の好き嫌い　36

第3章　身近な二者択一テーマで意見を表明する

1. 男と女、どちらが得か？ ……………………………………………40
2. 都会と田舎、どちらがいいか？ ……………………………………42
3. 冬と夏、どちらが好きか？ …………………………………………44
4. 犬と猫、どちらが可愛いか？ ………………………………………46
5. 日本語と英語、どちらが難しいか？ ………………………………48
6. テレビは有害か有益か？ ……………………………………………50
7. 日本は住みやすいか、住みにくいか？ ……………………………52
8. 占いを信じるか、信じないか？ ……………………………………54

第4章　政治・経済・ビジネスに関する意見を述べる

1. 民主主義に限界はあるか？ …………………………………………58
2. 日本人は働きすぎか？ ………………………………………………62
3. 政治家はどうあるべきか？ …………………………………………65
4. 天下りはなくならないか？ …………………………………………68
5. 日本経済はこれからどうなるのか？ ………………………………72
6. 「米」の自由化と「牛肉」の輸入 …………………………………76

第5章　文化・芸術・スポーツに関する意見を述べる

1. 「文明」と「文化」の違い …………………………………………82
2. 日本の芸術 ……………………………………………………………86
3. マスコミのあり方 ……………………………………………………91
4. 日本の国技 … 相撲 …………………………………………………93
5. 野球とサッカー ………………………………………………………96
6. ノーベル賞とイグノーベル賞 ………………………………………102

第6章　科学・技術・コンピュータに関する意見を述べる

1. 携帯電話の進化 ………………………………………………………108
2. メールとインターネット ……………………………………………112
3. 遺伝子操作 ……………………………………………………………116
4. 宇宙開発 ………………………………………………………………119
5. 生物の不思議 …………………………………………………………123
6. 20年後の科学の進歩を予想する ……………………………………126

第7章　教育問題に関する意見を述べる

1. 小学校の英語教育 …………………………………… 132
2. 大学における教育 …………………………………… 136
3. いじめと不登校 ……………………………………… 141
4. 校内暴力と家庭環境 ………………………………… 146
5. ゆとり教育と学校5日制 …………………………… 150
6. 教師の役割 …………………………………………… 154

第8章　環境問題に関する意見を述べる

1. 地球温暖化 …………………………………………… 160
2. ゴミ問題 ……………………………………………… 164
3. エネルギー問題と原発 ……………………………… 168
4. 生態系と動物愛護 …………………………………… 172
5. 交通渋滞と交通事故 ………………………………… 176
6. 環境はどのように守るか？ ………………………… 180

第9章　社会問題に関する意見を述べる

1. 少子高齢化社会 ……………………………………… 186
2. 国際化と情報化 ……………………………………… 189
3. 結婚と離婚 …………………………………………… 192
4. 性の問題 … 夫婦別姓やセクハラ ………………… 195
5. 職の問題 … 就職難やリストラ …………………… 200
6. 宗教とカルト ………………………………………… 203

第10章　医療問題に関する意見を述べる

1. 臓器移植 ……………………………………………… 208
2. 安楽死 ………………………………………………… 211
3. 中絶 …………………………………………………… 214
4. 生活習慣病とダイエット …………………………… 218
5. 癌とエイズ …………………………………………… 222
6. 健康法のいろいろ …………………………………… 226

第3部　発展編

第11章　民族と宗教と国際問題に関する意見を述べる
　　1．キリスト教とイスラム教とユダヤ教……………………………… 230
　　2．天皇について一歩進んだ知識……………………………………… 237
　　3．イラク問題とテロ…………………………………………………… 240
　　4．北朝鮮と核…………………………………………………………… 244

第12章　法律と憲法に関する意見を述べる
　　1．死刑制度の是非……………………………………………………… 250
　　2．憲法9条改正の是非………………………………………………… 253
　　3．裁判員制度…………………………………………………………… 257

第13章　コミュニケーションに関する意見を述べる
　　1．日本語と英語の違い………………………………………………… 262
　　2．日本人と外国人の発想の違い……………………………………… 266
　　3．言葉の使い方について考える……………………………………… 269

第14章　日本文化に関する意見を述べる
　　1．日本の西洋化・近代化と日本文化………………………………… 274
　　2．日本の宗教と日本人の宗教観……………………………………… 277
　　3．日本の年中行事、お正月・お盆…………………………………… 282

第15章　自分自身の生き方を述べる
　　1．私の人生観と世界観………………………………………………… 288
　　2．私のユニークな発想法と考え方…………………………………… 292
　　3．私の英語に対する考え方と勉強法………………………………… 300

終　章　意見表明の最強原則と力のつく勉強法
　　エピローグ……………………………………………………………… 310
付録1　面白雑学情報……………………………………………………… 312
付録2　考え方と生き方のヒント………………………………………… 313

本書の特長と使い方

本書の6大特長

その1　ジャンル別に意見表明のための「そのまま使える」例文を満載している。
その2　あるテーマに対する意見は一般的なものから、特殊なものまで、また、意見が二分する事象については、賛成意見と反対意見を必ず載せている。
その3　意見を表明するのに必要な基礎知識も英語で学べる工夫をしている。必要に応じ、意見の表現の前に英語による情報提供を施している。
その4　従来の表現集にはない、雑学、ジョークやそのほかのスピーチに必要なコツなどを駆使した表現も豊富に取り入れている。
その5　必要に応じ、「注」や「参考」、「表現のコツ」などを織り込み、知識や表現力を向上させるのに役立つ。
その6　例文自体から関連分野の情報を学ぶこともできるよう工夫されている。

本書の対象

1. 英語学習の中・上級者
2. 論理的な英語を話したい人
3. 英語のスピーチやディスカッションに関心のある人
4. ビジネスなどで外国人と話をする必要のある人
5. 発信型英語を教える立場にある英語教師

本書の記号の意味

[= ...]	同じ意味の語句や文
[⇔ ...]	反対の意味の語句や文
A／B	AとBが交換可能であることを示す
	例えばA／B CはACとBCを表す
注：	注意すべきこと
※	簡単なコメント
参考	参考にすべき情報を示す
表現のコツ	表現におけるコツを示す
→	注や参考や表現のコツなどで、日本語に対する英訳を示す
○	英文が正しいことを示す　［通常、正しい文は記号を何もつけない］
×	英文が間違っていることを示す

第 1 部
基礎編

第 1 章

論理的に話すための基礎表現

1 情 報 提 供 の 表 現

▶ **情報提供のための超基礎表現**

私は本で読んだのですが …	In a certain book, I've learned the following:
サムから聞いたのですが …	I have just heard from Sam the following:
ネットで調べたのですが …	I have just learned on the Internet the following:
一般に言われていることですが …	As is generally said, …
一般には余り言われていないのですが …	Though it is not so often pointed out, …
非常に面白いと思ったことですが …	What I think is very interesting is the following:
非常に重要だと思ったことですが …	Something I think is of great importance is as follows:
こんな話をご存知ですか？	Do you happen to know the following story?
面白いお話をいたしましょうか？	Let me tell you an interesting story.
あなたの認識は間違っています。	I am afraid your understanding is wrong. [=I am afraid you misunderstand the situation.]

あなたの情報には誤りがあります。	There is something wrong with your information.

▶ 具体的な情報提供

最初の夏季オリンピックは、冬季オリンピックより28年早い1896年に開催されました。世界大戦のため開催が中止された1916年、1940年、1944年を除いては、夏季オリンピックはそれ以来、4年に一度開催されています。	The Summer Olympics was first held in 1896, 28 years before the first winter game. Since then, it has been taking place every four years except for 1916, 1940 and 1944 due to World Wars.
90年代、日本では経済バブルが崩壊しました。企業は生き残りをかけて、大幅なリストラを行うしかありませんでした。そのため、何万人という人々が職を失ってしまいました。	Economic bubbles burst in the 90s in Japan. Companies had no choice but to undergo a major restructuring for survival in the market. Therefore, tens of thousands of people lost their jobs.
最近、多くの年金生活者が「オレオレ詐欺」の被害にあっています。被害者は大体60歳から80歳の方々です。警察は全力を挙げて被害の拡大を食い止めようとしています。	In resent years, thousands of pensioners have been cheated by the fraud known as the "'It's me' scam." The victims are mostly aged 60 to 80. The police are going all out to stop the spread of the damage.
京都はその昔1000年以上もの間、日本の首都でした。しかし、江戸幕府が崩壊した後の1869年、首都は、事実上京都から東京へ移行しました。 注:「事実上」は practically などと通常訳す必要はない。	Kyoto used to be the capital of Japan for more than a thousand years. Yet, in 1869 after the Edo Shogunate collapsed, the national capital was moved from Kyoto to Tokyo.

最近、ニートになる若者が増えるという傾向にあります。ニートとは、「young people Not in Education, Employment or Training」の頭文字語です。政府は、このような人々が経済に悪影響を及ぼすのではないかと警鐘をならしています。

There is a recent trend in which young people choose to become NEETs. NEET is the acronym for "young people Not in Education, Employment or Training". The government warns that such people may have a negative impact on the economy.

現在、発見されている素数で最大のものは、$2^{13466917}-1$ です。これは2004年2月29日の時点での情報です。桁数で表すと、4,053,946桁です。1cmに1つ数字を書くとして、この数値は約40kmの長さになります。
参考：1桁上げる take a figure up one place
　　　5桁の金額 a sum of five figures

The largest prime number found so far is the 13466917th power of two minus one. This is the information as of February 29, 2004. This is a number of 4,053,946 figures. If one figure were written in a space of one centimeter, the number would be about 40 kilometers long.

原口あきら氏は円周率10万桁を覚えた世界記録保持者です。10万桁の暗唱には約16時間かかります。語呂合わせで覚えるのですが、この中に約800の短編小説ができあがっているのです。

Mr. Akira Haraguchi is a world record holder who has memorized the pi to one hundred thousand places. The recitation will take about 16 hours. This will be recited by means of a game of making puns composed of about 800 short stories.

彼は「円周率は人生のバイブル。万物は真円を目指しているのではないか。唱えると自分の角が取れ、心が丸くなる」と述べています。
参考：英語のround は日本語のイメージとは異なり、「きつい」という意味もある。
　　→ He criticized me in round terms.
　　　（彼はきつい言葉で私を批判した）

He says, "Pi is a Bible for life. All things in the universe aim at the complete circle. The recitation of the pi will make us well rounded, sociable and give us a heart of gold.
注：A gives us a heart of gold（Aが心を丸くさせる→Aをすると心が丸くなる）
　　A has a heart of gold（Aは心が丸い）

参考：	How I wish a drink, alcoholic of course, after the heavy lectures regarding quantum mechanics...!									
単語の文字数	▶3.	1	4	1	5	9	2	6	5	3	5	8	9
	身	1つ	世	1つ	生	く	に	無	意味	い	わ	く
		7		9								
		泣		く								

英語の訳：量子力学に関する、その重苦しい講義の後では、一杯、もちろん、アルコールのヤツを飲みたいものだなあ！

2 意見表明の表現

▶ **意見表明のための超基礎表現**

私の意見は次のようなものです。	My opinion is this. [=What I have in mind is as follows:]
私の個人的見解は次の通りです。	My personal opinion is this. [=I personally think this way.]
これから私の率直な意見を述べさせていただきます。	Let me express my candid opinion. [=Let me speak out about my opinion.]
私の考えはあなたとは違います。私は次のような考え方をしています。	My idea differs from yours. I think this way.
私はそのようには考えません。私の考えはこうです。	I don't agree. What I think is this. 注：I don't think that way. とは言わない。
これについては、人によって意見がまちまちですが、私はこのように考えています。	This differs from person to person, but I think in the following way.
この習慣は、国によって異なりますが、基本的な部分は変わりません。	The custom varies from country to country, but is fundamentally the same.
そんな場合は、次のようにすべきです。	In that case, just do it the following way.
この問題に対しては、解決方法がいくつかあります。	There are several solutions to this problem.

この問題は難しく、なかなか解決方法が見つかりません。	It is hard for us to find a solution to this problem.
この問題の解決方法の1つを示します。	I will show you a solution to this problem.

▶ 具体的な意見表明

100円ショップが日本で人気を集めています。その成功の理由としては、日本が不景気であった1990年代に出店を果たしたことが考えられます。高価なものを買う余裕がなかった時期に、その低価格が消費者の心をつかんだのかもしれません。 注：may have p.p.「...したかもしれない」	"One-hundred-yen" shops have been successful in Japan. One possible reason for the success is that they appeared in 1990s, when Japan was in an economic recession. When people could not afford expensive items, the low prices may have appealed to consumers.
ヨーロッパ人はたいてい英語が得意とされますが、彼らがアジア人よりも賢いということではありません。それは、母国語の問題です。例えば、スペイン語は英語と共通した部分があるので、スペイン人にとっては英語が学習しやすいのです。同じ理由で、日本人には、もしかしたら韓国語が簡単に感じられるかもしれません。 注：mayより弱い意味がmight	Europeans are often good at English but it does not mean they are smarter than Asians. It is the matter of their first language. For instance, Spanish has some similarities with English so that English is easier to study for Spanish people. On the same score, Korean might be less demanding for Japanese.
飲酒運転法が強化されてからでさえ、飲酒運転による事故は減少していません。酒気帯び運転手の手でどんなに多くの人が殺されてもなお、自分は事故に巻き込まれないと信じて疑わない人がいるのです。たとえ少しでもお酒を飲む場合は、車を運転しないということを徹底しなければなりません。	Drink driving accidents have not reduced even after drunk-driving laws were strengthened. No matter how many people are killed by drunk drivers, there are still people who believe they would not be involved in an accident. You must make sure not to drive a car, even if you drink a little.

宇宙旅行という新時代が到来しました。旅行代理店が宇宙旅行の提供を始めたのです。驚いたことに、その代金は巨額で、志望者は何時間もの訓練を受けなければなりません。宇宙旅行は今や夢ではありませんが、莫大なお金と時間に余裕のあるほんの一握りの人々しか実現できないでしょう。

The new era of space travel has come. Some travel agencies began offering trips into space. Surprisingly, applicants have to pay a hefty fee and undergo hours of training. Although space travel is no longer impossible, only the few people who can afford such enormous amounts of money and have the time can enjoy it.

バレンタインデーは元来、恋人たちがお互いに愛情を言葉に表す日である一方で、日本では、女性が自分の好きな男性にチョコレートを贈る日となっています。日本の女性は結局、友人や仕事仲間に贈る義理チョコを含め購入するチョコレートは一つに収まりません。バレンタインデーは結局チョコレートメーカーの思惑により完全に商業化されていると私は感じます。
注：「...と感じる」は be under the impression that...、have a feeling that... などを用いる。

Saint Valentine's Day is originally the day when lovers voice their love to each other. In Japan women give chocolate to men they like on that day. Most of them eventually buy more than one chocolate as "giri choco," or obligation chocolate, due to an obligation to give it to friends or workmates. I am under the impression that after all, Valentine's Day is totally commercialized by chocolate makers.

3 順 接 と 逆 接

▶ **順接の基本パターン**

私は外国のことを知りたいから、よく海外旅行をしています。

(a) 等位接続詞を用いる。
I want to know about foreign countries, so I often travel abroad.
(b) 従位接続詞を用いる。
Because I want to know about foreign countries, I often travel abroad.
従属節は後ろに回してもよい。
I often travel abroad because I want to know about foreign countries.
(c) 接続副詞を用いる。
I want to know about foreign countries; therefore, I often travel abroad.
2文に分ける方法もある。
I want to know about foreign countries. Therefore, I often travel abroad.
2文目の文中に接続副詞が入る場合がある。
I want to know about foreign countries. I, therefore, often travel abroad.

▶ **逆接の基本パターン**

彼は言いたいことを言うタイプだが、憎めない性格です。

(a) 等位接続詞を用いる。
He tends to talk straightforwardly, but he is kind of a nice guy.
(b) 従位接続詞を用いる。
Though he tends to talk straightforwardly, he is kind of a good guy.
従属節は後ろに回してもよい。
He is kind of a good guy though he tends to talk straightforwardly.

(c) 接続副詞を用いる。
He tends to talk straightforwardly; however, he is kind of a good guy.
2文に分ける方法もある。
He tends to talk straightforwardly. However, he is kind of a good guy.
2文目の文中に接続副詞が入る場合がある。
He tends to talk straightforwardly. He is, however, kind of a good guy.

▶ 順接と逆接の応用例

教育を受ける女性の数が、何年もの間に確実に増えています。	The number of women who receive an education has been absolutely increasing for years.
よって、女性は家にいるものだという考えは支持されなくなり、多くの女性を様々な職場で見かけるようになりました。	**So,** the attitude that women should stay in the home has become unpopular and now women can be seen in various workplaces.
しかし、ビジネスの世界にはまだまだ女性への差別が根付いているようです。	**However,** there still seems to be much discrimination against women in the business world.

情報技術が急速に発達しています。1世紀前の人々にとって、今では、個人がコンピュータを所有したり、ネットサーフィンをしたりしていることは信じ難いでしょう。	Information technology has developed at a fast pace. People a century ago would not have believed it is normal now for an individual to own private computers and surf the Internet.
従って、私たちの生活はとても便利になりました。進歩を遂げた技術のおかげで、私たちは、家にいながらにして、買い物や仕事や銀行取引が行えます。	**Thus,** our lives became a lot more convenient. The advanced technology allows us to shop, work or bank without going out.

しかし、その便利さがゆえに、多くの人が面と向かっての人とのコミュニケーションを苦手とするようになりました。意外にも、技術の発展はこのような社会問題をもたらしました。	**Yet**, the convenience has led a lof of people to have trouble in communicating face to face. Unexpectedly, the advance of technology can lead to such social problems.

喫煙は、医学的に様々な身体疾患を引き起こすと証明されています。そして、マスメディアはこの喫煙の危険性を幅広く報道しています。	Smoking is medically proven to cause various physical disorders. Mass media has been extensively reporting the dangers of cigarette smoking.
従って、多くの喫煙者が禁煙を決意するに至りました。彼らは、自分の体が喫煙によっていかに蝕まれていたか再認識し始めました。	**Accordingly**, a number of smokers have decided to quit smoking. They have started to realize how badly their bodies have been affected by smoking.
それにもかかわらず、まだ喫煙し続ける人も中にはいます。そんな人々は、禁煙によるストレスのほうが、喫煙が健康に与える影響よりも大きいと考えているのでしょう。	**Nevertheless**, some smokers still keep on smoking. They may believe that stress caused by quitting smoking outweighs the bad effects of smoking on their health.

4　論理的展開の5つの手法

◎考えや意見を言うとき、使う単語を定義しないと、言いたいことが伝わらない場合があります。そこで、定義に関わる例文を挙げておきます。

▶ **定義に関する表現　（論理的展開の手法その1）**

その言葉の意味を定義しておきましょう。	Let me define the meaning of the word. [=Let me give a definition of the word.]
これは定義が難しい言葉です。	This is a hard word to define.
あなたは自由を「したいことをすること」と定義しています。	You define freedom as doing what you want to do.
果たしてこの定義が正しいでしょうか。	Do you think such a definition is correct?
その定義は正確ではありません。	That definition is not accurate.
蝙蝠（こうもり）は定義上、哺乳類です。	A bat is a mammal by definition. [=A bat falls under the mammal category.]

表現のコツ　定義は3レベルぐらいを使い分けよう

> 例えば、snowは次のような定義が使えます。
> - 初級レベル　white flakes falling from the sky in winter
> - 中級レベル　frozen particles of water vapor that fall to earth as white flakes
> - 上級レベル　atmospheric vapor frozen in crystalline form, whether in single crystals or aggregated in flakes

◎主張したいことは具体例を挙げると説得力が増すものです。具体例に関わる表現を学びましょう。

▶ 具体例に関わる表現 （論理的展開の手法その２）

具体例を挙げてみましょう。	Let me give you a specific example.
具体例を挙げて説明しましょう。	I will explain it by giving examples. [=Let me illustrate it.]
具体的に言えば、次のようになります。	To be more specific, what I want to say is this.
あなたのお考えを具体的に言い表してください。	Would you put your idea into concrete language?
私はまだ具体的なことは聞いておりません。	I have not yet heard anything specific.
彼女の行ったことを２、３挙げてみましょう。	I will give a few examples of what she has done.
成功例を１つ挙げましょう。	Let me mention a successful case. [=I will explain a successful case to you.]
これはほんの一例に過ぎません。	This is only one example.
そういう例はこれまでにありません。	There is no precedent for it. [=There has been no such precedent.]
同様の例をご存知でしょうか。	Do you happen to know any similar cases? [= ... know a similar case?]

◎主張を支えるのが、証拠（具体的で聞き手が知らない情報）と論拠（抽象的で聞き手も知っている情報）の2つです。

▶ **証拠と論拠に関する表現　（論理的展開の手法その3）**

証拠を1つ挙げましょう。	Let me give you a piece of evidence.
私は、そのことに関する新たな証拠を発見しました。	I discovered definite evidence concerning that.
彼女の言っていることが正しいことを証明する証拠を挙げましょう。 注：「証拠を挙げる」で動詞は give、produce、bring forward が用いられる。	I'll bring forward evidence to prove that she is right.
それに反対の証拠があります。	There is evidence to the contrary.
それは状況証拠に過ぎません。	That is only circumstantial evidence.
私は確かな証拠を握っています。 注：「確かな」は positive も使える。	I have certain proof of it. [=I have positive proof of it.]
その証拠は彼に不利ですね。	The evidence is against him. [⇔ The evidence is in his favor.（有利だ）]
あなたの主張には論拠がありません。	Your argument is groundless. [=You have no good grounds for saying so.]
あなたの論拠は大変薄弱ですね。	You are arguing on very tenuous grounds.

彼女は論拠がしっかりしています。	Her argument is well grounded.
彼は論拠をその点に置いています。	He founds his argument on that point. [=He bases his argument on that respect.]
論拠を示してください。	What is the basis for saying so?

◎主張や論拠が揃っていても、それらを用いてうまく推論 (reasoning) できなければ、つまり、上手に、それらを主張と結び付けなければ、言いたいことが相手に響きません。証拠や論拠を主張としっかり結びつけることが推論にほかなりません。推論に関わる表現を学びましょう。

▶ **推論に関わる表現　（論理的展開の手法その４）**

これまで述べた証拠から、私の考えが正しいと分かるでしょう。	According to the evidence I mentioned so far, you will find my idea is right.
その証拠だけでは、あなたの主張はまだ説得力がありません。	Considering that sort of evidence you showed me, I have to say your assertion is still unconvincing.
これらの資料に基づき、私は次のように推論します。	From these data, I draw the following conclusion. [=Based on these data, I infer as follows:]
私は、そういう状況だと推論しました。	I reasoned that such was the case.
私は彼女の言葉から、それについても同じことが言えると推論しました。	I inferred from her remark that the same thing was the case with that.
彼は常に合理的な推論を下す努力をしています。	He always makes efforts to make a reasonable inference.

その議論から何らかの結論を引き出すことは難しいでしょう。	It may be hard to draw a conclusion in some shape or other from that argument.
それは初めからわかりきった結論ですよ。	It is a foregone conclusion.

◎ユニークな言い方や相手を印象付ける言葉も、主張を成功させるための方法の1つです。

▶ 一歩進んだ論理展開の表現 （論理的展開の手法その5）

我々はよくこのことが目的のように扱ってしまう。	We often tend to deal with this as if it were an end.
これは常に、ある目的に対する手段であるべきです。	This should always be a means to an end.
あなたは、目的と手段を混同していますよ。	You are confused about an end and a means.
そんな考え方では、優先順位を逆転させてしまいますよ。	That way of thinking will lead to reversing the order of priorities.
その2つの話はつじつまが合っています。	The two stories make sense.
はじめは、その（過失の）責任を彼のせいにしていました。	Initially, I laid the fault at his door. 注：lay ... at a person's door 　　[=lay ... at the door of a person] 　　...を人のせいにする
あなたが悪い。あなたのせいですよ。	The fault is yours. [=The fault lies with you.]

それを説明していると、形容詞が足りなくなるぐらいになります。
※言葉では尽くせないことを強調する表現。

I am likely to run out of adjectives when it comes to describing it.

例を挙げたらキリがありません。
※例が多すぎることを強調する表現。

The list of examples could go on and on.

第2部
実践編

CD 収録

第2章
自分について伝えるための表現

1 印象的自己紹介の手法

▶ 自己紹介の基本表現プラスα　　　　　　　　　　CD 1 ➡ 01

私の名前は石井隆之です。	My name is Takayuki Ishii.
私には英語のニックネームがあります。	I have an English nickname.
私の英語名は、トーク・ストンウエルです。	My English name is Talk Stonewell.
英語のファーストネームがトークなのは、私は話好きだからです。	The reason why my English first name is Talk is because I like talking.
昔、外国人をガイドしているときに、そのように名づけられたのです。	I got that nickname when I was escorting people from other countries as a guide in the past. 注：I was called that way. とはあまり言わない。
英語のファミリーネームは、私の日本語の苗字の直訳です。	My family name in English is the direct translation of the one in Japanese.
これからはトークと呼んでください。	Just call me Talk.
私の趣味の中に京都散策があります。	My hobbies include going on outings in Kyoto.
この趣味は心を豊かにし、体を健康にします。	This hobby enriches my soul and promote good health.
私の専門は理論言語学です。	I specialize in theoretical linguistics.

言葉の不思議を探求するのが好きだから、言語学を研究しています。	Because I like to explore the mystery of language, I study linguistics.
私は、大阪は、枚方市の長尾というところに住んでいます。	I live in Nagao, Hirakata City, Osaka.
枚方を「まいかた」と読む人が多いです。確かに難読地名ですね。	Many people read this city as Maikata; yes, the name of this place is hard to read.
私の家の地番は、1－2－3です。そのような地番をわざと選んで住んだのかとよく聞かれます。	The street number of my house is 1-2-3. Actually, I am often asked whether I intentionally chose that number and lived at that address.

参考　「番地」を英語で表現する

お宅は何番地ですか。
　→ What is the street number of your house?
私は彼の家の番地を知りません。
　→ I don't know his street address.
彼は3丁目4番地5号に住んでいる。
　→ He lives at 3-4-5.
番地が飛んでいます。[家を探していて目当て番地がない]
　→ Some of the house numbers are missing.

▶ **自己紹介の実例**　　　　　　　　　　　　　　　　　CD 1 ➡ 02

こんにちは。私は、ロイヤーデパートでバイヤーをしております、豊田愛と申します。私の名前である「愛」とは日本語で「Love」を意味しております。両親は、私が人に愛される子に育ってほしいと願って、この名前をつけてくれました。だから、この名に恥じないよう、お客様に愛される商品の買い付けを心がけております。	Hello. I am Ai Toyota, the buyer for Royer department store. My given name, Ai, means "Love" in Japanese. My parents gave me this name hoping that I would be loved by people. In order to live up to my name, I try to buy goods that will be loved by our customers.

おはようございます。本日はお時間を割いていただきましてどうもありがとうございます。私は、原田悠一と申します。友人が蚊にかまれてしまい、あなたがその友人に「Are you itchy? かゆくはないです?」と聞いているところをどうぞ想像してみてください。アメリカ人の友人が、悠一は英語で言う「you」と「itchy」に聞こえると教えてくれました。これで私の名前を忘れずに覚えていただけたことと思います。

Good morning. Thank you for your time today. My name is Yuichi Harada. Please imagine that your friend gets bitten by a mosquito and you ask him or her "Are you itchy?" My American friend told me Yuichi sounded like 'you' and 'itchy' in English. I am sure you will not forget my name.

こんにちは。初めまして。私は家庭用品メーカー、カータスの細井太郎と申します。同僚は、私の仕事でのあまりの完璧主義者ぶりにうんざりしております。ですので、あなたも疲れさせてしまうのではないかと心配しているところです。どうぞお気を長くよろしくお願い致します。

Hi. Pleased to meet you. I am Taro Hosoi of the household product maker, Cartus. My fellow workers are sick of me being very much a perfectionist at work. I am afraid of making you tired, too. Please have a lot of patience with me.

表現のコツ 「よろしくお願い致します」は状況によって英語が異なる

> 日本語の「よろしくお願い致します」に当たる1つの決まった英語表現はありません。状況によって、次のものを使い分けましょう。
> → Please continue your favors toward us.（店の顧客などに対して）
>   I leave it to your best judgment.（相手の判断に任せるとき）
>   I trust it to your good offices.（相手に仕事などを頼んだとき）

2 趣味や興味に関する表現

▶ 趣味や興味に関する基本表現　　　　　CD 1 ➡ 03

私の趣味は切手収集です。	My hobby is collecting postage stamps. [=I am a philatelist.]
彼女は趣味と実益を兼ねて花を栽培しています。	She is raising flowers both for pleasure and for profit.
彼は仕事以外には何も趣味のない人です。	He shows no interest in anything outside his job.
我々は趣味がいろいろと共通しています。	We have many common interests.
趣味は人によって異なるものです。	Hobbies differ from person to person. [=Different people have different hobbies.] 注：「好み」の問題も含めてもう少し幅広い意味では次のように言える。 → Tastes differ. 　There is no accounting for tastes. 　（たで食う虫も好き好き）
彼女は天文学に非常に興味を持っています。	She takes a warm interest in astronomy.
この本は非常に興味がある本です。	This book is of absorbing interest.
その頃には、私は別のものに興味を持つようになっていました。	By that time, my interest had switched to another subject.

31

そのことに対しては、私は興味がなくなってきています。	My interest in it is waning. 注：waning の代わりに flagging または、dwindling が使える。

▶ 趣味や興味を述べる実例　　　　　　CD 1 ➡ 04

私は、新しいもの全て試してみたくなるたちです。読書、料理、ガーデニング、賭け事、スポーツ等、趣味は様々です。でも、今のところ、何よりも写真に凝っています。三度の食事より写真を撮ることにはまっています。	I am curious about everything new. My hobbies are varied, such as reading, cooking, gardening, gaming, playing sports and so on. But I am more into photography than other things at the moment. I would rather take photos of things around me than eat. 注：than other things は than anything else でも OK。
妻や子供は私の収集癖に愛想を尽かしております。ある部屋はマグカップで埋め尽くされており、またある部屋は靴でいっぱいです。これでも、私のコレクションからすると、まだ氷山の一角です。この収集癖は、A 型の典型的な性格だと思います。	My wife and children are sick and tired of my collecting mania. One room is full of mug cups and another is filled with pairs of shoes. These are only a couple of my collections. I suppose this is the common character of blood type A.
同僚には何か趣味を持つようにと言われてきましたが、どういう訳かどうしても何かにはまるということができません。私は、無趣味で生きていくことも不可能ではありません。おそらく、料理という唯一の趣味を仕事にしてしまったからでしょう。	Many of my workmates have encouraged me to develop other interests. However, I cannot devote myself to anything for some reason. It is not impossible for me to survive without a hobby. It may be because I turned my only hobby, cooking, into my career.

3 自分を売り込むトーク

▶ **自分を売り込むトークの実践例**　　　　　　　　　CD 1 ➡ 05

私のモットーは、「思い立ったが吉日」です。私は行動派の人間です。それで分かるように、いい考えが思いつくと、すぐに少しでも何か行動を起こさずにはいられません。ロンドンへ行こうと思い立った次の日には現地にいたということもありました。

My motto is that procrastination is the thief of time. As you see in that, I am a man of quick action. Whenever a great idea comes into my mind, I cannot help taking even a small action as soon as possible. Once I was in London only one day after the idea of visiting there had occurred.

自分を一言で表すと、楽天家だと思います。友人が待ち合わせに遅れてくると、あともう1章本を読み進められる時間ができたと思います。つまり、あまり癇癪(かんしゃく)を起こす性格ではないということです。

An optimist is a word for me. If my friend were late meeting me, I would think he gives me time to read one more chapter. The point is I do not lose my temper easily.

私は誰とでも友達になることができます。人に会うことは、私の趣味の一つです。様々な人は様々な考えを持っています。その考えを、私は偏見をなくすためにも知りたいのです。つまり、私は協調性を持って働くということにおいては誰にも負けません。

I can make friends with anyone. Meeting people is one of my favorite things to do. I enjoy learning other people's different ideas which help keep me from being biased. That means I come second to none in working in harmony.

▶ **ユニークな自己紹介　その1**　　　　　　　　　CD 1 ➡ 06

私は、島田紳助と同じ年齢です。
(1956年生まれの場合)
参考：他に1956年生まれの有名人に、野口五郎、桑田佳祐、小堺一機、竹中直人、田中康夫、トム・ハンクスなどがいる。

I am of the same age as Mr. Shinsuke Shimada.

私は、小室哲哉と同じ誕生日です。
（11月27日が誕生日の場合）
参考：小室哲哉は、1958年生まれ、他に11月27日生まれの有名人は、ブルース・リー（1940年）、杉田かおる（1964年）、村田兆次（1949年）がいる。

I was born on the same day as Mr. Tetsuya Komuro.
[=My birthday is the same as Mr. Tetsuya Komuro.]

※ちなみに、1956年11月27日は、私（筆者）の誕生日です。

ユニークな自己紹介　その２　　　　　　CD 1 ➡ 07

私は、動物界、脊椎動物門、哺乳綱、霊長目、ヒト科、ヒト属、ホモサピエンス種に属する人間です。
注：ホモサピエンスは「属と種」を一緒にした呼称で「ヒト」の学名になっている。Homoは「ヒト属」とも呼ばれる。英文ではgenus（属）という表現を使って再度説明している。

I fall under the species of Homo Sapiens, the family of humans, the genus of humans; the order of primates, the class of mammals, the phylum of vertebrates in the realm of animals.

私は、銀河系内の太陽系の第３惑星の地球における日本国は、大阪府枚方市長尾台１－２－３に住んでいます。
注：「銀河系」は the Milky Way（System）とも言う。

I live at 1-2-3, Nagao-dai, Hirakata City, Osaka, Japan on earth, the third planet of the solar system in the Galaxy.

※ちなみに、大阪府枚方市長尾台１－２－３は、私（筆者）の住所です。

4　身近なテーマの好き嫌い

▶ 動物・植物の好き嫌い　　　　　　　　　　　　　　CD 1 ➡ 08

チューリップは、私が一番好きな花です。花言葉でチューリップは思いやりを表します。ほとんどの女性が、チューリップのような花を贈られると喜ぶでしょう。

Tulips should be the flowers I love the best. In the language of flowers, they signify consideration. Most women would be happy if they were sent such flowers as tulips.

私は、ゴキブリが苦手です。あの黒光りした背中や、やけに早い動きが耐えられません。だから、巨大なゴキブリが生息していると言われるオーストラリアに行くのに夏は避けるようにしています。
注：「do ～をするのに夏を避ける」は、avoid summer to do ～よりも avoid doing ～ in the summer のほうが英語的である。

Cockroaches are not my thing. I cannot take jet-black backs and the extremely quick movements. This is the reason why I avoid visiting Australia in the summer where huge cockroaches exist.

▶ 数字の好き嫌い　　　　　　　　　　　　　　　　CD 1 ➡ 09

日本で幸運の数字とされているので、私の好きな数字は8です。8を漢字で書くと、末に広がっていて、物事が徐々によくなっていくということを表しています。

My favorite number is 8 since it is a lucky number in Japan. The Chinese character of eight broadens at the bottom, which we take to mean that things will gradually get better in the future.

日本人は数字の9や4を避けます。4は死と同じように「shi」と読み、9の読み方「ku」は苦しみを意味するからです。

Japanese people try to avoid numbers like 4 and 9. Four is pronounced 'shi', which is the same as death, and nine 'ku' indicates pain.

▶ 色の好き嫌い　　　　　　　　　　　　　　　　　　　　CD 1 ➡ 10

青が私の一番好きな色です。青は、地球や空や海の色です。その色を見ているだけで、私は落ち着いた平和な気持ちになります。

Blue has always been my best-loved color. It is the color of the earth, the sky and the ocean. Looking at the color gives me a calm and peaceful feeling.

基本的に私は、いつも黄緑色や明るいピンクといった薄い色よりもむしろ原色の方が好みです。私には薄い色は似合わないと言われます。

Basically, I would rather always go for primary colors than light colors such as lime green or baby pink. People say that these colors do not look good on me.

▶ 食べ物の好き嫌い　　　　　　　　　　　　　　　　　　CD 1 ➡ 11

私の好きな食べ物は、パッド・タイやパッド・シユウやトム・ヤン・クンといったタイ料理です。タイ料理は、とても独特な香りがします。タイ料理なら、四六時中食べられます。

My favorite food has to be Thai cuisine like Pad Thai, Pad Siew and Tom Yum Goong. It has such unique flavors. I can eat Thai food any time of the day and any season of the year.

私はとても好き嫌いが多いです。特に、生魚は一口たりとも食べられません。友人には、日本人として損をしていると笑われます。

I am a very picky eater. Particularly, I cannot take even a bite of raw fish. My friends laugh at me saying it is a serious disadvantage for Japanese.

▶ 歴史上の人物の好き嫌い　　　　　　　　　　　　　　　CD 1 ➡ 12

マハトマ・ガンディは、歴史上で最も偉大な人物だと思います。彼は、非暴力・不服従を唱えました。それは、多くの地域が紛争に苦しんでいる今こそ、私たちが考えなくてはならないことです。

Mahatma Gandhi is the greatest person in history. He preached nonviolence and disobedience, which we need to consider today when so many places are suffering from conflicts.

私は、アドルフ・ヒトラーは歴史上の人物として、偉大になりたかったのに、一番偉大とは逆の人物になったと強く思います。彼は、大勢の人々をあまりに理不尽な理由で殺したのですから。

I firmly believe that Adolf Hitler was the "least great" historical figure though he may have wanted to be the greatest. He had so many people killed for an unreasonable reason.

注：have ... killed は「...を殺された」ではなく、「...を殺させた」の意味になる。...の名詞句に his がついていると被害の意味。

表現のコツ　「理由」を形容する形容詞

　　有力な理由→ a strong reason
　　明白な理由→ an obvious reason
　　十分な理由→ a good reason、a sufficient reason
　　正当な理由→ a justifiable reason
　　もっともな理由→ a reasonable reason、a rational reason、a cogent reason
　　もっともらしい理由→ a plausible reason
　　表面的な理由→ an ostentatious reason
　　薄弱な理由→ a slender reason、a flimsy reason

第3章

身近な二者択一テーマで意見を表明する

1 男と女、どちらが得か？

▶ 男性の利点　　　　　　　　　　　　　　CD 1 ➡ 13

男性の利点はその体力にあります。例えば、スポーツを見てみると、男性は常に女性が出し得ない記録を生み出します。

The advantage of being a man is the great physical strength. For instance, if we consider sports, men always make records that are hard for women to reach.

男性の方が女性より多くの利点があります。男性は加齢を女性ほど気にする必要がありません。男性にとってしわはむしろ、個性を豊かにしてくれるものです。

Males have more advantages than females. They do not need to worry about aging as much as women do. Wrinkles rather add character for them.

▶ 女性の利点　　　　　　　　　　　　　　CD 1 ➡ 14

女性でいることは確実に多くの楽しみがあります。スカートをはいたり、化粧をしたり、ネイルアートをしたりと、普通男性がその良さを分からない様々なものを楽しむことができるからです。

Being female is definitely fun. Women enjoy various things that men do not normally appreciate, such as wearing skirts, make-up and painting nails.

定年まで家族のために働かなくてはいけない男性に対して女性は、働くか働かないか選択することができます。専業主婦は、専業主夫よりやはりまだ一般的です。

Females have a choice whether they work or not while many males work for their families until retirement. Full-time housewives seem to be still more common than at-home dads.
注：専業主夫は house husband ともいう。

▶ 男女の損得の問題から一歩進めた議論　　　　CD 1 ➡ 15

男性に対する社会の目は厳しく、日本では、まだまだ責任感の比重は女性に比べて大きいように思われます。

Our world is strict on men, which means it seems that in Japan the weight of responsibility is greater on the part of men than women.

それに比べて女性は一歩引いてもらえる暖かい扱いを受けているように思い、得な気がします。	In contrast, women are likely to be treated more considerately with some reserve, so I feel women are advantageously placed in our society.
しかし、最近は男女共同参画運動により女性が男性と対等に社会の責任を担う傾向が強くなるので、女性も甘えるわけにはいきません。	However, women cannot depend on special treatment these days because of the movement towards joint participation by men and women; women assume the same social responsibility as men.
社会の発展とともに、男女ともに自由が保証されるようになりましたが、同時に責任感も同じ比重の、真の男女平等の社会が実現することを私は望んでいます。	As society developed, the same degree of freedom came to be guaranteed for men and women. But I hope, simultaneously, that a society will come into being where the same amount of responsibility as men is imposed on women.
私は、男女平等社会を望むとはいえ、男女の区別をなくすことには反対です。男性には男性らしい仕事があるし、女性には女性らしい仕事があると考えています。	Though I believe that there should be no discrimination against women in our society, I do not believe that our society should ignore the distinctions between men and women. I think some jobs are better suited for men, and others for women.
もちろん、希望する仕事に就けない理由が女性だからという差別は良くないと思います。	Of course, I am against the situation where just because of the fact that they are women, they cannot find employment.

2 都会と田舎、どちらがいいか？

▶ 都会生活肯定派の意見　　　　　　　　　　　CD 1 ➡ 16

都会に住む利点は、その多様性にあります。レストラン、デパート、映画館など、何でも近くにあり、都会で退屈することはありません。

The advantage of living in cities is the great diversity. Everything, such as restaurants, department stores, and cinemas, is close by. We never get bored in cities.

都会の交通の便はとても整っているので、車を所有する必要がありません。それは、環境に優しい暮らしができるということです。

City transportation facilities are excellent, so you do not have to own a car. That means you can live in an environmentally-friendly way.
注：「環境に優しく」は ecofriendly も OK。

▶ 田舎生活肯定派の意見　　　　　　　　　　　CD 1 ➡ 17

田舎生活は都会暮らしよりもずっとくつろいだ気分にさせてくれます。生活はゆっくりとしていて、プライバシーが十分に守られます。そのような生活で、ストレスが溜まるということはないでしょう。

Country life can be more relaxing than city life. Life is slower paced and there is a lot of privacy. Such a life is almost stress-free.

田舎の一番いいところは、生活費がかからないということです。だから、ずっと夢に見ていたような家を手に入れることができるのです。

What is best about living in the countryside is that it is cheap to live there, so you can afford the house you have always dreamed of.

▶ 都会が好きという視点から発展した議論　　　　CD 1 ➡ 18

都会大好き！人が多いと嬉しくなります。様々なネオンやイルミネーションが心をワクワクさせます。

I love life in the city. I will be happy with so many people. Various sorts of neon signs and bright lights just excite me.

しかし、田舎は、落ち着く反面、寂しいです。又近隣の付き合いも複雑で、それが良い面と同時に難しい面も多くあります。
注：「両面がある」→ cut both ways

However, life in the country makes me feel lonely though it helps me regain my presence of mind. In rural life we are required to be neighborly, which cuts both ways.

だから、私は総合的に判断して、都会での生活が好きです。

Therefore, synthesizing the whole situation, I like city life better.

24時間開いている店もあり、色々と便利です。

It is convenient in many ways, since you can find around-the-clock shops easily.

ここで、「しかし」と声を大にして言いたいことがあります。便利であるということは、2つのマイナス面を秘めているということです。

But ... This is a big BUT. I have something very important to say. Convenience may cause and sometimes actually causes two disadvantages.

1つは、なんでも便利になったので、人間は怠け者になり、努力をしない人が多くなったということです。その結果、ほしいものが手に入らない場合に「キレる」という人も増え、人間は精神的に弱くなったのではないかと思います。
注：「精神的に弱い」を mentally weak としたら、通常「知的障害者」を意味する。

First, convenience has made people lazy and many have stopped trying; as a result, there has been an increasing number of people who will get quick-tempered when they cannot get what they want. I think people have became too sensitive.

もう1つは、便利なものは、危険を伴うということです。原発は電力を供給し、生活を豊かにしてくれますが、一歩間違って事故が起これば大変です。飛行機は便利で、大昔なら考えられないところまで、すぐに連れて行ってくれますが、墜落したら大事故になります。

Second, convenience may invite danger. For example, nuclear plants supply electricity, making our life rich, but its accidents will cause calamity. The plane which can take us to faraway places than in the past might bring about a serious accident when it crashes.

3 冬と夏、どちらが好きか？

▶ 冬が大好き派の意見　　　　　　　　　　　CD 1 ➡ 19

私はどちらかというと冬が好きです。雪景色より美しいものはないですし、スケートやスキーといった冬のスポーツより楽しいものはないと思います。

I would rather have winter. Nothing is more beautiful than landscape of snow. Nothing is more enjoyable than winter sports like skating or skiing.

冬の方が、気温に合わせて調節しやすいと思います。夏は限界があるものの、冬は寒ければ着る服を増やすだけでいいからです。

It is easier to adjust ourselves to the temperature of winter. We just put on more layers of clothes, unlike summer in which there is a limit.

▶ 夏が大好き派の意見　　　　　　　　　　　CD 1 ➡ 20

仕事が終わった後でも日が長いので、私は夏がとても好きです。オフィスから出て、空がまだ明るいのを見るのは最高です。

I'm a big fan of summer because there is still light in the early evenings. It is incredible to see the bright sky when I come out of my office.

夏が一番いい季節だと思います。夏にはたくさん着込む必要がないので、服にかけるお金を抑えることができます。

Summer is the best season of all. We do not have to wear as much clothing in summer, which makes it possible to save money on fashion.

▶ どちらも好きという立場から発展した議論　　　CD 1 ➡ 21

どちらも好きです。冬は身も心も引き締まり、夏は開放感があり、全てが可能に満ちているように、思わせる季節です。

I like both of them. In winter we are braced up physically and spiritually, while in summer we feel liberated and filled with potentiality in everything.

冬は雪景色がきれいで、夏は、海は青く、山は緑で鮮やかな景色に彩られ、どちらも、自然のよい面が最大限に発揮されている感じがします。

Winter provides us with beautiful views of snow, whereas summer is rich in blue seas and green mountains, which makes me feel that nature gives full play to its power.

「夏」という日本語は「熱」や「暑い」と語源的に近いようです。特に熱という言葉は、情熱を暗示し、私の性格そのものを表しています。

The Japanese word Natsu meaning summer is etymologically close to another Japanese word Netsu (heat) or Atsui (hot). Above all, Netsu is suggestive of passion, which represents my character.

「冬」は、「(エネルギーが) 殖［ふ］ゆ」から来ているようです。冬の間は、新たなる出発を暗示する春に向けて、エネルギーをためる時期ということです。その意味で重要な季節だと思います。

The word Fuyu seems to come from Fuyu, which means "energy increases." Winter is the season when we restore energy for the coming spring, which is symbolic of a fresh start. In this sense, winter is important.

表現のコツ　play を用いた注意すべき表現

彼女は感情を隠そうとしたが、つい笑みが口元にこぼれてしまった。
→ She tried to hide her feelings but a smile played about her lips.
ロープをしっかり引いて。というのは随分たるんでいるからね。
→ Pull the rope tighter, because there is too much play.
その大統領は自らのユニークな経済政策を実行に移すだろう。
→ The President will bring his unique economic policy into play.

4 犬と猫、どちらが可愛いか？

猫好きの意見　　　　　　　　　　　　　　CD 1 ➡ 22

私は、猫好きだと言わざるを得ません。猫の最高なところは、手間がかからないところです。猫は吠えないですし、散歩に連れて行く必要もありません。

I would have to say I am a cat person. The best aspect of cats is the low maintenance. Cats never bark and there is no need to walk them.

猫も犬も両方可愛らしいけれども、私は犬が苦手です。犬アレルギーを持っています。傍に寄るだけで、目も鼻もかゆくなって、涙が出てきてしまいます。
注：「涙が」で「涙」を主語にしない。

Both cats and dogs are charming but I cannot take dogs. I have an allergy to them. Being close to them, my eyes and nose feel itchy and my eyes start to tear up.
注：tear up の代わりに water でも OK。

犬好きの意見　　　　　　　　　　　　　　CD 1 ➡ 23

私は、どちらかというと犬好きだと思います。犬のほうが猫にはあまりない思いやりが見られて可愛く感じられます。

I suppose I am more a dog person. Dogs are lovelier than cats in terms of their attentiveness which cats normally don't show.

犬を飼うことで飼い主は健康的な生活を送ることができます。ほとんどの犬は散歩に連れていく必要があるので、意志が弱くても、散歩の機会を健康維持に当てることができます。

Dogs lead owners to healthy lives. Most of the dogs need to be taken on a walk. You can use the opportunity to keep fit even though you have a weak will.

犬と猫に関する一歩進んだ議論　　　　　　CD 1 ➡ 24

犬は人に対する愛情や、感情の表現は、飼ったことのない人でも感じ取れるほど、分かりやすいです。

We easily recognize dogs' affection toward us or emotions against us even if we have never kept them before.

猫は一見、何を考えているか、つかみづらいです。かなり気まぐれといったところでしょうか。

It is hard to understand what cats are thinking about at first. We may say they are quite capricious.

犬は太古に森を出て、草原で暮らすようになりました。その結果、敵から身を守るため、群れを成して生きるようになったので、協調性が重要になったのです。だから、人間にも忠実な生物となっているのです。

Dogs came to live in the grassy plain after coming out of the woods in the remote past, as a result of which they began living in crowds so as to protect themselves from enemies. This life demanded cooperation. Therefore, dogs became obedient to men.

これに対し、猫は森にとどまったので、何にも頼らず生きていけたのです。だから、現在でも身勝手な振る舞いをするのです。それが反って可愛いとみなされることが多いです。

In contrast, cats stayed in the woods; therefore, they could live independently. That is the reason why they behave selfishly even now. Many people love cats all the more because they are selfish.

犬と猫の体も、根本的に異なる点を知っておくべきです。例えば、犬は体内でタウリンというアミノ酸を合成できますが、猫はできません。

We should know that dogs and cats are fundamentally different. For example, dogs can make taurine, a kind of amono acid, in their bodies, but cats cannot.

だから、ドッグフードにはタウリンがほとんど含まれていません。これを猫に食べさせ続けると、猫はタウリン不足で、失明する危険性があるということを知っておきましょう。

参考：タウリンは別名アミノエチルスルホン酸で、イカや蛸に多く含まれる。構造式は $NH_2CH_2CH_2SO_2OH$

Therefore, there is almost no taurine in dog food. If you have your cat eat it, it comes to be lacking in taurine. You should know that there is a danger that lack of taurine can make it lose its eyesight.

5 日本語と英語、どちらが難しいか？

日本語が難しい理由　　　　　　　　　　　　　　CD 1 ➡ 25

日本語は、その書記体系のために英語より難しくなっています。3種類の文字があり、ひらがなとカタカナがそれぞれ46文字と常用漢字1945文字となります。この複雑な文字体系を習得するには、相当な努力が必要とされます。

Japanese is harder to learn than English due to its writing system. There are 3 styles of characters; 46 letters each for hiragana and katakana and 1945 kanji in common use. It requires a lot of effort to master this complicated writing system.

その複雑な敬語表現のために、日本語を習得するのはとても困難とされます。日本語を第2言語として勉強する人たちにとって、いつ、誰に、どの形態の敬語を話せばいいのかを判断するのが複雑なようです。

Japanese is very demanding to master because of the puzzling honorific expressions. Second language learners of Japanese seem to find it complicated to judge when, to whom and what form of the language to apply.

英語が難しい理由　　　　　　　　　　　　　　CD 1 ➡ 26

英語は、文字と音声が複雑な関係にあります。例えば、「sign」という単語の「g」は無声語のため発音しません。このように、英語では音声が文字と一致しません。これが英語を難しくさせています。

There is a complex relation between letters and sounds in English. For example, you do not pronounce the 'g' of 'sign,' as it is a silent letter. Thus, sounds sometimes do not match letters in English. This makes English difficult.

英語は始めやすい言語だけれども、日本人にとっては発音しづらい単語があるということが次第に表面化してきます。「r」「v」「th」等の日本語にはない音が、英語には存在します。これが、日本人は優れた文法力のわりに、会話力が乏しい理由です。

English is easy to start but it turns out to be too hard to pronounce some words for Japanese. English has some sounds that the Japanese language does not have, such as 'r', 'v' or 'th'. This is the reason of their low oral skills for their grammatical competence.

日本語と英語の難しさから一歩進めた議論

日本語は英語よりも難しいか？という質問に、私は、どちらともいえないと答えます。

I usually answer yes and no to a question whether Japanese is more difficult than English.

日本語が難しいのは、文字の種類と数の多さ、特に漢字の使用と複雑極まりない敬語の存在のためです。

Yes to the question means that Japanese has many kinds of characters, especially Chinese characters, and very complicated honorific expressions.

英語が難しいのは、発音体系の複雑さと語順の厳しさのためです。

No to the question means that English is characterized by its complicated sound system and its strict word order.

英語は表現力が豊かなのに、どうしても表現できないことがあります。

Though we can usually express almost anything in English, there are some things impossible to express.

たとえば、順番を聞く疑問詞が存在していないのです。例を挙げると、「レーガン大統領は第何代大統領ですか」がうまく聞けないのです。
注：実際には次のように表現できます。
　→ワシントンは初代大統領です。レーガン大統領は？
※この答えは、第40代大統領です。

For instance, there is no interrogative which asks about the order. Taking a typical example, we cannot easily ask a question of "Where does Reagan stand in the list of presidents?"
→ Washington was the first president. How about Reagan?

疑問詞に関して言うと、日本語にはその複数形らしきものが存在しています。たとえば、「だれだれ」「いついつ」「どこどこ」は複数を尋ねる疑問詞のようです。英語には、疑問詞の複数形は、基本的には存在していません。

With regard to interrogatives, Japanese is greater because it has something like their plural forms. Take "Dare-dare", "Itsu-itsu", "Doko-doko" for example; they are all expecting more than one answer. But in English there does not exist plural forms of interrogatives.

6 テレビは有害か有益か？

▶ テレビは有害ではないと主張する　　　　　　　　　　CD 1 ➡ 28

テレビは有害ということはありません。私たちは、娯楽、ニュース、教育、天気等の情報をむしろテレビに頼っています。不適切なシーンを含んだ番組もありますが、どの番組を見るか私たちは選ぶことができます。

Television is not harmful for us. We rather depend on television for entertainment, news, education or weather. Some shows might hold inappropriate scenes but we can choose which program to watch.

テレビは有害なものではありません。むしろ、安くて便利な娯楽です。もしテレビが有害なものであるとすれば、他の全てのメディアも有害であるということになります。

Viewing television is not meant to be harmful to us. It is rather a cheap and convenient entertainment. If TV were hazardous, all other media could be so, too.

▶ テレビは有害だと主張する　　　　　　　　　　　　　CD 1 ➡ 29

テレビは悪影響を及ぼします。ほとんどのテレビ番組は虚像のものであるのにも関わらず、現実も同じようになると信じる人がいます。テレビは、そのような人々に現実と虚構の判断をしづらくしているのです。

Television has negative effects. TV shows are mostly virtual and yet some people believe that real life also works that way. Watching TV makes it difficult for them to judge between reality and virtual reality.

最近のテレビ番組の半分以上が、何らかの形で暴力に関連しています。テレビの暴力シーンに触発された若者もいると言ってもいいかもしれません。この点で、テレビは私たちに害を及ぼすものであるかもしれません。

More than half of recent TV programs are somehow related to violence. It can be said that some young people have been encouraged by violent scenes on TV. In terms of this, TV could be harmful for us.

▶ テレビの功罪から発展した議論　　　　　　　　　　　CD 1 ➡ 30

報道の有り方、内容と、見る側の受け止め方、利用の仕方で、有害にも有益にもなります。

Whether TV is helpful or harmful depends on how TV broadcasting is conducted, what content it conveys, how viewers feel and in what way they use it.

テレビで育った現代っ子が、簡単に人を殺し反省できないのも、テレビのもたらす有害な一部分ではないかと思ってしまいます。	I even think one of the many harmful aspects of TV is best illustrated by the sad incident of a young person brought up in our TV age killing others easily without any reflection.
しかし、ストレスの多い現代社会において、テレビは数々の楽しい番組（ショーやドラマなど）を提供してくれます。	However, TV has a positive ring if we see that TV provides various enjoyable programs including shows and dramas in the age of a stressful society.
同時にテレビ番組をうまく選ぶことにより、いろいろな有益な情報を得ることができるという点で、すばらしい貢献をしているとも言えます。	At the same time we can safely say that it contributes a great deal to our society in the sense that a wide variety of useful information is obtainable if we choose TV programs carefully.
ここで、注意すべきことがあります。テレビで流される情報が正確なものでない可能性も念頭に置く必要もあるのです。政治家や官僚、また、スポンサーである大企業などが、報道内容を制限する、あるいは改変する可能性もあるからです。	Here we have to note that we should bear in mind that not all the information may be correct. There is a fair possibility that politicians, bureaucrats, or big businesses act as sponsors restricting or modifying information broadcast on TV.
正しい情報を得るためには、できる限り、いろいろな情報源を比較することでしょう。テレビだけでなく、ラジオ、新聞、雑誌、ネットなどを通じて、客観的な情報を得る努力をすべきでしょう。	Comparison of many sources of information like radio, newspapers, magazines or the Internet in addition to TV makes it possible to get correct and objective information; we need to make such efforts.

7 日本は住みやすいか、住みにくいか？

▶ 住みやすい国だと述べる　　　　　　　　　　　　　　　CD 1 ➡ 31

日本は住みやすい国です。なぜなら、戦争放棄の憲法によって戦争を禁じているからです。この戦争に対する態度が、日本が住みやすい国であるという理由になります。

Japan is a country comfortable to live in because any war is prohibited by the war-renouncing constitution. This attitude toward war is the reason why Japan is a livable country.

海外から帰国した際に、日本はなんと非のうちどころのない国であろうと再認識しました。電車やバスは常に時刻表通り発着し、停電はすぐに回復します。これは、日本人の国民性の表れでしょう。

Returning from overseas, I realized how perfect a country Japan was. Trains and buses are always on time. Electricity is restored in a minute after blackouts. This is the indication of the national character.

▶ 住みにくい国だと述べる　　　　　　　　　　　　　　　CD 1 ➡ 32

日本人はその勤勉さで知られています。仕事をしすぎたとしても、誰も驚きはしません。ゆったりとした生活を求める人々には日本は住みよい国とは言えないかもしれません。

Japanese people are famous for diligence. No one would be surprised even if you overwork. For those people who seek a laid-back lifestyle, Japan may not be a comfortable country to live in.

日本が住みやすい国だとは思えません。他国に比べて、生活費が高いからです。日本で理想の家を買おうと思っても、一生働いても買えないこともあります。

There is some doubt that Japan is a comfortable country to live in. The reason is its high living cost compared to other countries. It is sometimes beyond your lifetime salary to own the ideal house in Japan.

▶ 日本に住むことを一歩進んで考える　　　　　　　　　　CD 1 ➡ 33

最近は、日本を脱出したいと考える人が多く、現実に、日本脱出を実行している人もいます。

In recent years many Japanese have come to think of escaping from Japan, and in reality, some of them put it into practice.

しかし、住みにくい問題があるなら、逃げるのでなく、住みやすくなるよう、自分なりに努力をするべきではないかと私は思います。	However, I think that if you have some problems in your life, you have to make every possible effort to turn your life for the better in your own way.
住みにくさの一番の原因は、3つあげられると思います。「金」「時間」そして「人間」にかかわるものです。	There are three main reasons why Japan is uncomfortable to live in: money, time and human-related things.
まず、金銭的な視点から、日本の物価は世界の標準より高いということです。	In the first place, from the viewpoint of money, we can say prices in Japan are higher than the world standard.
また、ゆったりとした時間がないというのが2点目です。残業しないといけないぐらい仕事が多かったり、逆に仕事がなくても早く帰りにくい状況があったりします。	The second point is that we don't have enough time. It is common to work overtime or to feel pressure to remain at work even if there is no work to do.
最後の点、これがまた無視できませんが、人間関係の重要性です。他人に対して気を使わないといけないのが、日本文化です。気を使わないタイプの人間はレベルが低いとみなされる傾向があります。 注：Last but not least の用法に注目。	Last but not least, the importance of human relations is the norm. In Japanese culture, we have to always be considerate of others. We are seen as unsophisticated if we are not attentive to others' feelings toward us.
理想的には、「相手に対して気を使っているように見えないように、気を使う」という高等な技が必要で、これには息が詰まる人もいるのではないかと思います。	Ideally, a profound art of being seemingly less considerate but in actuality more considerate of others is needed, which, I think, makes some of us feel a lot of stress.

8 占いを信じるか、信じないか？

▶ **占いを信じる人の意見**　　　　　　　　CD 1 ➡ 34

占いを信じることに問題はないでしょう。本当に未来を言い当てる才能を授かった人はいます。その人が本物かどうかをきちんと見極めていれば、占い師を信じていいと思います。
注：「...かどうかを見極める」は英語では、「...であると確認する」と訳す。

It is fine to believe in fortune-telling. There are people who are really gifted to tell what lies ahead. As long as we see carefully that they are genuine, there is nothing wrong with giving credit to them.

私は占いを信じています。以前、偶然に出会った占い師の方に、私は歌手になると言われました。そして、それは実現したのです。彼女を信じるほかにこのことを説明することはできないと思います。

I do believe in fortune-telling. A fortune-teller I had come across by chance told me that I would be a singer. Then, it came true. I cannot explain this fact unless I believe what she said.

▶ **占いを信じない人の意見**　　　　　　　CD 1 ➡ 35

私の経験から占いはただのでっち上げられたものだと思います。今まで私が出会った占い師は誰一人として悪い予想はしませんでした。彼らは、必死に私を喜ばせようとしていただけです。

Fortune-telling is just made up, from my experience. All of the fortune-tellers that I have ever met told me things that were very encouraging. They were desperately trying to please me.

占いとは娯楽の一つだと思います。全ての決断を占いに委ねている人もいますが、そのお金と時間を、自分でよりよい未来にするために使ったほうがいいと思います。
注：entertainment の「娯楽」の意味は不可算名詞、one of entertainments としない。

Fortune-telling is only for entertainment. Some people reach a point where they make every single decision based on fortune telling. They had better spend the precious time and money on something to make their future better for themselves.

占いについて一歩進んだ意見

私は、占いを信じません。参考にするときがあっても100％信じることはありません。	I do not believe in any divination. From time to time, I use it just for reference, but I will not believe 100 % of it.
2つ理由があります。1つ目の理由は、人が他人の過去、未来を完全に知ることは、不可能だということです。これは神のみが知っているのです。	I have two reasons for it. The first reason is that others' past or future is impossible for us to know. This is something only God knows.
2つ目は、占いを信じると、それだけに頼って生きることになり、自分で問題を解決できなくなる可能性があるということです。	For the second reason, total reliance on divination caused by a strong belief in it will deprive you of your power to solve problems for yourself.
占いの内容に一喜一憂することになり、たとえば、悪運が続けば、精神的なダメージが最悪の状態になります。	You may come to spend most of your life in suspense, now optimistic, now pessimistic. If you have a spell of bad luck, your spiritual damage will be at its peak.
いいことを言われた場合だけ信じ、悪いことを言われたら信じないことが大切でしょう。これが占いの理想的な用い方です。	It is important to believe something good but not to believe something bad. This is the ideal use of fortune telling.

参考 占いの英語のいろいろ

手相占い	palmistry, chiromancy [kai...] cf. 手相見（palmist, palm reader）		
人相占い	divination by the features cf. 人相学（physiognomy）		
夢占い	oneiromancy / oneiroscopy / divination by means of dreams		
姓名判断	onomancy	風水	Feng Shui
トランプ占い	cartomancy	数字占い	arithmancy

第4章

政治・経済・ビジネスに関する意見を述べる

1 民主主義に限界はあるか？

▶ 情報を伝える　　　　　　　　　　CD 1 ➡ 37

日本は民主国家でその首長、および国政の代表者は選挙によって選ばれます。地方政治の代表者も選挙で選ばれます。

Japan is a democracy, where its political leaders and representatives are elected by vote. So are the representatives of local governments.

物事を決めるために議論をし、賛成、反対の意見をよく聞き、人の意見を尊重しながら結論を出すのが民主主義の基本的な形です。

The basic idea of democracy is that in order to make decisions people discuss given matters while respecting other people's opinions before drawing conclusions.

議論の最後に多数決をとります。それで最多数の意見を結論とします。もちろんその際にも少数意見を尊重し、それを考慮しながら結論を出すのがよい民主主義といえるでしょう。

At the end of the discussion they take a vote and the opinion that gets the most votes is adopted. Good democracy is the one in which people allow for minor opinions when reaching the final decision.

民主主義下では法の支配という考えも重要な要素です。物事は前もって決められた法律に従って行なわれるべきで、それをやぶった者は法によって罰せられたり、それによる損害を弁償する、という考え方です。

Equally important under democracy is the rule of law. Things should be carried out according to the laws adopted earlier, and if anyone breaks them, he or she should be punished by the law or pay for the damage.

▶ 現在の状況の把握と分析　　　　　CD 1 ➡ 38

民主主義では意思決定に時間がかかると言われています。時間をかけて充分な議論の末に決定を下すのはいいことですが、ときには困るときもあります。

In a democratic system it takes much time to make decisions. It's fine to reach a decision after a long enough discussion, but sometimes it poses difficulties.

とりわけ憲法などの高位の法律が現実とのギャップを生じ、その変更が急がれるときには困ります。例えば近年では北朝鮮によるミサイルと核爆弾の実験が行なわれました。そしてその仮想攻撃対象に日本も入っています。	In particular, when a higher level law like the constitution doesn't match the reality and comes to need quick revising, then a problem arises. One example is the recent experiments of missiles and nuclear bombs by North Korea. And Japan is one of its prospective targets.
日本は現状の憲法では戦争および戦争装備を放棄しているために、直接的に北朝鮮に対して軍事的な行動で予防を張ることはできません。そのために憲法を改正する必要があると多くの人は主張します。	Since the current constitution prevents Japan from fighting a war or having weaponry for that purpose, it would be impossible to make military preparations against North Korea. Many people insist that the constitution be revised to do so.
このように緊急の事態であっても即時に必要な行動が法律によって制限される例です。	As above, even in an emergency, necessary urgent actions could be hampered by the law under the circumstances.
また、近年の滋賀県の新幹線駅誘致問題のように県政と市政が同じ問題に関して対立するというようなことも起こってきます。これは民意を反映させる選挙の制度が完全なものではないことのひとつの表れかもしれません。	In a political brush surrounding the building of a new Shinkansen station in Shiga Prefecture, the Prefectural administration and the city administration are on the opposite sides of the issue. This might be a reflection of the fact that the electoral system is still defective.
市長選では駅建設推進反対票のほうが多かったにも関わらず賛成派の市長が当選しました。不正があったわけではありません。反対票は2人の候補者で割れてしまったからです。	In the mayoral election, though there were more votes against the promotion of the station building, the candidate in favor was elected. It's not that there was any fraud. Votes out of favor were divided by two candidates.

59

しかし、このように対立が起こるのが民主主義のいい面だとも言えます。	However, such confrontation should be another desirable aspect of democracy.

▶ 別の観点（刑事手続きの面）から　　　　　　　　　　CD 1 ➡ 39

法の支配はとりわけ刑犯罪に関して重要な面を見せています。裁判を受ける権利、三審制、罪刑法定主義、物的証拠無しには有罪にならない、などの原則は国民が安心して生活を送るためにはなくてはならない概念です。	The rule of law plays an important role, particularly in the field of criminal proceedings. The right to a trial, the three-stage judgement system the principle of legality, and the idea that no one can be convicted without physical evidence and so on, are concepts imperative for people to live in peace.
違反事項と罰則ははっきりと明文化されていて、公布されている必要があります。これが守られない国は民主国家とは言えません。	Illegal acts and penalties must be clearly stated in writing and made public. Without this, a country can never be a democracy.
反社会的な行為が行なわれることがあります。その行為が非合法であると法律上明記されていないと、犯罪とは認められず罰することができません。これでは被害者などを守ることができないのでまずいことになります。	A person may commit an act that may be antisocial; however, unless the act clearly is illegal, the person cannot be charged or punished. It being true, we can't save victims of such acts, and it's too bad.
コンピュータやインターネットが発達した社会では法には規定されていない悪質な行為が起こることもあります。この点まずいのではないでしょうか。	In a society where computers and the Internet are well developed, malicious things can happen that are not stipulated in the law. This is a potential problem of a democratic society, isn't it?

結論

多様な価値観を認めながらその中で生活をしていくのが民主主義です。そして善悪の判断を含めいろんな決定をしていかなければなりません。

In a democracy, one is expected to respect a variety of values. And one is expected to make many decisions including judgments about what is right and wrong.

封建社会や独裁国家ではひとり、あるいは一握りの指導者が政策決定をし、民衆はそれに従います。しかし民主国家では全員が政策決定に参加します。

In a feudal society or dictatorial nation, one or a handful of leaders make decisions on policy, and the people follow. But in a democracy, people are participants in the decision making process.

多様な価値観の中で、どの人の意見を取り入れ、どの意見を排除していくのか。これは簡単に決められることではありません。時代とともに変わることもあるかもしれません。これが民主主義の特典ではありますが、同時にここに民主主義の限界もあるような気がします。

It is very difficult to decide which opinions to accept and which ones not to accept amongst a wide variety of values. The proper decision may change at different times. This is where democracy is good, and it seems to be the limitations of democracy at the same time.

2　日本人は働きすぎか？

▶ 情報を伝える　　　　　　　　　　　　　　　　CD 1 ➡ 41

日本人は昔から勤勉といわれています。	Japanese have been reputed as hard-working.
日、米、英、独、仏を比較したある統計では過去半世紀の労働時間数は 1993 年か 1994 年くらいまでは日本は他国を大きく上回っています。その後、英米は日本と同レベルまで増えますが、独、仏は依然として下回っています。	Some surveys contrasting Japan, the U.S., the U.K., Germany and France for the past half a century say the working hours of Japanese workers were far more than those of the other countries untŠ 1993 or 1994, after which the US and UK equaled the Japanese level, though the hours worked in Germany and France remained much lower.
リストラとも関係のある問題です。1990 年初期から続く不景気で、働きたくても働けない人がいることも事実です。 注：「リストラ」は worker displacement とも表現できる。	This has something to do with corporate restructuring. It's also true that there are stŠl many jobless people looking for jobs due to the recession of the early 90's.

▶ 考えを述べる　　　　　　　　　　　　　　　　CD 1 ➡ 42

日本人は欧米の人たちと比べて仕事と私生活の間に線を引くのが下手です。	Japanese are poor at separating work and private time, compared to Americans and Europeans.
あるテレビ番組でも日本人と結婚した北欧の女性が、夫が仕事を家に持ち帰ってしているのに不満を漏らしていました。	On one TV program a North European woman complained about her Japanese husband bringing home his work from the office.

企業経営者にとっては都合のいいことです。このことが70年代、80年代の日本の目覚しい発展となったのでしょうが、一方では過労死などの根源にこの日本人の姿勢があるのだと思います。

This characteristic works in company management's favor. It must have helped Japanese economy boom in the 70's and 80's, but it's assumed that this attitude of Japanese toward work is at the root of death caused by overworking, or karoshi.

日本の労働組合は企業内組合で会社の中にそこの社員で組合を作ります。ゆえに組合と会社が協調していかなければならない部分があり、日本経済の発展に寄与した面もあるが、労働者の労働時間を抑えにくい構造にもなっていると思います。

In Japan labor unions are within the companies, consisting of employees working there. Therefore, in some cases the union and the management have to work in cooperation. In some respects this has contributed to Japan's economic development, but it also makes it difficult to check the number of hours workers are working.

儒教の教えが根付いている日本では君主に対する忠誠心が強いです。ひとつの会社に生涯勤める終身雇用の元でもあります。
cf. Confuciusは「孔子」、Confucianは「儒教徒」。ちなみにconfusionは「混乱」。

In Japan where Confucianism is influential, the follower has strong loyalty to the master, which explains why we have the lifetime employment system.

▶ 未来の予想　　　　　　　　　　　　　　CD 1 ➡ 43

日本人も仕事に対する考えが変わってきています。額に汗して働くことが美徳だというのは古い人の考えですが、ライブドア事件や村上ファンドに代表されるようにうまく資本を動かして利益を得ればよいという考えの人も増えてきています。それがこれからの日本を象徴しているように思えます。

The Japanese attitude toward work has been changing. That it's a virtue to work with perspiration on the brow is an old-fashioned idea. As seen in the Livedoor case or in the Murakami Fund, people who pursue profit by manipulating capital at any cost are on the rise, which I think shows the course Japan will take in the future.

日本は昔に比べ資本を操作する傾向になってきているので、よく働く日本人は減っていくでしょう。	As Japan leans more towards capital manipulation, Japanese will be less willing to work as hard as they have in the past.
それは正社員の減少、派遣社員などの増加現象にも見られます。仕事を必要に応じてやっていけるシステムが発展すればそれを利用していき、より多くの余暇を持つようにすることもいいことです。	Fewer full-time workers and more temporary workers are one aspect of it, too. If there's an employment system that a worker only works according to his needs, it wouldn't hurt to use it and have more leisure time.
企業側も必要に応じて人を雇えて便利な部分もあります。	It would benefit the employer, too because it'd make it possible to hire only as a need arises.

▶ 結論

かつて働きすぎと言われた日本人たちのおかげで日本は現在の繁栄を得ることができたのは事実です。	It's true that the current prosperity is on the shoulders of Japanese once called "working too hard."
それによる経済発展をもって「エコノミックアニマル」とよばれた時期があります。しかし、他人の目はどうでもいいでしょう。	They were once described as "economic animals" owing to the resultant economic boom. We should not care about how others look at us.
そうしなければ我々は生き残っていけません。	We could not live otherwise.
勤勉でありながらも仕事と私生活の区別をうまくできる環境を作っていきたいものです。	I hope we could create surroundings where people can be diligent and keep work and private life separate as well.

3 政治家はどうあるべきか？

▶ 情報と意見を伝える　　　　　　　　　　CD 1 ➡ 45

民主国家では政治家は選挙によって選ばれます。

In democratic countries politicians are elected by vote.

政治家の職務は法律や条例などを作ること、条約を承認したりすることです。時には重要な犯罪事件に対して容疑者を糾弾することも行います。

Their jobs include making laws and by-laws, ratifying treaties, and sometimes impeaching suspects in serious criminal cases.

政治家は公務員であり、すべての国民に平等に奉仕する立場にあります。しかし、自分が代表する地域の利益を図るのも仕事です。

Politicians are public servants, required to serve the whole population equally. It's also their job to serve the localities they represent.

政治家は本来非常に重要な仕事であり、給料は充分に保証されています。

A politician has a very important job and his or her income is secured.

政治家は判断を下すときには特定の人の利益を代表するのではなく、全体の利益を重視しなければなりません。

When making decisions, they must not consider the benefit of certain people, but rather weigh the benefit to the whole population.

法律に従って行動するのはもちろんですが、なによりも優先すべきは常に人々の福利厚生です。

No doubt they must abide by the law, and put the well-being of the people above all.

テレビなどで支出が多くて赤字運営の議員が出ているのを見ます。収入は保証されているべきですが、議員本人は自分が苦しくても市民が幸せならそれもよしとするほどの人であるべきです。

On TV, we see Diet men whose offices are running in the red. Though their income should be secured, a politician should be able to feel happy if people are happy regardless of his own condition.

考えを述べる　　　　　　　　　　　　　　　　　　CD 1 ➡ 46

実際には人のために働いているんだから人よりいい目をしても当たり前だ、と思っている政治家が多いような気がします。最近では知事が業者とつるんで自分の身内の業者に不法に便宜をはかるという事件がありました。

It seems many politicians think that because of their position it's beyond question that they deserve a rich life. Recently a governor hooked up with private businesses and tried to illegally benefit a relative.

民間企業の人たちも、人のために働いているんですよ。その結果利益を得ているんで、政治家と同じなんです。勘違いするべきではないでしょう。

People working at private firms work for other people, too. And they get income for it as politicians do. Politicians should not have the wrong idea.

政治家に関して思うこと　　　　　　　　　　　　　CD 1 ➡ 47

政治家は任期を過ぎて次に落選してしまうと収入を失う可能性があります。家業がある人はいいのですが、元々サラリーマンの場合は同じ所に再就職は難しいでしょう。

A politician, if his term ends and he loses the election, can end up losing income. It wouldn't present a problem if he has a family business to go back to, but he would have difficulty getting back to his former job if he was originally a company employee.

そういう意味でいろんな面で保証は厚くされているべきです。

In this sense he should be assured various perks.

でないと政治家になることが経済的に無理な人がでてきます。民主国家では熱意のある人は誰でも政治家を目指すことができないといけません。

Otherwise for some people it's financially impossible to be a politician. In a democratic country, anybody who aspires to be a politician should be able to try to be one.

しかし政治家にはお金を持っている人がけっこういるように思えます。

However, we get the impression that there are many rich politicians.

政治家としての給料以外にも支援団体からの寄付金や後援会を通しての各種催しものなどからの上納金などがあり、その使途は不明なものがけっこうあるようです。	Besides their salary as politicians, they receive donations from support groups, and proceeds from events they hold through support groups. How the money is used is often unclear.
最近では元首相が利益団体からの1億円にものぼる金を届出無しに受け取った例があります。また、アメリカのラスベガスで何億円もの金をすった元国会議員もいます。	One example of such is a case in which an ex-prime minister received up to 100 million yen from an interest group without making the mandatory report to the authorities. Another one is a case of a politician who spent several hundred million yen in Las Vegas in the US.
政治家は自分の利益のために働くのではいけないと思います。既成の政治家には襟を正して業務を遂行してもらいたいし、将来に向けては能力があるだけでなく清く、誠実な政治家が仕事に就ける環境を創っていくべきだと思います。	I don't think that a politician should work for his own benefit. I hope the present politicians carry out their jobs in a square manner. And in the future it's urgent that we create an environment where not only able but clean and sincere politicians will run for office.

▶ **政治家はどうあるべきかに関する意見** CD 1 ➡ 48

政治家はお金の絡む仕事です。きれいごとではやっていけないこともあるでしょう。不正なお金には関わらない毅然とした態度と強い精神が要求されるでしょう。個人個人がその自覚を持つことが重要です。	Politics always comes with money. And sometimes it can be difficult to keep clean. Therefore, one has to have a firm stance and a strong will not to take any dirty money. Each politician should take this to heart.
お金に目がくらむと特定の人たちに利益を誘導してしまうことになります。すべての人を公平に取り扱うのが政治家です。	Money can blind a person, who then could end up favoring certain people. Dealing fairly for the benefit of all the people is the statesman.

4 天下りはなくならないか？

▶ 情報を伝える　　　　　　　　　　　　CD 1 ➡ 49

天下りには社会的な弊害がつきまといます。	Amakudari, or golden parachute from public office, always brings about social afflictions.
問題点のひとつは、民間企業と官僚の癒着の原因になることです。	One problem is that it's a cause of intimacy between private sectors and bureaucracy.
民間企業では公共事業に関する仕事獲得を有利に進めるために官庁の有力者の退職後に自分の会社に条件のよい職を用意します。また、官庁は少しでも待遇をよくしてもらうために官庁勤務中には企業へ便宜をはかろうとする。これが癒着の原因です。	This means a company provides a good position for a retired official so as to get an edge in getting a contract related to public works. And officials try to favor the company so that they can get good working conditions after they join it. This is the root of the problem.
もうひとつの問題点は特殊法人への天下り。公社、公団の退職を繰り返しそのたびに退職金をもらう官僚もいるそうです。もちろん退職金は公費から出ています。	Another problem is re-entrance to the so-called Special Corporation, the corporation with a special status. I hear there are some officials who enter and retire from one public corporation called Kosha or Kodan after another and each time get a retirement allowance. It is paid from the public budget.
退職金の総額が億を超えていた例もテレビで放送されていました。	One case in which the total allowance one official got exceeded 100 million yen was reported on TV.

人材の斡旋や仲介に官庁の権限が効かされ、それゆえ有能でない人物が要職につくことがあります。民間企業でも公社、公団でも不必要な人材を抱えることになります。	The public offices exercise their influence to introduce their workers to good positions when the workers retire. As a result, incompetent workers can get important positions. Thus companies and public corporations can have unneeded personnel.
天下りをなくすことが発案され、政治の場で議論されることがあります。	Eradication of the Golden Parachute is sometimes proposed and discussed at the political arenas.
アメリカでは一部の高級官僚が退職後に関係企業に就職することは法律で禁じられています。	In the USA, some high-ranking officials are prohibited by law from joining private companies after retiring.
中央省庁から民間企業への天下りは2003年までの5年間で3027人、また特殊法人、許可法人、公益法人へは43％ほどが就職していることがわかっています。	It's known that for the 5 years until 2003, 3027 officials retired from central public offices and joined private businesses, and some 43 % of the retired were hired by special corporations, licensing corporate bodies and public-service corporations, or welfare corporations.

▶ 考えを述べる　　　　　　　　　　　　　　　　　　　　　　　　　　CD 1 ➡ 50

官民の癒着で一部の民間企業が利益を受けるのはよくないです。また一方では公的なお金が使われています。	It's unfair that a private firm benefits from too intimate relations with the bureaucracy. At the same time tax payers' money is being spent.
不況で民間で働く人たちが厳しい生活を強いられる中、一部の官僚たちが公金で私服を肥やすようなシステムは許しがたいものです。	It's never tolerable that some officials pocket money from tax, while workers of the private sector are barely getting by in the recession.

法律で規制すべきものですが、官民の癒着に加え、政治家も官僚に頼らなければならない構造ができ上がっており、二の足を踏んでいるのです。	Such intimacy must be banned by law, but political make-up is such that politicians have to rely on bureaucrats for things, so they think twice about introducing such a law.
つまり、政官民の黄金の三角形があるのです。この民は一般の民間人は関係なくトップに立つ経営者だけですので政官財というのが正確です。	This is to say there's a so-called golden triangle between the political, bureaucratic and business worlds. The business world here is not general businessmen but large corporations' owners. To be exact it is politicians, bureaucracy and corporate owners.

▶ **未来の予想** CD 1 ➡ 51

政官財の癒着があるとさまざまな困難が予想されます。	With the intimacy between politicians, bureaucrats and business ownership, various hurdles are expected ahead.
法的にはいろんな障害があり規制が難しくとも、道徳的に悪いことならやめるというのが美しい日本人です。	Not doing what's morally wrong is a Japanese virtue, or the beautiful part of Japanese culture, even though it may be difficult to regulate it by law.
安倍首相は「美しい国へ」をスローガンにしていますが、詰め込み教育が優先して、道徳教育の程度の低い日本ではそれも当面は難しいようです。	PM Abe put up "Beautiful Japan" as his slogan. It is difficult to achieve for the moment given the dominant cramming and deteriorating moral education in schools.

▶ **提案を述べる** CD 1 ➡ 52

天下りを断つためには政治家の、特に政府内閣に参画する政治家の英断が必要でしょう。しかしそれは期待できません。	It would take a brave decision of politicians, particularly those who are members of the Cabinet to put an end to the Golden Parachute. But it's the farthest thing from happening.

かつてアメリカのレーガン大統領は命令に逆らった航空管制官を一度に一万人以上解雇したことがあります。

Once President Reagan of the USA fired more than 10,000 aviation controllers, who had refused to follow orders.

その後航空事業はどうなったのかは知りませんが、この世の悪を断つには自分の懐具合を省みない人の思い切った決断が必要でしょう。

I don't know what happened after it, but I believe it takes an unselfish person and his radical decision to get rid of the real evil of this society.

5 日本経済はこれからどうなるのか？

▶ 情報を伝える　　　　　　　　　　　　　　　　　CD 1 ➡ 53

日本は、今や800兆円、地方自治体や、特殊法人を合わせると1000兆円を超えると言われる借金の「赤字大国」です。

Japan is now a deficit giant where the amount of debt is 800 trillion yen, and if the deficits of local governments and special corporations are included, the total amount is said to surpass 1000 trillion yen.

一方で、現在日本はイザナギ景気を上回る好景気だと言われています。イザナギ景気は1960年代、いわゆる高度成長期の一時期の景気動向です。

On the other hand, it's now said Japan is enjoying a good economic situation, even better than that of the Izanagi economy, which was part of the high economic growth in the 1960's.

新聞紙上でも大企業、銀行をはじめ収益の上がっているニュースがよく見受けられます。

The newspapers often report that the profits of large companies and banks are up.

しかし、一般の人の実感はまったく逆のものです。とりわけ関西地区ではますます景気は冷え込み、この先数年は上向かないだろうと言う人もいます。

But the general public feels the reality is contrary to the reports. In the Kansai district in particular, business is further slowing and some even say it'll take some more years for it to turn up.

今回の好景気は経済の成長率は高くなく単に好景気のサイクルが長いというものです。

The good economy this time is not because it shows high economic growth but because it's been lasting so long.

日本は80年代のバブル経済後の失敗反省により、企業がリストラ、投資の控えなど慎重、堅実に経営を進めるようになり、その結果景気が上向き経済動向に表

After bungling and regretting their activities during the bubble economy in the 80's, companies engaged in more cautious and solid

72

れています。中国やアメリカなどへの輸出も順調で、さらに経済を押し上げています。

management like streamlining, and reserved investment, which resulted in an economic up-turn suggested by the economic indices. Good exports to China and the US help lift business too.

一方雇用はどうかというと、リストラが進む一方、雇用の形態も正社員以外のアルバイト、派遣社員などが増えました。

Looking at employment, while restructuring is in progress, companies are adding many temporary workers and contract workers instead of hiring full-time employees.

人件費の面からも企業はコストを下げることに成功しています。しかし、可処分所得のすくない消費者を生み出すことになっていて、いわゆる格差を助長することにもなっています。
注：「人件費」は labor cost とも言う。

Companies have successfully cut down personnel expenses. But it produced consumers with low disposable incomes further widening the income gap.

国内需要の成長が現在の景気動向の順調さに表れているわけではないのです。消費の実感が景気動向とかけ離れているわけです。

The current good economic condition doesn't mean we have high domestic consumption, which explains the reason why consumers' perceptions are far removed from the economic indices.

企業の売上、利益に対する姿勢や社員雇用の形態の変化はかつての経済大国日本のそれとは違った形で、根付いてきました。また企業は各種の規制緩和により起こる激しい競争に勝ちぬくべく統合などにより競争力を付けています。

The way companies look at sales and profit, and the employment system have changed much since the time Japan was an economic giant. The current one has taken root. Companies have gained a competitive edge by merging and other measures to survive fierce competition resulting from deregulation.

一方では所得などの格差が起こり問題視されています。	On the other hand, resultant disparities in income are considered a problem.
安倍首相が言うように格差が固定せずに、つねに第二、第三の機会が得られる社会になることが成功の鍵で日本経済の本当の意味の発展につながることでしょう。	Sharing Prime Minister Abe's view, I hope for a society where the disparity is changeable and a second chance is always there, which should be the key to success leading up to a real advancement of the Japanese economy.

▶ 今後の心配について述べる　　　　　　　　　　　　　　CD 1 ➡ 54

今後の未来が心配です。企業の利益が上がれば、それが従業員の給料に反映され、お金が社会に循環し、購買力が上がるでしょう。	I'm worried about the future. If the company increases its profits and employees' wages are increased, then they have more disposable income and have strong buying-power.
そのサイクルが途中で切れている感じですので、消費者の購買力が上がりません。そこで個人商店などの中小企業にはお金が回ってきません。	But I feel this flow is broken somewhere, keeping people's buying power from rising. Thus money won't come around to small and middle-sized businesses like private shops.
近頃人気のある雇用形態の非正社員化は人々の生活様式に変化をもたらし、画一的なサラリーマン的生活から脱皮する人が増えていい面もあると思います。	The temporary employment system, which is popular these days, has brought about a change in lifestyle which has given many people the freedom to quit being company employees.
しかし、日本は儒教的な「二君に仕えず」の考え方がまだ支配的で、職をよく変わる人はあまり見られません。	But in Japan where the Confucian teaching "Don't serve two masters" is influential, a person who often changes jobs isn't respected.

よりよい条件を求めて仕事を転々とすることは本来個人の権利と思いますが、社会はまだそれを受け入れる体制がありません。ゆえに正社員でない人は仕事にあぶれやすいのではないかと思います。
参考：職を転々とすることは、job-hopping、はしご酒をすることは、bar-hopping、宴会などであちこち歩き回っておしゃべりすることは、table-hopping。

The society is not ready yet for that though I believe it's a right to change jobs for ever better working conditions. That explains why temporary workers find it difficult to get a job.

経験が生かされない社会、第二第三の機会の与えられない社会では成長は見込めません。

In a society where experience doesn't help, a second chance is not given, and one can't expect to progress.

元自社社員を再雇用する会社はあるようですが、これは雇用条件が限られています。

Some companies reinstate their ex-employees but the requirements should be limited.

▶ **自由競争に関する意見**　　　　　　　　　　　　　　　　CD 1 ➡ 55

自由な競争で超金持ちが出る社会になってきました。しかしそのお金が、社会全体に循環することも考えていかなければなりません。

Japan is becoming a society of free competition producing super rich people. At the same time we have to come up with ways to circulate their money in the whole society too.

経済のシステムの自由競争化の目的はその結果として人が幸せになることにあると思います。自由競争そのものが目的ではないと思います。

I think the objective of a free competition economic system rests in making people happy. Free competition itself is not the final goal.

6 「米」の自由化と「牛肉」の輸入

▶ 情報を伝える　　　　　　　　　　　　　　　　　　CD 1 ➡ 56

自由貿易国として GATT 加盟国の日本政府は基本的には外米の輸入を開放の方向で動いています。
注：GATT=General Agreement on Tariffs and Trade

The government of Japan, a member of GATT, is working to open the Japanese market to foreign rice.

牛肉の輸入は狂牛病の影響で禁止になりました。

Beef imports were banned after mad cow disease came to light.

輸入は、2006年はじめに再開されています。しかし、まだ禁止の部位が輸入肉に入っていたので再禁止になった事件がありました。

They were resumed earlier in 2006, but after a while it was banned again because still-banned parts were found in imported beef.

▶ 米の自由化に関する考えを述べる　　　　　　　　　CD 1 ➡ 57

輸入は、自国の生産物の不足分を補うための手段だと思います。

Importing is a means of making up for the shortage of the agricultural products produced in a country.

自国の農家を圧迫する結果になるような輸入はその国自体にとって問題です。

The import resulting in the suffering of the country's farmers will pose a problem to the country itself.

だから私は、日本において、米の自由化には反対です。

Therefore, I am against the liberalization of rice in Japan.

▶ 牛肉の輸入について　　　　　　　　　　　　　　　CD 1 ➡ 58

自由主義の国ではどの商品を買うのかは本来消費者が決めることであるので、原則的には牛肉の輸入再開は悪いことではないと思います。

Under the free market system, it's up to consumers to decide what to buy, so I think basically it's never a bad thing to reopen the market to imported beef.

その商品に対する正しい情報が本当に正しく消費者に伝わっているかが問題です。	However, I wonder whether we actually have access to the right information of the products or not.
例えばＡ地産の産物でも、Ｂ地で何らかの手を加えることでＢ地産と表示できるというような話を聞いたことがあります。 参考：アメリカ産の和牛が存在する。	Why I wonder about it is that I once heard no matter where the product originates, if it is processed at B locality, it could be branded as a product from B.
本当に人体に悪いものならば政府が責任を持って止めるべきです。今回の狂牛病の牛を恐れての輸入禁止を解禁にするのはテレビなどを通して見ているとアメリカの圧力に折れている印象は否めません。	The government must check anything harmful to health at any cost. Recent TV coverage of this matter gives the impression that the Japanese government bent to America's demand that Japan import beef from the US.
輸入肉を販売する業者は事実をはっきりと明記するべきです。	Dealers of imported beef should announce the fact clearly.
そして政府は狂牛病が蔓延すればどうなるのかをいつでも国民にはっきりさせておくべきです。 注：狂牛病は専門的には、bovine spongiform encephalopathy と言う。	And the government should keep the public informed of what would happen if the mad cow disease became rampant.
米はかつて許可を持つ米屋の専売でしたがこれは一種の独占と言えます。いまではどこでも米を売ることができるようになり、消費者は選択の幅が広がりました。	Once rice retailing was exclusively in the hands of licensed rice shops, which could have been kind of a monopoly. Now anyone can sell rice and consumers have a larger choice as to where to buy.

牛肉輸入開始では国内生産業者が、米輸入自由化でも国内業者に厳しい競争を招いたように、困難にさらされることも事実です。	It's true that a resumption of beef imports puts domestic beef producers in trouble, just as opening up the domestic market to imported rice creates more competition for domestic rice farmers.
しかし自由経済社会では解放された状態が自然な姿で、その中で競争力を磨いていくのが社会発展の推進力となります。	But the real free economy is the one where every item is open, and having a competitive edge is something that drives the society ahead.
その中で特別な問題が察知されたときのみ政府が介入すべきでしょう。 注：only を伴う句や節が文頭に来た場合は、その後の文は疑問文のような倒置が起こる。だから should there be... という形になっている。	Only when there is a problem should there be government intervention.
しかしながら米などの主要な食物は戦略的な面から見ても海外への依存率は低く保つのが独立国としての当然の姿勢で、政府としての責任と思います。	However, staples like rice are important from the strategic viewpoint and we should not depend much on overseas producers for them. It's the government's responsibility.

▶ 提案を述べる　　　　　　　　　　　　　　　　CD 1 ➡ 59

日本の米は輸入物と違い日本人の趣向に合っています。	Japanese rice, unlike the imports, fits the Japanese taste.
たとえ自由競争が原則とはいえ、万が一外米の競争力に負けて日本の米農家が破綻してはおいしい米が食べられなくなるし、もちろん戦略的にもまずいです。	Though it's true that free competition is the life of the society, if Japanese rice farmers lose to imported rice and go bankrupt, we could no longer eat delicious rice and it'd be very bad strategically.

そこで、日本の米と米生産技術を海外にも輸出して日本米生産地域を国外にも作りましょう。	Then why don't we export Japanese rice and rice producing technology and expand Japanese rice producing areas abroad?
それにより米の価格も下がり、国内の米農家にも競争力を持つ必要がでます。	With that the price of rice would fall, making Japanese rice farmers more competitive.
日本の農家が破綻しないように政府もうまい援助方法を考えなければなりません。	The Japanese government would be required to come up with good ways to help them economically.

第 5 章

文化・芸術・スポーツに関する意見を述べる

1 「文明」と「文化」の違い

▶ 文明と文化の違い　　　　　　　　　　　　　　　　CD 1 ➡ 60

文明は普遍的なもの、文化は個別的なものです。	Civilization is universal, while culture is specific or particular.
メールやインターネットが可能な現代は、1つのコンピュータ文明の時代といえます。文明が1つなのは、コンピュータが、世界のどこでも同じスタンダードで用いることができるからです。	We can safely say that the modern age of the Internet and email is the age of a single computerized civilization. The reason why there is one civilization in the world is that computers can be used around the world under the same standards.
なお、文化は、歴史的にも地理的にも個別的なものです。飛鳥文化や平安文化という言葉があったり、日本文化やニューギニア文化などの言葉がありますね。飛鳥文明や日本文明とは普通言いません。	And culture is specific both in history and geography. There are expressions like Asuka culture and Heian culture, or Japanese culture and Papua New Guinean culture. In general, we don't have such expressions as Asuka civilization or Japanese civilization.
文明は物質的なもの、文化は精神的なものだという考え方もあります。 注：spiritualistic は spiritualism（唯心論）の形容詞形。	Another theory concerning the difference between the two is as follows: civilization is materialistic, whereas culture is spiritual.
文化人類学者の梅棹忠雄氏は、「文明とは腹の足しになるもの、文化とは心の足しになるもの」という名言を発しています。	The cultural anthropologist Tadao Umesao made a witty remark. civilization is something for our stomach, while culture is something for our spirit.

角川必携国語辞典によれば、「文明とは新技術で世界に広がるもの、文化とはそれぞれの土地が文明を受け入れて、自分たちの自然条件の下で生み出された生活全体を指し、世界には広がらない」ということです。

According to the *Kadokawa Hikkei Japanese Dictionary*, civilization is new technology that can spread across the world and culture is the whole system of life under particular local conditions after some portion of civilization is introduced into their own land. The culture will not be exported to the world.

文明は、さまざまな文化において技術的に高度に発達した部分を総合的に捉えたものです。

Civilization refers to the overall system of highly developed technological aspects of various cultures.

文化は技術的な側面では、優劣がありますが、それぞれに特徴があり、価値があると思います。たとえばアフリカのマサイ族は高度な文明がなくても、価値のある文化を持っているといえます。

Cultures may be different in levels of technology, but each culture has its own characteristics and values. For example, the Maasai in Africa can be said to have no highly developed civilization but their own valuable culture.

「文化」に対応するコンセプトは、「自然」だといえます。

We can say that culture contrasts with nature.

人間が自然に対して何らかの働きかけを行って、人工的に発展させたすべてのものを文化として捉えることができます。

All the things produced by certain actions taken toward nature and then developed artificially by humans are regarded as part of culture.

人間が自然に対して、最初に起こした文化は、土を利用した文化、すなわち農業です。だから、「農業」の英語は、アグリ（＝土）とカルチャー（＝文化）の合成語なのです。

The first culture humans created by modifying nature was the culture of earth, which is agriculture. Therefore, the English word for agriculture consists of "agri," which means earth, and the word "culture."

文明と文化に関する意見

文明が発達した現在、さまざまな種類の環境破壊が表面化しています。文明はこれ以上発達してはならないのではないかと思います。	In present society where civilization was developed, various kinds of issues of environmental destruction have come to the fore. This situation even makes me feel that there should not be any more civilization.
今こそ、昔の良さを振り返り、文明を考え直すのが重要です。	Now is the very time to think and rethink civilization by recollecting the positive aspects of the past.
日本人は日本文化、特に、日本の伝統文化を知らない人が多いのが現状です。	The present situation is that many Japanese do not know Japanese culture, especially about traditional aspects of Japan.
日本人は国際人であることの重要性を強調する傾向にありますが、本当の国際人は、自国の文化を愛し、同時に他の国の文化にも理解がある態度を持った人のことをいうのではないかと思います。	Generally speaking, Japanese people tend to emphasize the importance of being internationally minded people, and people of the true global mind should love their own culture and simultaneously, understand cultures of other countries to some extent.
自国の文化を愛するためには、その文化のことをよく知るべきでしょう。	To love one's own culture is to know the culture in more detail.
英語が世界語だからといって、英語のコミュニケーション能力だけが素晴らしくできても国際人とはいえないでしょう。	We cannot easily say that those only with an excellent communicative ability of English are internationally minded.

| 日本のことを馬鹿にする英語ペラペラの日本人を、外国人はあまり好みません。 | Foreign people do not like Japanese very well if they are able to speak English quite fluently but hold the Japanese culture in contempt. |

| 訥弁（とつべん）だけれども、日本のことが好きで、それゆえ日本文化をよく知っていて、話題が豊富な日本人のほうが好かれます。
注：「訥弁」be rather awkward in one's speech とも言える。 | Those Japanese who love Japan and therefore know a lot about its culture with an ample stock of topics are preferred even if they do not have a glib tongue.
参考：if以下は簡単には if they cannot easily explain the topics とするとよい。 |

| これは私の経験からはっきり言えることです。 | I am confident from my experience that this is surely the case. |

表現のコツ　「馬鹿にする」の表現のいろいろ

```
...を馬鹿にする    → hold ... in contempt / hold ... in low esteem / hold ...
                    cheap
                    think meanly of ... / make light of ... ［軽視する］
                    make fun of ... = make jest of ... ［からかう］
                    make a fool of ... / make a mockery of ...
                    have a low opinion of ... ［低く見る］
                    look down on ... ［見下げる］
                    speak insultingly of ... ［...を馬鹿にしたようなことを言
                    う］
馬鹿にして言う      → say jeeringly / say in derision
```

2 日本の芸術

▶ 情報を伝える　　　　　　　　　　　　　　　　　　CD 1 ➡ 62

日本の伝統芸術としては、能、歌舞伎、文楽、水墨画、浮世絵、日本庭園、枯山水などが挙げられます。

Traditional art forms of Japan include Noh performance, Kabuki theatrical art, traditional puppetry, India-ink drawing, traditional wood-block genres, Japanese pond and plant gardens, and dry landscape gardens.

能は、14世紀に観阿弥とその息子世阿弥によって完成された総合的な古典芸能で、ゆっくりとした象徴的な動きと表情があまりない能面が特徴です。

Noh is an overall classical dance-drama perfected by Kan'ami and his son Zeami in the 14th century, which is characterized by its slow symbolic movement and emotionless masks.

歌舞伎は、16世紀を起源とする日本の代表的舞台芸術で、ダイナミックな動きと華美な隈取が特徴です。

Kabuki is a representative Japanese theatrical art dating from the 16th century which features dynamic movement and emphatic makeup called Kumadori.

歌舞伎は人間劇、能は仮面劇であるのに対し、文楽は人形劇です。「文楽」は江戸の寛政年間に人形浄瑠璃を始めた植村文楽軒に由来します。

Kabuki is a play, Noh is a masque, but Bunraku is a puppet show. The name Bunraku originated in Uemura Bunrakuken, who started a primitive puppet show during the Kansei era of the Edo period.

水墨画は墨絵とも称し、全てが墨のみで描く伝統的な絵画で、単純性と微妙さが特徴です。

Suiboku-ga, also called Sumie, is a traditional drawing in which everything is depicted only in black India ink. This art form is characterized by its simplicity and subtlety.

水墨画は枯山水の二次元化で、枯山水は水墨画の三次元化といえます。（庭画一致）	Suiboku-ga drawing is a two-dimensional embodiment of Karesansui gardens, while the Karesansui garden is a three-dimensional realization of Suiboku-ga.
無声の詩が水墨画で、有声の画は漢詩であるといえます。（書画一致）	We can say that India-ink drawing is voiceless poetry, whereas Chinese poetry is voiced drawing.
日本の庭は3つに分類できます。築山といわれる池と植物のある庭、枯山水といわれる石と砂だけの庭、さらに茶庭があります。	Japanese gardens are classified into three categories: pond and plant gardens called Tsukiyama, rock and sand gardens called Karesansui, and tea gardens called Chaniwa.
築山庭園は、その中を散歩するよう設計されていることが多いので、回遊式庭園と呼ばれています。	Pond and plant gardens are often designed for taking a walk in them; therefore, they are called Kaiyu-shiki Teien directly translated as strolling gardens.
枯山水とも呼ばれる石庭は、考えるための庭です。	Rock and sand gardens, also known as dry landscape gardens, are for meditation.
たとえば竜安寺は、七五三形式による3つの石のグループから成る石庭を持っています。	Ryoanji Temple, for example, has a rock garden containing three groups of stones, seven, five and three stones respectively.

しかし、その庭の前に座るとすべての石を見ることはできません。これは不完全の美を示しています。我々はまた、人間は限られた視点から物を見る傾向があるのに対して、仏はもっと高い視野からすべてを見ることができるということを示しているともいえます。	However, if you sit in front of the garden, you cannot see every stone, which shows the beauty of imperfectness. We can also say this shows that humans tend to see things from their limited perspective, while Buddha can see everything from a higher perspective.
浮世絵は、文字通りには、「浮世の絵」です。	Ukiyoe is literally pictures of the floating world.
浮世絵の特徴は3つに絞れます。	Ukiyoe can be summarized into three characteristics.
まず、風俗画で、江戸幕府が認めた由緒正しい狩野派の絵に対立します。	First, it is a genre painting that is in contrast with the painting of the Kano School that was dominant during the Edo period.
次に、木版画で、絵師、彫師、摺師（すりし）の3者が必要です。	Second, it is a wood-block print, which requires three people: a painter, a sculptor, and a printer.
最後に、ヨーロッパの印象派に多大な影響を与えたという点を特筆すべきでしょう。	Finally, worthy of special mention is that this exerted a great influence on European impressionism.

▶ 日本の芸術に関する意見　　　　　　　　　　　　　　　　　　CD 1 ➡ 63

日本の芸術は、奥が深いので、日本人であれば、そのうちの何でもよいので鑑賞するか、実際に趣味として実践するのがよいと思います。	Japanese arts are so profound that I think it is a good idea for us Japanese to be aware of them or put even one into practice as a hobby.

特に定年後は、何か趣味をもっていることが、充実した生活に不可欠だと思います。	Especially after retirement, having some hobby will be indispensable for making your life richer, I think.
伝統文化だけでなく、現代文化にも注目すべきでしょう。	We should pay attention to modern arts as well as traditional arts.
たとえば現代の日本のアニメには、優れたものがあると思います。だから、世界全体に広めるとよいのではないかと考えています。	For example, some modern Japanese animations are wonderful, I believe. Therefore, we should introduce them to the other parts of the world.

▶ 日本の芸術の特徴に対する意見　　　　　　　　　CD 1 ➡ 64

日本の芸術は、全体として、2つの特徴を持っていると思います。	Art forms in Japan have two features as a whole.
1つは、自然を重視するということです。自然というものを最も自然な形で、人工のものの中に表現するという技術が見られます。	One is that Japanese art places emphasis on nature. In any Japanese art, a technique of expressing nature most naturally in something artificial can be seen.
もう1つは、シンプルを重視する点です。豪華絢爛なものもありますが、ただ単純性に価値をおくものがほとんどであるような気がします。	The other is that it emphasizes simplicity. Though there are arts showing pomposity, most of them seem to simply lay emphasis on simplicity.
「侘び」や「さび」という原理も、シンプルであることの重要性を中心としています。	The principle called Wabi, refined poverty, or Sabi, rustic simplicity, centers on the importance of simplicity.

実践編　第5章　文化・芸術・スポーツに関する意見を述べる

侘びは、「華美」に詫びることといえます。日本の芸術では、これが茶道の重要原理になっています。	We can say that Wabi is a sentiment to apologize for pomposity. In the field of Japanese art, tea ceremony has this feeling as an important principle.
一方、「侘び」という華美に対する対立心自体にも詫びる感情が「寂び」だという興味深い説があります。	On the other hand, there is an interesting theory that the Sabi sentiment is to apologize even for the Wabi frame of mind, which is in sharp conflict with Kabi.
この「寂び」は、日本の芸術では、松尾芭蕉が大成した俳諧の原理になっています。	Sabi is, in Japanese art, the principle of Haiku perfected by Matsuo Basho.
とにかく、我々日本人は、どんなものでもよいから、日本の芸術を鑑賞し、または実際に趣味として行ってみるべきではないかと思います。	At any rate, I think it might be a good idea for us Japanese to appreciate even one of the Japanese art forms, whatever it may be, or to take it as a hobby.
きっと学ぶことが多いだけでなく、思わぬ感動が得られるでしょう。	I think it will surely make us moved in an unexpected way as well as enable us to learn many things.

参考 「侘び」と「寂び」の英語

> 微妙な差はあるとはいえ、これらの概念は、英語では表現しにくいのですが、「貧しさ」や「単純さ」や「さびしさ」というマイナスイメージと「洗練されていること」や「優雅さ」というプラスイメージといった2つの対立する概念を同時に表している点に注意すべきでしょう。
> → refined poverty, quiet elegance, rustic simplicity

3 マスコミのあり方

▶ 雑誌に関する意見   CD 1 ➡ 65

新聞は客観的に事実を報道する義務がありますが、雑誌は事実関係がはっきりしないグレーゾーンを扱います。それが雑誌の存在意義だと思います。	Newspapers are under the obligation to report facts objectively, while magazines deal with the gray zone where things are not yet established as facts. This is the very significance of the existence of magazines, I think.
週刊誌の役割としては、新聞やテレビの報道を分析する機能があると思います。新聞やテレビは、報道できないことがあり、真理がぼけたり、わかりにくかったりすることがあるからです。	The role played by weekly magazines is, I think, to analyze what is said in the reports written in newspapers or broadcast on TV. This is because the facts and figures become unclear or hard to understand due to the restrictions in the content of newspaper reports.
新聞ですべてを知ることはできません。つまり、新聞は発行部数が多いことも原因して、多方面にいろいろ気を使わないといけない側面があるのです。だから、新聞報道は制限されます。	We cannot know everything by reading newspapers. In other words, newspaper companies have to be considerate of various sectors of the world because of their large circulation, and therefore, there will be a limitation in press reporting.
雑誌が新聞の書けない部分を担当するといってもいいでしょう。	We can say that magazines will take care of the area in which newspapers cannot adequately cover.
しかし、どのマスコミも、伝え方によって社会に悪影響を与える可能性があります。	However, any mass communication can exercise a negative influence on the society depending on how reporting is done.

やはり、正しく真実を、誇張することなく、伝えることが重要であるのは言うまでもありません。

It is needless to say that the truth should be reported accurately without exaggeration.

▶ マスコミといじめ　　　　　　　　　　CD 1 ➡ 66

学校におけるいじめは、現在における深刻な問題です。最近は、いじめによる自殺が頻繁に報道されています。

Bullying at school is a serious problem of our present age. There have been frequent broadcasts about suicides resulting from bullying recently.

テレビ局によっては、同じ情報を強調して何度も報道しがちで、皮肉にも、これが自殺の連鎖反応を起こしている気がします。
注：「自殺の連鎖」は copy-cat suicides とも表現できる。

Some TV stations tend to emphatically broadcast the same kind of information repeatedly. I kind of feel that this sort of broadcasting may ironically trigger a chain reaction of suicides.

マスコミは報道の内容と方法の両方に、気をつけるべきではないかと思います。

The press should be careful both in what they report and how they report it.

参考：いじめ問題は、1年に1クラスに数件は起こっていると思われるので、全国の小中高校では、小さないじめ問題まで含めたら年間1000万件ぐらいになり、一方、未成年の自殺者は300人ほどで、いじめによるものは、はっきりしていないものの30件ほどなので、このことを考えると、いじめイコール自殺というように即断できない。

cf. Since each class of primary, junior high or senior high school is thought to have several bullying problems a year, the total number of such problems might be about 10 million if we include the smaller ones. On the other hand, the annual number of the minors who commit suicide is about 300, out of which about 30 is concerned with bullying though the exact number is not clear. Considering the above situations, we cannot always relate bullying to suicide immediately.

マスコミにおける過激な報道は慎むべきだと私は思います。

I am of the opinion that overemphasized information should not be broadcast by mass communication organizations.

4 日本の国技…相撲

▶ 情報を伝える　　　　　　　　　　　　　　　　CD 1 ➡ 67

日本において、組み合う格闘技を総じて相撲と呼ぶことができる。だから、腕を組み合えば腕相撲、指を組み合えば指相撲となるのです。

In Japan, Sumo is a generic term for all the martial sports in which you grapple with each other. Therefore, Sumo with the use of arms is called arm wrestling, and the one with the use of fingers is called finger wrestling.

相撲はそもそも神事です。古事記には、神様同士の相撲的な記述があります。

Sumo was originally a divine ceremony. In *Kojiki*, or *The Record of Ancient Matters*, there is a description of Sumo between the two deities.

タケミナカタの神がタケミカヅチの神の腕をつかんで投げようとした記述があります。その際、タケミカヅチが手をツララに、さらに、剣に変えたため、つかめなかったとされています。

In the story, the deity called Takeminakata tried to throw another deity called Takemikazuchi. At the moment of the catch, Takemikazuchi suddenly changed his arm into an icicle and then a sword, which made the throw impossible.

ちなみに、タケミカヅチの神は、奈良の春日大社に祭られています。

Incidentally, Takemikazuchi is enshrined in the Kasuga Grand Shrine in Nara.

日本書紀には、神様ではなく人間同士の最古の相撲が記述されています。垂仁天皇7年7月7日（旧暦）に野見宿禰（ノミノスクネ）と当麻蹴速（タイマノケハヤ）の戦いです。

In *Nihonshoki*, or *The Chronicle of Japan*, there is a description of the oldest Sumo between humans. On the 7th day of the 7th month in the 7th year of Emperor Suinin, Nomi-no Sukune and Taima-no Kehaya fought.

宿禰は、相撲の始祖とされています。 注：始祖は他に次のような表現がある。 　→ the father、the founder、 　　the progenitor	Sukune is regarded as the originator of Sumo.
相撲は古くは大陸から渡来した葬送儀礼と、東南アジアから伝来した豊穣儀礼の2つの性格が交じり合ったものと考えられます。	Sumo is considered to be a mixture of the funeral ceremony derived from the continent and the harvest festival originating from Southeast Asia.

▶ 相撲の特徴について一歩進んで考える　　　　　　　　　　　CD 1 ➡ 68

相撲は、ほとんど裸で行われます。確かに着用するのはまわしのみです。	Sumo wrestlers wrestle almost naked. What they wear is only the loincloth.
神道的な発想では、裸という状態は、神聖で、神に近いと考えられます。だから、裸で生まれる赤ん坊は、神と同様、穢（けが）れがなく、神聖なものと考えられているのです。	In Shintoistic philosophy, the state of being naked is sacred; therefore it shows the Sumo wrestlers are closer to deities. That's why a baby born naked, of course, is considered sacred as a deity, who is free from evil.
子供の宮という漢字で書く「子宮」から生まれた神聖な赤ん坊は、まず世の中の汚れにさらされるので、生後7日目にその穢れをはらうため、神に清めてもらうことになります。 注：2行目のwhichの先行詞はa womb。 ※お宮参りは通例生後1ヶ月前後に行う。	The sacred baby born out of a womb, the Japanese word for which consists of Chinese characters: shrine of a child, is supposed to be taken to a shrine on the seventh day after birth, since he or she is contaminated with evil around this world after birth.
相撲がほとんど裸で行われるので、それ自体で神聖だとみなされます。	Since Sumo is performed naked, it is regarded as sacred in itself.
神を祭る日本のお祭りで、裸祭りが多いのは、裸が神聖だという考えによるものだと思います。	I think the reason why there are many nude festivals which enshrine deities in Japan is that nudity is divine.

裸祭りは、世界に例を見ないようです。アフリカの諸部族は、ほとんど裸で祭りが行われますが、裸を強調しているのではなく、通例、裸に色を塗るなりして、華麗さを目立たせているのです。

There seem to be almost no such naked festivals in the world as in Japan. It is true that some African tribes perform festivals almost naked. However, they don't emphasize their nudity, but highlight the pomp of their body by painting in many cases.

▶ 現代の相撲について感じるところを伝える　　　　CD 1 ➡ 69

近頃は、外国人が「相撲取り」になり、素晴らしい成果をあげている関取がいます。

These days foreigners become professional Sumo wrestlers and some of them are crowned with great success.

日本のしきたりに則って技を磨き、大関、横綱と昇進していくのは立派で、感動的でもあります。
参考:「大関」は champion、「横綱」は grand champion と訳せる。

The way they train themselves according to Japanese tradition and then get promoted gradually to Ozeki, or even to Yokozuna, is quite impressive and something that I take a lot of pride in.

その反面、日本人の相撲取りの成り手が少なくなったのでは？と寂しくなります。

On the other side of the coin, I feel a little shocked about the present situation where there are few Japanese who want to become Sumo wrestlers.

確かに、国技としての相撲に外国人が入り込んでいるのは、国際化が相撲業界にも押し寄せた結果でうれしいことではあるが、日本人の横綱がいてほしいという気持ちもあります。

It's true that the emergence of many foreigners in the field of Sumo as a national sport of Japan is creditable in the sense that internationalization has covered the Sumo world, but I feel there should be a Japanese grand champion.

5 野球とサッカー

▶ 野球に関する情報　　　　　　　　　　CD 1 ➡ 70

野球は、北米のアメリカ、カナダ、中南米のメキシコ、キューバ、ドミニカ、ニカラグア、パナマ、プエルトリコ、コロンビア、ベネズエラ、そして東アジアの台湾、韓国などで盛んです。

参考：ヨーロッパではサッカーのほうがずっと盛んです。

Baseball is popular in the U.S. and Canada in North America; Cuba, the Dominican Republic, Nicaragua, Panama, Puerto Rico, Colombia and Venezuela in Middle and South America; and countries like Taiwan and South Korea in East Asia.

cf. In Europe, football, which is called soccer in America, is much more popular.

野球の起源は、よく知られていませんが、英国の球技であるタウンボールがアメリカに持ち込まれて、それが変化発展したものだと言います。

Though the origin of baseball is not exactly known, it is generally believed that the Town Ball, a ballgame in England, was introduced into America and changed and developed.

ベースボールを「野球」と訳したのは、第一高等中学校（現在の東大教養学部）のベースボール部員の中馬庚（ちゅうまかなえ）氏で、1894 年刊行の部史にその言葉が現れます。

The person who first translated baseball into Japanese as "Yakyu" was Mr. Kanae Chuma, a member of the baseball club at Dai-ichi High Secondary School, presently the Liberal Arts Department of Tokyo University. The word appears in the club's history published in 1894.

野球（のぼーる）という雅号を用いた正岡子規が、翻訳したという俗説は誤りです。しかし、子規は野球用語を数多く翻訳した功績で、2002 年には殿堂入りを果たしています。

The popular explanation that Masaoka Shiki, who used a pen name of No-ball, translated the word baseball as Yakyu is wrong. However, Shiki entered the Sanctuary of Baseball because he rendered remarkable services to the cause of popularizing baseball through his many translations.

野球用品に対する出費は、2004年度は、990億円で、ゴルフに次いで、球技関連スポーツ用品の全出費の15%を占めています。しかし、全スポーツ用品（スキー、スケートや剣道用品も含まれる）に対する出費のわずか4.8%に当たるということです。

The total annual expenditure for baseball goods was 99 billion yen as of 2004, accounting for 15% of the total expense for the equipment for sports using balls and was second only to the amount spent for golf equipment. However, this baseball-related expense corresponds to only 4.8% of the total expenditure for all the sports, which include skiing, skating and Kendo.

参考 野球における和製英語

日本語の野球用語	正しい英語
ウイニングショット（決め球）	money pitch
オーバースロー（上手投げ）	overhand pitch cf. overthrowは「暴投」
オープン戦 （公式試合の前後の非公式試合）	preseason game / exhibition game
ゲームセット（試合終了）	The game is over.
ゴロ	ground ball
ショート（遊撃手）	shortstop（SS）
スタメン	starter
ストッパー（抑え投手［守護神］）	closer ［こちらのほうが普通］ cf. stopperはサッカーの用語
スピードボール（速球）	fastball cf. speedballは「コカインとモルヒネを混ぜた注射」と混乱するので避けたほうがよい。
スリーベース（三塁打）	triple
セーフティバント	a drag bunt
タイムリーヒット	an RBI single cf. RBI（=runs batted in）は「打点」
タッチアウト	tagged and out
チェンジ	end of inning / Inning is over.
デッドボール	hit by a pitch
トンネル	to let it go through one's legs
ノック	fungo
フォアボール（四球）	base on balls / a walk

実践編 第5章 文化・芸術・スポーツに関する意見を述べる

▶ サッカーに関する情報　　　　　　　　CD 1 ➡ 71

FIFA が認定している最古のサッカーは紀元前 206 年ごろの中国までさかのぼります。

The oldest soccer authorized by FIFA dates back to around 206 B.C. in China.

中世ヨーロッパの農村では、村同士で 1 つのボールを互いの村まで運ぶという遊びがあったといいます。

In the Middle Ages in Europe, between two farming villages, there was a game of carrying a ball from one village to the other and vice versa.

スポーツとしてのサッカーは、イングランドにおけるパブリックスクールが成立させたといわれています。

It is said that soccer was first established as a sport when public schools in England started playing the game.

ちなみにパブリックスクールは、その名に反して、公立学校ではなく、私立学校です。

By the way, public schools are not public but private in conflict with their name.

現在のサッカーの競技人口は、FIFA によると、世界全体で約 2 億 4 千万人とされています。

The population of soccer players is about 240 million in the world, according to FIFA.

▶ 野球とサッカーを比べる　　　　　　　　CD 1 ➡ 72

両スポーツとも、体と頭を使って競い合う楽しいスポーツです。

Both sports are really fun because both require physical strength and mind power.

両者を比べると、日本ではまだまだ野球の方がファンは多いように思えます。それだけ野球は日本に定着していると思います。

Comparing both, it seems to me that baseball has more fans in Japan than soccer. I think baseball is deeply rooted in Japan.

サッカーは、基本的には足を使うことを中心とするスポーツなので、明らかに足のスポーツといえますが、野球は、バッターの役割が大きいので、バットを握る手が重要となり、手のスポーツともいえると思います。	Since soccer centers basically on the use of feet, it is clearly defined as a sport of feet. But in baseball, the batter's role is important, which means the hand used for holding a bat is important; therefore, it is a sport of hands.
識者の中には、西洋を足の文化、日本を手の文化と規定している人がいます。私もその意見にある程度賛成です。	Some learned people say that the west belongs to the Foot Culture, and Japan to the Hand Culture, and I agree to some extent.
ヨーロッパやアメリカの歴史をひも解くと、民族や国民はよく動いています。	In European history, its races or peoples frequently moved.
参考：太古は狩猟文化が中心であったということもあり、古代のヨーロッパが足を重視する足の文化に属していたということに異論はないと思います。	cf. In ancient times, hunting culture formed the nucleus of the society. I am sure that there is no divergence of opinion about the insistence that ancient Europe belongs to the Foot Culture, which emphasizes the use of feet.
だから、スポーツの分野でも足のスポーツであるサッカーが盛んになったのです。	Therefore, in the field of sports, soccer, the sport of the foot, became popular.
正式にフットボールという点からも、サッカーはまさに足のスポーツということになります。	Soccer is the best example of a sport of the foot, since it is properly called football.
一方、日本は、やはり手の文化です。	On the other hand, Japanese culture falls under the Hand Culture.

足を使って大移動するようなことのない農耕文化を主とした日本では、手際よくボールを手で投げる投手から、上手に手でバットを振り、ヒットを飛ばす野球、つまり手のスポーツが人気を博したのもなんとなく分かります。

In Japan, where agrarian culture was central to its life in the past, there was not a great drift of the population. I sort of understand that in this kind of country, a "hand sport" like baseball has gained popularity, because it requires the skill of hands holding a bat to hit the ball.

参考 日本語における「手」の表現と、その英語

英語表現に hand（手）がほとんど用いられない点にも注意しましょう。
手紙 letter　手形 bill　手帳 pocket notebook　手本 model
手柄 merit　手際 skill　手心 consideration　手口 method
手品 a juggler's trick　手ほどき initiation　手ごたえ response
手さばき manipulation　手続き procedure　手数料 commission
手取り net income　手出し meddling　手掛かり clue　手違い mistake
手切れ金 a solatium for severing connections
手軽に easily　手近に close by　手堅く firmly
手ごわい tough　手っ取り早い prompt; rough and ready
手玉に取る lead a person by the nose
口八丁手八丁 excel in both speaking and writing
上手 skillful　下手 unskillful　切手 stamp

▶ 蹴ることについての面白い意見　　　　　　　　　　　　CD 1 ➡ 73

ボールを天に向けて蹴り上げることは、男性的なしぐさといえます。だから蹴鞠（けまり）は男性の貴族がたしなんだのではないでしょうか。

The act of kicking a ball toward heaven is regarded as a masculine gesture. Don't you think that Kemari, a game of kicking a ball upward, was enjoyed by noble men?

これに対し、ボールを地に落とす行為は、女性的で、だからこそ、手まりは女性が行います。

In contrast, the action of letting a ball hit the ground is feminine; that is the reason why women enjoy playing at bouncing a handball, which is called Temari.

一般に天に男性である神がいると考えるので、天は男性原理で、地球は命をはぐくむので、地は女性原理です。だから、天の父や、母なる自然という言葉があるのです。	Generally speaking, in mythology a male god exists in heaven, so heaven is masculine. The earth gives birth to living things, so it is feminine. This idea is supported by the existence of the phrases like Heavenly Father and Mother Nature.
蹴鞠は、ボールが天に向かうので、男性の遊び、手まりはボールを地に向けるので、女性の遊びなのです。	Kemari is for men because the ball goes up, while Temari is for women because the ball goes down to the earth.

参考 男性原理と女性原理

　　古来日本音楽の代表的楽器「笛と太鼓」については、男性原理と女性原理が、見事にうまく組み合わさっています。笛はその形状が攻撃性を暗示する男性原理で、太鼓は形状がふくよかさを暗示し女性原理ですが、笛から出る「音」(ね) は女性原理で、太鼓から出る「音」(おと) は男性原理です。「ね」という言葉は、「・・・ね」というと女性的、「おと」は男につながり男性的であるのは分かりますね。

　　翻訳：We can see elegant reciprocation of male and female principles in Japanese classical musical instruments: flutes and drums. Japanese flutes belong to the male principle in its shape suggestive of aggressiveness, and Japanese drums to the female principle in its shape indicative of plumpness. Moreover, the sound called 'ne' from the flutes corresponds to the female principle, and the sound called 'oto' from drums, to the male. Interestingly, 'ne' attached at the end of a sentence is feminine, and 'oto' part of the word meaning a man, otoko in Japanese, is of course masculine.

6 ノーベル賞とイグノーベル賞

▶ 情報を伝える --- その1（ノーベル賞）　　　CD 1 ➡ 74

ノーベル賞は、ダイナマイトの発明者として知られるアルフレッド・ノーベルの遺言に従って1901年に始まった世界規模の賞です。

The Nobel Prize is a worldly acknowledged prize which began in 1901 according to the will of Alfred Nobel, who is known as the inventor of dynamite.

ノーベル賞には、物理学賞、化学賞、生理学・医学賞、文学賞、平和賞、経済学賞の6部門があります。

The Nobel Prizes are classified into the following six sections: Nobel Prize in physics, Nobel Prize in chemistry, Nobel Prize in physiology or medicine, Nobel Prize for literature, Nobel Peace Prize, Nobel Memorial Prize in Economic Science.

最初の3部門は科学分野における最高の栄誉であると考えられています。

The winning of the first three sections is considered to be the greatest honor.

ノーベル平和賞は、政治家が受賞した場合には、賞の権威に対する毀誉褒貶（きよほうへん）が激しいという側面もあります。

When politicians get the Nobel Peace Prize, a variety of criticisms concerning the dignity of the prize may occur.

自然科学の大きな分野と言える数学にノーベル賞がないのは、ノーベル自身が知人の数学者を嫌っていたためなど、諸説があるが、詳細は不明です。

One of several reasons given for the absence of the prize in math, a major branch of natural science, is that Nobel himself hated a mathematician he knew; however, the truth is not known.

ビタミンB1の発見で、クリスティアーン・エイクマンがノーベル生理学・医学賞を受賞していますが、その栄養素の発見者は、日本の農学者であった鈴木梅太郎博士です。	Dr. Christiaan Eijkman was awarded with the Nobel Prize in physiology and medicine for the discovery of vitamin B1, but the actual discoverer of the nutrient is Dr. Umetaro Suzuki, an agriculturist in Japan.
彼の論文が日本語のみで書かれていたので、長い間欧米に知られていなかったのです。	Because his papers were written only in Japanese, his accomplishments had not been known for a long time by Westerners.
鈴木博士のビタミンB1の発見のきっかけとなったのは、日本人に最も身近な米の研究です。	The research on rice, one of the most familiar foods in Japan, led to Dr.Suzuki's discovery of the vitamin.
日本人では、湯川秀樹が1949年に物理学賞を受賞したのが初めてです。彼の受賞理由は、中間子の存在の予想です。	The first Japanese prize winner was Hideki Yukawa, who received the Nobel Prize in physics in 1949. The reason for his winning the prize was predicting the existence of mesons.

参考 ビタミンB１不足で起こる病気とその英語のつづり

> ビタミンB1不足で起こる病気の１つとして有名なのが脚気ですね。この英語は、２つのつづりの繰り返しです。他に繰り返すパターンの英語もついでに挙げておきましょう。
> 　　beriberi　脚気（かっけ）
> 　　bulbul　ヒヨドリ
> 　　agar-agar　寒天
> 　　tartar　1. 歯石　2. 酒石（ワインの発酵の際にたまる沈殿物）
> 　　pooh-pooh　…を軽くあしらう、馬鹿にする

参考 日本人のノーベル賞受賞者

年	物理学賞	化学賞	生理学 医学賞	平和賞	文学賞	経済学賞
2002	小柴 昌俊	田中 耕一				
2001		野依 良治				
2000		白川 英樹				
1994					大江 健三郎	
1987			利根川 進			
1981		福井 謙一				
1974				佐藤 栄作		
1973	江崎 玲於奈					
1968					川端 康成	
1965	朝永 振一郎					
1949	湯川 秀樹					

▶ 情報を伝える --- その2 （イグノーベル賞）　　　　CD 1 ➡ 75

イグノーベル賞 (Ig Nobel Prize) とは、「人々を笑わせ、そして、考えさせてくれる研究」に与えられる、ノーベル賞のパロディ的な賞です。Ig Nobel は「あさましい」という意味の ignoble と掛けています。

The Ig Nobel Prize is a parodical prize of the famous Nobel Prize. This prize is given to the research which makes us laugh and think. The words "Ig Nobel" pan on "Nobel" and "ignoble," which means not good or honest.

授賞式は毎年10月ハーバード大学で行われ、本物のノーベル賞受賞者たちも出席します。

The awarding ceremony is held at Harvard University in October every year. Some real Nobel Prize winners attend it.

この賞を不名誉と感じる受賞者もいますが、脚光のあたりにくい分野の地味で地道な研究に焦点を当て、科学の面白さを再認識させてくれるという点で、意味のある賞だと考える人もいます。	Though some people feel this prize is dishonorable, others think it is meaningful in the sense that it leads us to realize how interesting science is by focusing on some slow but steady study, or "sturdy" study, which is usually not in the limelight.
2006年の栄養学賞受賞者の受賞理由は、「フンコロガシが食べ物である糞の好みにうるさいことを説明したこと」であるとしています。	A reason for awarding the winner the prize in the science of nutrition is that he explained academically that dung beetles are particular about the types of dung they eat.
また、数学賞受賞者の受賞理由は、「集合写真を撮る際に誰も眼をつぶっていない写真を撮るためには、何人いる場合何枚取れば確実かを計算したこと」です。 参考：集合写真の中でも「記念写真」は、souvenir picture という。	The winner of the math prize is said to have been awarded because he calculated how many pictures should be taken and how many people should be in the picture if you want to insure that everybody's eyes are open.
日本人の受賞者と受賞理由を幾つか挙げましょう。	Let me introduce to you Japanese Ig Nobel prize winners and the reasons for their awards.
1997年に、経済学賞が「たまごっち」開発者に与えられ、授賞理由は「数百万人分の労働時間を仮想ペットの飼育に費やさせたこと」です。	The Economics Prize went to the inventor of Tamagocchi in 1997 and the reason for the award was the fact that the amount of the workloads of several million people was spent in growing a virtual pet.

2002年に、平和賞が犬語翻訳機「バウリンガル」の開発者に与えられ、授賞理由は、「人と犬に平和と調和をもたらしたこと」であったそうです。

In 2002, the Peace Prize was given to BOWLINGUAL, the translating machine of dogs' language, and the reason for the award is said to have been that it brought about peace and harmony for both humans and dogs.

2004年には、カラオケ発明者に対して、平和賞が与えられています。授賞理由は「カラオケが、人々が互いに寛容になる手段を提供した」ということです。マイクの取り合いで果たして寛容になるのかな？という気もしますが・・・。

In 2004, the inventor of Karaoke was awarded with the Peace Prize. The reason for the award was the fact that Karaoke offered the chance for people to be generous. I wonder if people will really become generous in case that they struggle for microphones.

最近では、2005年にドクター中松が栄養学賞を受賞しました。その理由の1つに、「35年間にわたり、自分の食事を写真に収め、3日前の食べ物が頭の働きや体調に影響を与えることを突き止めたこと」があります。

The recent winner was Dr. Nakamatsu, who won the prize for science in nutrition in 2005. One of the reasons for the award is that he took pictures of all the dishes he ate over the period of 35 years and detected the fact that foods eaten three days before would influence brain functions and bodily conditions.

第6章

科学・技術・コンピュータに関する意見を述べる

1 携帯電話の進化

▶ 情報を伝える　　　　　　　　　　　　CD 1 ➡ 76

大きなBOXで肩に掛ける携帯電話が、今や、手の平に納まるミニサイズになり、特定の人しか持たなかった物が、低学年に至るまで、皆が持っている今日この頃になりました。

The cellphone, once the size of a big box carried on our shoulder, has become very compact and can be held in a hand. And although they were once owned by a very limited number of people, almost everybody, even school children in the lower grades, has one now.

携帯を自宅に置き忘れた日は、丘の上に上がった河童のように感じます。

I will be like a fish out of water if I leave my cellphone at home.

ハンディーな携帯電話もこの10数年で急速に広がり1993年にはほんの3%ほどだった普及率は2003年には94%にまで伸びました。

Handy cellular phones have rapidly spread in the last 10 years, and its diffusion rate, which was 3% in 1993, is up to 94% in 2003.

生活は多方面で便利になっています。公衆電話では探さなければならないし、小銭がなければかけられない不便さがあります。ポケットベルも結局公衆電話に頼らなければなりません。
注：「小銭」は、small change だが small を省略できる。さらに、small money, loose money, broken money でも可。

They have made life easy for us in many areas. Pay phones, you have to look for, and they can't be used without change. The pager is useless without pay phones.

ビジネス社会では携帯電話は仕事の効率化、迅速化に大いに役立っています。

Cellular phones play a useful role in improving efficiency in the business world.

子どもが犠牲になる事件もニュースでよく見かけます。

Many cases where children are victims are reported.

自分の子がどこにいるのかいつも連絡を取れるようにしておくには携帯電話はいい手段です。子どもに持たしている親もけっこう多いです。	The cellular phone is a good way to keep track of your kid's whereabouts. Many parents have their children keep one these days.
今では携帯電話はEメールやインターネットの端末としての役割が重要です。	Another important role of the cellular phone is as a terminal for e-mail or the Internet.
そのほかにもゲーム、自動販売機の支払用の器具、カメラなどいろんな役割を果たしています。	Besides, it functions as a game console, a paying device for vending machines, a camera, etc.

▶ 携帯電話の害について   CD 1 ➜ 77

携帯電話の害もあります。	Cellular phones have their demerits.
電磁波の悪影響がそのひとつです。アメリカやヨーロッパでは1回に話す時間や、1日に使う回数が制限されているようです。	The bad effect of their electric magnetic waves is one of them. In the US and Europe, the period of time one talks at one time and the number of times one uses it in a day are restricted.
その影響で右脳の働きの低下やコミュニケーション能力が劣ってきているとも言われて大問題です。	It also, it's rumored, has the effect of slowing the function of the right brain and degrading communication skills. It's a serious problem.
また精密機械にも悪影響を与えるそうです。心臓のペースメーカーを狂わす可能性があるので、人ごみでの使用などには要注意です。	It's also known that it has a negative effect on precision machines. One has to be careful about its use in a crowd because it can cause pacemakers to run amuck.

109

飛行機内や病院内なども機器類を狂わすといけないので禁止になっています。	They are also prohibited on airplanes and in hospitals where they can interfere with machines.
機器への影響は確実に証明されたものではないという声もあります。	Some say they haven't been proven to have a bad effect on machines.
しかし、危険の可能性があるのなら使用は控えるのが賢明な選択です。	But it would be wise to refrain from using it, if there is the slightest chance of danger.
公共の場所での電話での話し声は意外に気にさわるものでもあります。	The sound of telephone talk in public places is unexpectedly annoying.
マナーの問題が大きいのですが、その最たるものが運転中の携帯電話の使用です。	Manners are in question. The worst of it is the use of the cellular phone while driving.
携帯電話を探したり、かけたりする動作は著しく運転の集中力を低下させるのでやめるべきです。	It must be avoided because looking for the phone or using it distracts one while driving.

▶ 携帯電話のこれからを論じる　　　　　　　　　　　CD 1 ➡ 78

携帯電話の果たす役割は現在多岐にわたり、現代人にはなくてはならないものになっています。	Cellular phones play a range of roles and are indispensable for the people today.
電車に乗っても必ず何人かの人が携帯電話を操作しています。電車で電話として使用するのはマナー違反ですが。 注：マナーは manner ではなく、manners	For example, on the train you always see some people use them, though it's a violation of manners to phone on the train. cf. manners の代わりに social rules も OK。

110

携帯電話の進化によって人の生活スタイルが大きく変わっているのは事実です。	It's true that the development of the cellular phone has changed our lifestyles.
これが吉とでるか、凶とでるかは今のところわかりません。	It remains to be seen whether it is for the better or the worse.
少なくとも携帯電話がなかった時期に戻るのはもう難しいようです。	The least I can say is that it's nearly impossible to go back to pre-cellular phone times.
最近のソフトバンクモバイルの申し込み殺到による受付の停滞に見られるように、多くの人が利用するものなので、少しの障害が社会に大打撃を与えます。	As seen in the case of the current SoftBank Mobile temporary reception malfunction after people rushed to apply, cellular phones are used by a great many people, so even if something small goes wrong, it can inflict an enormous damage on the society.
そういうことを見通しながら賢く利用していかなければなりません。	Let's make the most of the cellular phone with the above in mind.

2 メールとインターネット

> 利点や欠点を考える　　　　　　　　　　　　CD 1 ➡ 79

メールは、通常電話ができない夜中とか相手が忙しい時間帯に、相手に情報を伝えることができるので便利です。	E-mailing is convenient because we can send messages during the late night when you cannot telephone the other party or in cases when he or she is busy.
電話では直接言えないようなことも、メールの形だと言いやすいという側面もあります。	We can point out that email makes it easy for us to directly say things which may be hard to say by phone.
しかし、人が出会って話すようには相手に通じず、表現不足で誤解を招くことも時々あります。	However, we cannot communicate so well as we meet, sometimes ending up misunderstanding each other.
携帯電話の問題でもあるのですが、公共の場所や乗りもの内でメール、インターネットをする人が増えています。	It could also be a problem of the cellular phone. An increasing number of people are doing e-mail and Internet in public places.
人間関係の減少、質の低下は社会的問題です。	The weakening and degrading of interpersonal relationships are a social problem.
外に出て物理的に人と接しても、直接のコミュニケーションは一切ないという状況が見られます。みんなインターネットやメールに没頭しているからです。恐い気がします。	People go out and mingle physically but don't communicate directly at all, because everyone is absorbed in the Internet or e-mail, which is horrifying.
インターネットのいいところは、どんなところにいても、いろんな情報を得られることです。	What's good about the Internet is you can get information about things anywhere.

どこで映画を見ることができるか。安い車は手に入るか。新しい本はいくらか。とかどんな情報でも手に入ります。	Where can I see the movies? Are cars available at reasonable prices? How much is the new book? Whatever info you want is available.
また、自分が知りたいことを質問することもできます。例えば医学のことで知りたければ、医学に関する掲示板を探して質問をすればいいのです。	You can ask about whatever you want to know about. For example, to learn about medicine, you go to a bulletin board about medicine and ask a question.
ただ、簡単に誰もが入り込めるし、自分から情報を流せるので情報が氾濫して、ほしい情報にたどり着くのに時間がかかりすぎてしまうという問題はあります。各種の検索エンジンは情報の整理をし選択しやすい努力はしていますが、なかなか満足できるものができるにはまだ数年かかるでしょう。	Anyone can have easy access to it and post info onto it, which causes it to be flooded with info. As a result, it takes too long a time to get what you want. Search engines work hard to place information in good order, making it easier to get, but I think it will take another several years to satisfy many people.
コンピュータウイルスは最悪です。今では大切な情報をコンピュータに保存している人はたくさんいます。その情報を破壊されてしまってはパニックです。大企業から色々な学校までコンピューターによるところが大きい時代です。	Computer viruses are bad news. Now many people keep precious information in their computers. They'd panic if it's destroyed. Everyone from large firms to all kinds of schools rely much on computers nowadays.
コンピュータそのものがそうですが、とりわけインターネットは諸刃の剣の部分があると感じています。生活は非常に便利になりますが、一度何かが狂うと取り返しのつかないことになるということです。例の 2000 年問題はその一例だと思います。 参考：Y 2 K は Year 2 kilo が語源	The Internet is a kind of a double-edged sword, not to mention the computer itself. It makes life convenient for us, but if something goes wrong, then all goes wrong. I think that it makes it very difficult to recover the information. The "Y2K" problem was just one example.

メール・インターネット社会の課題について語る

メールは、作業を簡略化します。例えば仲間に伝言を伝えるのに電話やファックスだと伝える人の数だけの操作をしなければなりませんが、メールだと一度で済みます。	E-mail simplifies work. For example, with telephone or fax, a telephone is needed for everyone that you want to communicate with. But with e-mail one can send info to many people at once.
同時に費用も低く抑えられます。また、速度も速いし、何よりもコンピュータ上で作成した物、文章、図面、表など、そのまま即相手に送ることができます。	And the cost is low and it's fast, and above all, you can send things you create on your computer such as sentences, figures, charts, etc.
一度に無制限の人のコンピュータ端末に情報を送れるので、コマーシャル媒介としても有効です。	Since one can send info to an indefinite number of computer terminals at once, it's quite useful as a medium of advertisement.
ゆえに知らない人でも他人のアドレスさえ手に入れば情報を送れるので、いわゆる迷惑メールが増えます。	Thus if one only gets someone's address, one can send an email to that person, and it causes the number of spam e-mails to increase.
迷惑メールに関してはウィルス対策関係のソフトなどと同様に制限するソフトがあるようですが、法の面からも統制していくべきと思います。	As for spamming, very much like anti-virus software, there are software programs that bar spam emails, but I hope authorities prohibit them by law, too.
情報を入手するかしないかはあくまで受け取る個人に任せられるべきです。	It should be up to the individual whether or not to receive info.

法律で罰せられる可能性が出てくると自由な情報の行き来を妨げ、表現の自由などにも関わる問題になります。	With the possibility of being punished, one would feel it difficult to send info, hampering a free exchange of info, which could be a problem in terms of freedom of expression.
中国などの全体主義国家ではインターネットやメールは反体制分子がコミュニケーションの道具として使うことを恐れて政府はネット上での政府批判などに対して制限をかける方向です。	In totalitarian countries like China, the governments are afraid that dissidents will use the Internet and email as a medium of communication, so they try to inhibit anti-government comments on the net.
インターネットの発達は中国経済の発展にとっても歓迎するべきことでしょうが、反面あまりに自由に意見の交換ができて、政府にとっては諸刃の剣のようです。	Development of the Internet should be welcomed by China in terms of economic advancement, but at the same time it allows a free exchange of views. It is a double-edged sword for the government.
これは自由主義社会でも似た面があります。最近アメリカで政府関係のサイトで核爆弾を製作する方法が誤って掲載されてしまったニュースもありました。	A similar problem is observed in free countries too. Recently in the US, in a state-run site, a manual of how to make nuclear explosives was posted by mistake.

▶ 結論を述べる　　　　　　　　　　　　　　　　　　　　　　　　CD 1 ➡ 81

どんなに科学技術が発展しても、常に人間が冷静で賢く技術を利用するようにならなくてはなりません。	We, human beings, have to stay wise and in control of technology, no matter how developed it might be.
技術に翻弄され、将来自分を失う人間が増えることを心配しています。	I'm worried the day may come when people will be controlled by technology and lose their individuality.

3　遺伝子操作

▶ 情報を伝える　　　　　　　　　　　　CD 1 ➡ 82

遺伝子操作というとクローン人間ということがすぐ頭に浮かびますが、必ずしもそういう未来のフィクションばかりの話ではありません。

We tend to associate human cloning with gene manipulation. But it's not always a fictitious futuristic story like that.

天然災害によって不作の年があると食糧不足になったりしますが、遺伝子組み換えによって冷害、水不足など各種の災害に耐えうる植物をつくり、食糧不足の解消に役立ちます。

When a natural disaster hits, we can suffer a food shortage. By splicing genes we can produce plants tolerant of problems such as cold weather and water shortages, which should help solve the food shortage.

医療では現在臓器移植の問題がありますが、自分の細胞を使って自分の臓器を補足することも可能になるでしょう。

Now the medical world faces the problem of organ transplants. It will be possible to provide a new organ grown from your own cells.

また遺伝子操作ではガンやその他の難病を将来治すことができると言われています。

With gene manipulation it's said that difficult diseases like cancer could be cured in the future.

植物を遺伝子操作し、環境の汚染に対応していく考えもあるそうです。

There's also a plan to reduce environmental contamination by manipulating genes of plants.

▶ 遺伝子の技術への期待　　　　　　　　CD 1 ➡ 83

遺伝子の技術で期待するところはガンの克服です。

Gene technology can very likely help cure cancer.

今までにこの死の病気ガンに対する研究は多くなされてきて、克服できる率も上がってきてはいるようですが、決定的なものはないようです。	There have been many research studies on this deadly disease, and the recovery rate has been rising. Yet we still don't have a perfect cure.
ガンは自分自身の一部が変化する病気なので外科手術、化学療法や放射線では自分自身も痛めてしまう可能性があります。	Cancer is caused by the transformation of cells inside your body; therefore external treatments such as surgery, chemotherapy and radiation can hurt you.
遺伝子を使った治療では、自分自身の体組織を取り出し、その遺伝子を操作してガンに強い組織に変えて体にもどします。そしてガン細胞を撲滅する。これは期待できそうな気がします。	In gene therapy, first you pick up your own body tissue and splice its genes to change it into one resistant to cancer and replace it in your body. Then cancer is gone. I think you can count on it.
同じように今まで不治だった病気が治せるようになるのではないかと期待します。	In the same way I hope other incurable diseases could be treated and cured.

▶ 遺伝子操作の危険性　　　　　　　　　　　　　　　CD 1 ➡ 84

遺伝子操作は人間の領域ではないと思います。	Gene manipulation is something which must not be done by humans.
思い上がった人間のすることで、遺伝子操作が進展すれば、人類の破滅にも繋がりかねません！	This shows how arrogant humans are as a species. There is a danger that if gene manipulation progresses, the human species could become extinct in the future.
遺伝子操作が恐れられるのは生殖系細胞における場合でしょう。	Gene manipulation is most fearsome when applied to reproductive cells.

異常な機能や欠損した機能を修復するための治療的な遺伝子操作は問題ないが、クローン人間作りや、強化型戦闘員を作るための遺伝子操作はやめてもらいたいです。

Therapeutic use of it is welcome for purposes to fix abnormal or missing functions, but stop the research to create human clones or strengthen soldiers!

また国家が介入して優性遺伝子のみを使用して子孫をふやすというような操作も恐いです。
参考:遺伝学における「優性」は dominance

It would also be horrifying if the government picked out dominant genes and used them to create super humans.

まだまだ議論が必要です。

Further discussions are needed.

表現のコツ 「議論」を用いた印象的な表現

議論が沸騰しました。
→ The debate was in a ferment.
議論が紛糾しました。
→ Contending voices were heard on all sides.
その問題については議論が分かれています。
→ Opinion is divided on this issue.
そんな議論ではだめですね。
→ The way you argue does not hold water.
議論百出してうまく結論に至らなかった。
→ We could not come to a successful conclusion due to endless disputes.
そのことで議論に花が咲いた。
→ That occasioned hot discussion.

4 宇宙開発

▶ 情報を伝える　　　　　　　　　　CD 1 ➡ 85

初期の宇宙開発は米ソの競争の中で発展しました。	Early space exploration developed in the race between the USA and the USSR.
1957年に旧ソ連は人類初の人工衛星スプートニクの打ち上げに成功しました。	In 1957, the then Soviet Government successfully launched the first artificial satellite "Sputnik" in history.
その後も米ソを中心に月探査機や惑星探査機が送られたり、有人飛行を試みたりと宇宙開発は進みました。	After that, space exploration progressed as both the USA and the USSR launched lunar and planet probes, and began launching manned flights.
1961年には旧ソ連がガガーリンを乗せた史上初の有人宇宙船ボストーク1号を打ち上げます。	1961 saw the then USSR launch Vostok 1 with Gagarin on it, the first manned space flight in history.
1969年アメリカのアポロ11号が月に到着しアームストロングらが人類で始めて月面を歩きました。	In 1969 America's Apollo 11 landed on the moon and Armstrong and the other crew members became the first humans to walk on the moon.
1970年頃から米ソは一国では多額の費用を費やす宇宙開発は難しいと考え、協調の方向に向かいます。	Around 1970, both countries, finding space exploration too costly for one country to continue, leaned toward cooperation.
今ではアメリカにヨーロッパ、日本、カナダ、それにロシアといった国々が参加し、国際宇宙ステーション（ISS）の建設が行われています。	Now, construction of the international space station is under way, joined by the USA, European countries, Japan, Canada and Russia.

| これからの宇宙開発は、人類共通の大きな事業となっていくのです。 | Space exploration of the future is a huge project for all mankind. |

▶ 宇宙開発に関する意見　　　　　　　　CD 1 ➡ 86

| 米ソが宇宙開発競争をしている時代は戦略的な意味が大きかったと思います。ロケットの発射はミサイルの発射と密接に関係しています。 | The space exploration race between the USA and the USSR had much strategic meaning. Rocket launching had much to do with missile launching. |

| また宇宙から人工衛星を使って他国を偵察することも可能です。 | It's possible to spy on other countries using an artificial satellite. |

| 現在は国際協調に重点が置かれています。全人類発展のために宇宙開発が進むことを願います。 | Importance is placed on international cooperation today. I hope space exploration will progress for the development of the whole of mankind. |

| かつてコロンブスやバスコダガマが新大陸を求めて大海原を航海したように、宇宙に新地を求めて旅立つのは人間の本分でもあります。 | Like Columbus or Vasco da Gama who sailed the oceans looking for a new land, it's human nature to go to space looking for a new world. |

| 実際の宇宙開発に直接関係ありませんが、ホーキング博士に代表される理論物理の世界の宇宙研究も目の離せない興味深いものです。 | Although not directly related to physical exploration, the field of theoretical physics represented by Dr. Hawking keeps attracting our attention. |

| この分野の研究で、ブラックホールやワープによる宇宙旅行などが予想されています。 | In this field of study, black holes, warp travel and the like have been conceived and predicted. |

宇宙開発の費用の問題

費用のかかることでもあるので、他の分野の事柄の進展をさまたげてでも促進するべきではないとの批判もあります。

There are criticisms that since it's costly, you should not promote it at the expenses of the development of other things.

宇宙開発は膨大な費用がかかるので、今の段階ではまだ他分野にお金をかけるべきだという意見があります。例えば医療、エネルギー源の開発、地球温暖化など環境変化への対応、恒久的平和の確立、貧困の廃絶など地球規模で費用をさかなければならない項目はたくさんあります。

Because space exploration costs are enormous at the moment, the money should be spent on other areas such as medicine, development of energy sources, measures against environmental anomalies like global warming, establishment of permanent peace, and the eradication of poverty, which would require a large sum of money on a global scale.

宇宙開発に対する肯定的意見

人類がもし半永久的に繁栄し続けるなら宇宙開発は絶対に避けて通れないものと思います。

If humans are to advance forever, space exploration is a must.

いずれは宇宙へと人類の住処を求めていかなければならないでしょう。

Sooner or later we would have to set out for space seeking new habitats.

実際に人類は月に立ち、地球軌道上で各種の研究をするようになりました。

In fact, man set foot on the moon and conducted a variety of experiments on the earth's orbit.

また、アメリカの飛ばした宇宙船は土星、冥王星など宇宙の果てと考えられていた惑星の調査データも送ってきて、なお宇宙を旅しています。

And a space craft the U.S. launched has sent us data on Saturn, Pluto and the other planets, which had been thought to be the end of the universe, and is still traveling in space.

テレビドラマ「スタートレック」のようにいつか人類が宇宙を飛び回る時代が来るでしょう。	The time is sure to come when people will travel freely in space like in the TV drama "Star Trek."
この夢が人類を進歩させるのです。	Such a dream drives humans forward.
宇宙開発は人類発展の起爆剤です。	Space exploration is the detonator of human development.

表現のコツ 「起爆剤となる」を表現する

> 動詞の trigger が使用できます。
> この事件が革命の起爆剤となった。
> → This incident triggered a revolution.

5　生物の不思議

▶ 動物のトリビア的情報を伝える　　　　　　　　　　　CD 1 ➡ 89

モグラはかなりの大食漢で、1日に自分の体重と同じ分量を食べます。さらに、10時間以上食べないと飢え死にします。	A mole is a big eater which eats its weight in food every day. Moreover, it will starve to death if it is kept from eating for ten hours.
象の鼻は4万本の筋肉からできています。さらに、においをかぐ能力は犬よりも優れているといわれています。	The elephant's trunk is made up of 40,000 strings of muscles. Furthermore, its sense of smell is said to be far greater than that of a dog.
マッコウクジラの脳は9キロもあり、人間の1.4キロに比べると、約7倍の重さです。しかし、脳の重さを体重で割ってみると、0.00018となり、この数値は人間の場合の約200分の1です。	The brain of a sperm whale weighs 9 kg, and in comparison with the weight of a 1.4 kg human brain, it will be about seven times heavier. However, the weight of the whale's brain divided by its whole weight is only 0.00018, which corresponds to one two-hundredth of the human brain.
ハリセンボンという魚が存在します。この魚の針の数を数えた人がいました。実際には、千本ではなく、612本でした。	A porcupine fish is called Hari-senbon, literally translated as 1,000 needles. A person once counted its needles, whose number actually totaled 612, not 1000.
魚にも珍名さんはたくさんいます。オジサンというひげの生えた魚や、タコノマクラというとげのない海胆（ウニ）が存在しています。	Many fishes have unique names. For example, there is the Ojisan (bearded man), or Takono-makura (octopus's pillow), which is a needleless sea chestnut.

参考 海の生物を表すユニークな英語

雲丹（ウニ）　sea urchin、sea chestnut
水母（クラゲ）　jellyfish　　ヒトデ　starfish
イソギンチャク　sea anemone　タツノオトシゴ　sea horse

▶ 植物のトリビア的情報を伝える　　　　　　　　　　CD 1 ➡ 90

ヘチマは江戸時代初期に中国から渡来しました。	A sponge cucumber was introduced from China in the early Edo period.
ヘチマは漢字では「糸瓜」と書きます。	The sponge cucumber is written in Chinese characters, which literally mean thread cucumber, or Ito-uri in Japanese.
もともと、文字通りイトウリと呼ばれていましたが、トウリと呼ばれるようになりました。	It was originally Ito-uri in Japanese, and gradually came to be called Touri, which is similar in sound to Ito-uri.
この言葉の最初の「と」は、いろは歌では、「へ」と「ち」の間にあります。だから、「へ」と「ち」の「間」（マ）ということで、ヘチマと名づけられたということです。	The first letter of the word Touri, "To", is between "he" and "chi" in the classical Japanese alphabet song called Iroha-uta. Therefore, it is called Hechima, which means "between 'he' and 'chi.'"
江戸時代の人たちの洒落が生み出した言葉なのです。	This is a word made by the sophisticated wit of the Edo people.
話は変わりますが、門松は、めでたい植物である松竹梅からできています。 注：「話は変わるわけではないが」といって話を変える。	Not to change the subject, Kadomatsu, or the New Year's bamboo decoration, is made up of auspicious plants called Sho-chiku-bai, or pines, bamboos and Japanese apricots.

竹が目立ちますが、松の枝や梅の小枝も使用されています。	The bamboo is outstanding but pine branches or plum sprigs are also used.
松は陽木の長、竹は陽草の長、梅は陽花の長といわれています。	Pines, bamboos and Japanese apricot trees are the heads of yang trees, yang grasses and yang flowers respectively.
松竹梅は、偶然、植物の主要な3分類をまとめた表現です。松は裸子植物、竹は被子植物単子葉類、梅は被子植物双子葉類に属するので、植物学的にも、松竹梅は、釣り合いの取れたセットとなります。	Sho-chiku-bai is coincidentally the set of three main categories of plants. Pines, bamboos and Japanese apricot trees are classified as gymnosperms, monocotyledons and dicotyledons respectively. Therefore, botanically, Sho-chiku-bai is a well-balanced set of plants.

参考 植物の「珍名さん」

> もっとも短い名前 → 「イ」 畳表に使う藺草（イグサ）のこと、英語ではrush
> もっとも長い名前 → 「リュウグウノオトヒメノモトユイノキリハズシ」で21文字。
> 変わった名前 → 「バクチノキ」「クシャミノキ」「ショウベンノキ」「ボロボロノキ」「ナンジャモンジャノキ」「アイヌソモソモ」「ママコノシリヌグイ」「クソカズラ」「ウナギツカミ」「ブタノマンジュウ」など枚挙に暇がない。

表現のコツ 「枚挙に暇がない」を表現する

> 「枚挙に暇がない」という表現も、実はいろいろあり、枚挙に暇がないのですが、そのいくつかを挙げてみましょう。
> → be too many to mention
>   be too numerous to mention
>   there is really no end to the list of ...
>   it is virtually impossible to exhaust the list of ...
> ちなみに上の「参考」で挙げた、「変わった名前」のところは、次のように英訳をスタートできるのです。
> → Though it is virtually impossible to exhaust the list of strange plant names, let me show some of them:

6　20年後の科学の進歩を予想する

▶ 一般的に予想されていることを伝える　　　　　　　　　　CD 1 ➡ 91

ロボット化が進んで、一家に一台ロボットが存在していると予想されています。	It is expected that the progress in robotization will result in each family having one robot.
ロボットは、家の中を自由に動き回り、色々な仕事をします。	This robot will move freely around the home, doing various kinds of jobs.
例えば、朝には家族全員の健康チェックをします。ロボットの頭の上に手を置けば、簡単なチェックができるのです。	For example, each morning it will check the health condition of each family member. Just by putting your hand on the robot's head, quick physical exams will be possible.
ロボットは、その健康状態に最適の食事のメニューを考えて、ネットワーク化された、台所機器に命令します。	The robot will find out the most suitable menu for each health condition and give orders to the kitchen equipment network.
食べ物は、簡単なものなら、全自動で調理されます。複雑な調理はロボットが担当します。	The equipment will be able to easily cook simple meals automatically. More complicated cuisine will be prepared by the robot.
ロボットは、料理のほかに、掃除や洗濯その他の仕事をします。	This robot will do many other jobs like cleaning the house or washing clothes.

▶ バーチャルリアリティについての情報　　　　　　　　　　CD 1 ➡ 92

聴覚の分野では、録音などを通じてCDやラジオやテレビ番組で、いろいろな音を再現することが可能になっています。	In terms of the sense of hearing, it is now possible to reproduce various sounds through CDs or radio and to record TV programs.

視覚については、人類はテレビやビデオ、さらにはＤＶＤなどを発明し、あたかも本物を見ているが如き体験ができます。	As for the sense of sight, humans invented TV, videos and DVDs, which make it possible for us to experience the virtual reality of looking at pictures that almost seem quite real.
そのほかの感覚について、本物の体験と変わらないというバーチャルリアリティは、これから発展すると思います。	A virtual reality related to the other senses may be possible in the future.
コンピュータで予め、必要な情報を入力しておくと、自然のある場面における匂いを再現できる可能性があります。	There is a future possibility of any smell being reproduced in the suitable situation if all the necessary data were entered into a computer.
例えば、匂いを合成できる薬品を複数置いておき、適切なコンピュータプログラムにより匂いを合成するわけです。	For example, several chemicals which can synthesize smells could be stored in the computer so that any smell could be produced instantly through proper programs.
これを応用すれば、例えば、テレビで焼肉パーティの映像が出ると、本当に焼肉の香りがするというテレビを開発できるということになるでしょう。	The application of this system could make it possible for us to enjoy the same smell of grilled beef as in the scene of a barbecue party in a TV program. This kind of virtual reality TV may be possible in the future.
さらに、触覚のバーチャルリアリティも研究が進められていると聞きます。 注：「触覚」は the sense of touch のほかに、tactual sense、tactile sensation ともいえる。	Moreover, I hear that there have been some virtual reality research projects on the sense of touch.

例えば、手を触れると、本物を触った感触が得られるというような仕組みの研究です。

For instance, the mechanism in which we can feel real things without actually touching them when we put our hand onto something is a theme of some research.

▶ 科学の発達に関する意見　　　　　　　　　　　　　　CD 1 ➡ 93

極端な予想としては、20年後、自動車が空を飛んでいるというものがあります。

A rather extreme expectation in the future is that in 20 years cars may be flying.

このことは笑い飛ばすことはできません。というのは、我々は20年前、今のような、メールができ、インターネット接続ができ、写真が撮れ、テレビが映り、テレビ電話が可能という多機能携帯電話が出現するなどとは思わなかったからです。

We cannot laugh the idea away, because few people ever predicted today's situations where by means of even one portable phone, we can e-mail somebody, have easy access to the Internet, take pictures, enjoy watching TV and talk by video phone.

思いもよらないことが20年後起こっていても不思議ではないのです。

We cannot say in our modern age that it is unusual to have something in 20 years that never occurred to most of us.

しかし、なんでもかんでも世の中が便利になりすぎると、問題が生じるのではないかと心配になります。

However, I am worried that serious problems will occur if everything becomes too convenient in our lives.

その問題は2つの側面から論じることができます。

We can discuss this issue from two different perspectives.

1つは、人間そのものに関することです。簡単に言えば、人間が怠け者になるということです。

One is related to humans themselves. In short, we will become lazy with a capital L.

2つ目は、自然環境に関する問題です。便利になればなるほど、地球を汚すことになります。地球環境がおかしくなり、天変地異が起こる可能性があります。
注：天変地異は、説明的には extraordinary phenomena in heaven and earth、詩的には the disturbances of the elements といえる。

The second problem refers to our natural environment. The more convenient the world becomes, the more contaminated the earth becomes. This may cause natural disasters.

現在でも、温暖化やオゾン層破壊、大気汚染、水質汚染など、自然環境の悪化は深刻です。

In our modern age, the environment is seriously damaged. We can name many examples like global warming, ozone depletion, air pollution, and water pollution.

我々は、常に冷静に物事を判断し、残された諸問題を解決し、より良い未来を創造することを第一に考える必要があるでしょう。

We need to give top priority to a creation of a better future through constant calm attitudes we take to think about how to solve residual problems.

表現のコツ　with a capital ... の表現

「with a capital ＋文字」で、その文字から始まる単語の意味を強調するイディオムをつくります。

彼は馬鹿正直だ。
→ He is honest with a capital H.
彼女は根っからの保守主義者だ。
→ She is a conservative with a capital C.

第7章

教育問題に関する意見を述べる

1 小学校の英語教育

▶ 早期英語教育の情報と賛成意見を伝える　　CD 2 ➡ 01

語学教育は一般的に早く開始すればより効果的だといわれています。	Generally, it's said the earlier one begins to learn a foreign language, the more efficient it is.
最近では小学校でも英語教育が取り入れられるところがあり、外国人の講師が会話などを教室で指導するケースもあるようです。	Recently, some elementary schools have adopted English lessons and in some cases foreign teachers teach conversation in the classroom.
小学生くらいの子どもは発音などに対して非常に素直でアメリカ人先生の発音を非常に早く吸収します。	Kids at the primary school level take to things like pronunciation naturally so they pick it up very quickly.
だから、私は早期英語教育に賛成です。	Therefore, I support early English education for children.
英語が国際的に使用されている重要な言語であることも、見逃せない事実です。	The fact that English is now used worldwide is also an important undeniable fact.

▶ 日本語こそ重要という意見があることを述べる　　CD 2 ➡ 02

小学生時代にはもっと日本語自体の能力を先に高めるべきだという意見もあります。ただでも日本語が乱れているといわれる時代なのでなおさらですね。	Another opinion is that in primary school children should improve their Japanese first. This is a valid point, given the fact that many Japanese don't mind speaking messy Japanese.
現状の中学からの開始で充分という論もあります。	One theory is it's early enough if one starts in secondary school like now.

開始は現行でいいが、ただ方法は変えて文法、単熟語暗記式の学習から口語、コミュニケーション中心の方法に変えていくべきだという意見もあります。

Another opinion is that starting English in secondary school is OK, but that the method should change from the current teaching style centering on memory of grammar and words and phrases to the one emphasizing oral practice and communication.

▶ 早期英語教育について思うこと　　　　　　　　　　CD 2 ➡ 03

どちらにせよ、学校での英語学習はもっと実用性を重視したものにするべきです。

In either case, more importance should be placed on practical English.

近い内に日本も外国人の流入は避けられない日が来るでしょう。ある程度の英語を話せることは日本人の生き残りにもかかってきます。

In the near future there is expected to be an influx of foreigners into Japan. Japanese survival depends partly on whether we learn to speak some English or not.

できるだけ早い時期に英語に慣れることは悪いことではありません。

It can never be bad to familiarize yourself with English early.

▶ 早期英語教育に対する反論　その1　　　　　　　　CD 2 ➡ 04

英語が唯一の国際語ではありません。早期学習に反対はないが、選択の余地のあるものにすべきです。

English is not the only international language. I'm not against an early start, but I'd suggest students be given choice.

つまり、早期学習は奨励しても学習そのものは学校以外の外部に任せます。

To be more precise, though school should encourage an early start, they should leave the lesson up to an outside entity.

例えば英会話学校などに安く入れるようにする。それを受けるかどうかは個人の自由がいいです。	For example, they could see to it that a student can enter an English conversation school at a reduced rate. And it's up to each student whether they take it or not.

▶ 早期英語教育に対する反論　その２　　　　　CD 2 ➡ 05

英語教育の早期導入が受験競争の低年齢化をもたらすのではないかと心配です。	I suspect that the early introduction of English teaching may bring about severe competition for entrance exams at an early stage.
ビジネスに利用されない真の国際化を念頭に置いた英語学習の早期化なら、何が何でも反対ということはありません。	I am not totally against the early start of English, if it is elaborately planned under the concept of true internationalization without being capitalized on by business.

▶ 早期英語教育に対する反論　その３　　　　　CD 2 ➡ 06

早期英語教育という理念自体は良いことなので賛成します。	Early English education is good in itself, so I agree with it.
しかし、現在の状況では、実施がほぼ不可能です。	However, it is impossible to implement early English education at the moment.
その理由は、３つあります。	There are three main reasons for it.
１つは、実力のある日本人英語教員が不足している点です。	One reason is the lack of Japanese English teachers skillful at communicating in English.

2つ目は、外国人教員を大量に採用することが、人材不足に加え、採用にコストもかかるという点です。	The second reason is the estimated high cost of employing foreign teachers in addition to the shortage of staff.
3つ目に、他の教育が犠牲になるということです。英語教育を受けている間は、他の学習ができなくなるからです。	The third reason is that this will sacrifice the teaching of other subjects. This is because other lessons are physically impossible to offer while English classes are being given.

表現のコツ 「犠牲」を用いた表現

> 彼は公共の利益のために自己の利益を犠牲にするタイプの人だ。
> → He is the type of person who sacrifices his personal interest for the public good.
> 彼女は休暇を犠牲にして、仕事を仕上げました。
> → She made the sacrifice of her vacation in order to finish her work.
> cf. She sacrificed her vacation in order to finish her work. のほうが普通。
> その研究者は、かなりの犠牲を払ってその研究を深めた。
> → The researcher went deep into the study of it at a considerable sacrifice.
> 上司は会社の改善のために尽くしたというが、自分を犠牲にしたのだろう。
> → Our boss says that he devoted himself to the betterment of the company but I feel that he victimized himself after all.

2 大学における教育

▶ 情報を伝える　　　　　　　　　　　　　　　　　　　　　CD 2 ➡ 07

大学とは、学術の中心として、広く知識を授け、深く専門の学芸を教授・研究するための学校です。	A college is a school where we are given general education and technical skills based on research programs as an academic center.
日本では 1877 年（明治 10）に、国立大学として東京大学が初めて設立されました。	Tokyo University, established in the 10th year of the Meiji era, was the first national university in Japan.
種智院大学は、日本の有名な僧、空海が 828 年に庶民のために設立した私立学校、綜藝種智院が起源です。	Shuchiin University originated from the Shugeishuchi-in, a private school set up for commoners in 828 by Kukai, a famous Buddhist priest in Japan.
日本では、大学生の学術レベルの低下がよく指摘されています。	In Japan, it is often pointed out that the academic level of Japanese university students has been going down.
2007 年に、志願者数が入学者数と一致する、いわゆる「大学全入時代」が到来しました。	The age of the so-called "All Applicants Can Enter Colleges," by which I mean the number of applicants to colleges would equal that of their entrants, came in 2007.

▶ 現在の状況の把握と分析を述べる　　　　　　　　　　　　　　CD 2 ➡ 08

近年の大学生は、一般常識が欠けている面が多く見受けられます。このことは、実際に大学で教鞭をとっている先生方からも指摘されています。	Recent college students are lacking in common knowledge in many cases. This fact has been often talked about by college teachers actually teaching them.

大学生に限らず、大人一般に言えるのですが、漢字が書けない人が増えています。この理由は、幸か不幸か、IT技術の急な発達により、コンピュータを通じて文章を書くことが増えているからでしょう。

There has been an increasing number of those adults in general, including college students, who cannot write Chinese characters. This may result from the current situation where they mainly use their computers when writing something, fortunately or unfortunately thanks to the rapid developments of the IT industry.

コンピュータ上で文書を作成した場合、自動的にひらがなが漢字変換されるので、コンピュータに頼っている限り、意識して漢字を書く機会がありません。このことが、大人の漢字能力を下げている主な理由であると考えられます。

If you work on the computer writing documents, hiragana letters are automatically converted to corresponding Chinese characters; therefore, you are not given chances to write Chinese characters consciously yourself as long as you rely on your computer. This is regarded as one of the main reasons adults are lacking in their ability to write Chinese characters.

多くの大学では、TOEIC対策を英語教育に導入しています。その理由は、就職時にTOEICのスコアが大きな役割を果たすからです。
注：play a large roleの代わりにplay a large partも使える。

Many universities introduce TOEIC-test-centered English classes into their English education courses. The reason is that the students' TOEIC scores will play a large role in their finding employment.

TOEICのスコアが高いからと言って、英語能力が高いとは断言できません。例えば、英語で商談ができるとは限りません。TOEICで聴解力や読解力を測れても、会話力を図ることはできないからです。

We cannot say those who have high TOEIC scores are high in English abilities. For example, they cannot always have excellent business talks in English.
This means that TOEIC tests can only measure listening and reading abilities, but not a faculty for speaking English.

会話能力があり、英語で商談できるからといって、企業はその人材を無条件に採用するとは限りません。やはり最終的には、「人間力」がものをいいます。私がいう人間力とは、「人望」と「協調性」と「勤勉」と「判断力」の4拍子揃った人格のことです。

Those who are able to speak well and have business talks smoothly cannot always find acceptable employment. After all, the faculty as a human plays an important role. What I call human faculty is a personality with four basic features: popularity, cooperativeness, industry and a good sense of judgment.

▶ 未来の予想について述べる　　　　　CD 2 ➡ 09

大学生に英語を中心とした語学力とコンピュータ操作をはじめとする IT 関連の技術力の向上が益々期待されるでしょう。国際化時代であり、かつ、情報化時代である現代社会に対応する優秀な人材を企業が求めることは間違いないからです。

The enhancement of language abilities mainly in English and improvement of IT-related skills including computer operations are to be expected on the part of college students. This is because companies in general seek those who are excellent enough to adjust themselves to our modern society, because we are now living in an intercultural and information-oriented age.

暗記のみに頼ってきた受験生時代の影響から、「指示待ち人間」が増えています。

People who tend to wait until they are ordered to do something have been increasing in number, as a result of the examination hell under which they depend only on memorization.

言いかえれば「考える」ということをしない人が大学から大量発生することになるわけで、これは日本社会全体に悪影響を与えるでしょう。
注：have a bad influence の have の代わりに exercise や exert も使える。

In other words, the number of those who haven't formed a habit of "thinking" will mushroom from universities. This trend will have a bad influence on the Japanese society as a whole.

コミュニケーションを強調するあまり、文法を軽視する大学英語教育はうまくいかないでしょう。文法を気にしていたらしゃべれませんが、文法を身につけないとしゃべれないという事実を知るべきです。

College English education in which the teaching of grammar is disregarded as a result of the excessive emphasis on communication will end in failure. We should know the fact that we cannot communicate unless we learn a good knowledge of grammar, though we cannot speak if we are worried too much about grammar.

▶ 提案を述べる　　　　　　　　　　　　　　　　　CD 2 ➡ 10

大学は真の意味での国際人を養成すべきです。真の意味での国際人には、「異文化の理解」と同時に「自国についての知識をしっかりと持ち合わせていること」が要求されます。例えば、日本人においては、日本文化や日本社会についてよく知っているということが挙げられます。

Universities should produce cross-cultural communicators in its true sense. Such people are required to have a good knowledge of their own countries as well as a deep understanding of other cultures. For instance, in the case of the Japanese, they should know much about Japanese culture and society.

現代の日本の大学生は、日本の伝統文化についてはあまり知りません。その文化を正しく世界に発信する国際人として、伝統文化に関すること、例えば、茶道や華道、能や歌舞伎などにもっと関心を持つべきでしょう。

The present Japanese college students are not well-versed in Japanese traditional culture. They should have a keener interest in things traditional like tea ceremony or flower arrangement, Noh or Kabuki, as those internationally-minded people who send some correct cultural information about Japan to the world.

大学生に求められる基礎的な力は、「論理的に考える」ということに尽きるでしょう。「論理的思考能力」を身につけると将来、どこに就職しても何とかやっていけるものです。というのは、論理的に思考できれば、正しい判断力・決断力が沸いてくるからです。	The only basic ability required of college students is to think logically. Logical thinking enables them to manage to do their jobs pretty well in any working place, because the ability to think logically will lead them to get adequate judgment and decision-making ability.
大学英語教員は、同じ科目を教える者同士で、授業参観すべきです。なぜなら、そうすることにより、よりよい教授法を確立することにつながり、授業運営上の問題点を解決する助けになる可能性が見出せます。	College English teachers teaching the same kind of classes should observe their fellow teachers' classes. This is just because such class observation will encourage them to establish better teaching methods and to help them get some hints in solving the problems they find in class management.
TOEIC対策が重要だからといって、学生に問題を解かせて、説明させるような授業をすべきではありません。理由は簡単です。授業が単調になり、学生にとって面白くないものになる可能性が高いからです。技能のみならず、教養も身につく工夫に富む授業を展開すべきだと私は思います。	The teaching style in which students are made to answer questions and then give explanations is not recommendable, even though TOEIC-oriented English teaching is important. The reason I say this is quite simple. This kind of teaching style tends to be monotonous and often boring to the students. I think it important for the teacher to tax his or her ingenuity in teaching English from various perspectives to enhance the level of the students' culture in addition to their development of English skills.

3 いじめと不登校

▶ 情報を伝える　　　　　　　　　　　　　　　CD 2 ➡ 11

学校でのいじめは今日本では深刻な問題になっています。いじめを原因として不登校、さらには自殺のニュースがテレビではあとを絶ちません。

School bullying is a serious problem now in Japan. News items about school refusal and suicides resulting from bullying appear on TV endlessly.

さらに悪いことには学校側によるいじめ隠蔽（いんぺい）の傾向があることです。

To make matters worse, some bullying cases have been covered up by school authorities.

文部科学省の調べでは平成 15 年にはいじめ発生数が公立の小中高校、特殊学校を含め 23,351 件報告されました。
注：M.E.C.S.S.T.=Ministry of Education, Culture, Sports, Science and Technology（略称＝ MEXT）
※正確にはこれは公立の小中高に対する調査。

According to a study by M.E.C.S.S.T., in the 15th year of Heisei, 23,351 bullying cases were reported in junior high and high schools and schools for the handicapped.

また同年国公立小中高の不登校者数が 126,212 人になっています。

In the same year, in state-run and other public schools, 126,212 students refused to go to school.

いじめの内容には言葉での脅し、冷やかし、仲間はずれ、集団無視などがあるが、ひどい場合には暴力やたかりなどもあります。

Bullying includes verbal threats, derision, exclusion from groups and group silent treatment, and in very bad cases, physical aggression and coercion.

不登校の原因には友人や教師との関係、学業の不振などの学校での問題もありますが、親子関係や病気など、個人に起因するものもあるようです。

Among the causes of school refusal are relationships with classmates or the teacher, bad grades, which are related to school life, and relationships with parents and illness, which are related to home.

いじめや不登校はアメリカにもある問題です。ある報告では全米で毎日約160,000人の子どもが登校拒否をしています。	School bullying and school refusal exist in the US too. One report says across the US about 160,000 children refuse to go to school every day.

▶ いじめと家庭環境の関係性　　　　CD 2 ➡ 12

いじめは、まずその子の家庭環境が原因しているのではないかと思います。	I think that bullying is directly attributable to the home environment.
家庭でコミュニケーションが不足したまま育った子供は、空気が読めなくなり、いじめられる性格となるのではないでしょうか。	Those children who are brought up in families that lack communication within their families cannot behave properly according to the situation, resulting in forming characteristics often targeted by bullies.
また、子供に罵声を浴びせるなど不適切なコミュニケーションを体験した子供は、いじめっ子になってしまうのではないかと感じます。	On the other hand, I kind of feel that those who had improper communication with their families and who were harshly criticized as children often have a tendency to become bullies.
家庭内のコミュニケーションは、子育てにおいて極めて重要です。	Communication at home is of vital importance in childrearing.
いじめが明らかになれば、今度は、学校と家庭との間のコミュニケーションを密にする必要があるでしょう。	Once bullying is identified, it is necessary to keep the lines of communication open and encourage parents and teachers to communicate as often as possible.

▶ 不登校について思うこと　　　　　　　　　　CD 2 ➡ 13

学校に自分の居場所を見出せない状態にあるときに、不登校が始まります。

Children who do not feel like they fit in at school often start refusing to go to school.

教師は生徒の状況をできる限り知る努力をすると共に、どんな状況の時でも温かく生徒を見守り受け入れる必要があります。

Teachers should try to understand all the situations about the pupil in question, and at the same time, make every possible effort to get the student involved in school activities and make the student feel accepted.

いじめが不登校の原因になっている場合もあるでしょう。

Bullying may be one of the reasons for refusing to go to school.

▶ いじめ問題を解決するには？　　　　　　　　CD 2 ➡ 14

教師に生徒の生活状況をすべてチェックさせるのではなく、専門の職を置いて生徒の生活を指導するのも方法だと思います。この立場の人は専門の知識、能力だけでなく人格もそれなりに伴った人を採用しなければなりません。

Not relying on teachers for checking students' private lives but having someone like a counselor do so instead is a good idea. Of course, this person needs not only expertise and skills but a personality fit for the position.

2方向からこの問題を見なければなりません。いじめられる側の子や不登校の子にも何か原因はないかを探らなければならないということです。

You need to take the matter from two angles, meaning there might be causes on the part of the bullied and refusing too, which you should also look into.

▶ いじめ問題と発想の転換　　　　　　　　　　CD 2 ➡ 15

学校を何とかしようというのはひとつの方法ですが、私の場合は子どもが学校そのものに行く必要がないと思っています。

It's one option to change schools, certainly. I don't necessarily think you have to go to school.

問題がなければ行っていればいいのですが、子どもがいじめにあったりすると、学校へは行かせないのも方法でしょう。	If nothing is wrong, it's OK to go. But if your kid is being bullied, one option is not let him or her go to school.
子どもをどうにかしようと思う前に、親の方が考えを変えればいいわけです。学校に行かなくでも子どもは育ちますよ。いや、むしろ行かない方がいい子に育つかもしれないですよ。	It might be good for the parents to change their way of thinking before doing something that could affect the child's future. The child might grow to be a better person without school.
まったく発想を変えてみてはどうでしょう。	How about looking at it from a completely different perspective?
大学に行くまでは親や塾が勉強の面倒を見てやればいいのです。実際にそういう家族の話も聞いたことがあります。	Either the parents or a cram school can take care of their study until they reach university age. I have actually heard of a family doing that.
いじめられっ子は、本当は強い子だと思います。親に苦しみを訴えることなく、耐えているからです。	A bullied child is really strong spiritually because he or she has put up with the situation without appealing to his or her parents for their help.
いじめられていると、解決の糸口がないように思いますが、その期間は人生のほんの一部です。いじめっ子を十分見返すことができますよ。	While you are being bullied, there tends to be no solution to the problem. However what you are now experiencing won't last forever. The period of bullying is just a small part of your whole life; therefore, you can triumph over your bullies later in your life.

私は、小学校のころ、いじめられていましたが、いじめっ子たちをかわいそうに思っていました。今はいじめさせてあげるが、将来は立派になって、君たちが私を尊敬するようになるだろう！と心に言い聞かせていました。悔しいから、今度は誰かをいじめてやろうとは思いませんでした。	When I was an elementary school pupil, I used to be bullied and used to feel sympathy for the bullies. I made it a rule to tell myself that I would be so great a man in the future that the bullies would respect me though I now let them bully me. I did not think I would bully others later out of chagrin.
人をいじめてしまう子は、本当は心が弱い子ですね。かつて誰かにいじめられたから、今誰かをいじめてしまう。	The children who are prone to bully another child are really chicken-hearted. They tend to bully him or her if they were once bullied.
また、いじめられないように、他人をいじめてしまう。	Or they are likely to bully him or her so that they may not be bullied instead.
むしろいじめっ子たちに対して、いじめはいけないと怒るのではなく、いじめっ子の気持ちを理解し、真の意味で救ってあげるといじめはなくなる可能性があると思います。	I think it better for us not to only scold by telling them not to bully others, but to understand them to save them in its true sense. Then bullying may disappear.

表現のコツ　「〜になる、育つ」の grow

「大きくなって看護婦になる」は grow up to be a nurse です。up を用いない場合は、「大人になる」という含みがありません。また、「grow into、grow out of、grow + 形容詞」の形も重要です。

彼女は彼を好きになり始めた。
→ She is growing to like him.
夕方に近づくにつれ影が長くなる。
→ As the evening draws near, shadows grow longer.
20歳になる前に彼がその悪い習慣をやめると思いますよ。
→ I expect him to grow out of the bad habit before 20.

4 校内暴力と家庭環境

▶ 情報を伝える　　　　　　　　　　　　　　　　CD 2 ➡ 16

ある調査では 2003 年の一年間で公立の小中高校の学校内外での暴力行為の発生数 35,392 件が報告されています。

A survey says in Heisei 15, 35,392 cases of physical aggression were reported in and around primary and high schools.

別の調べでは暴力への対応としてすべての教師が何らかの対応をしたと答えているが、保護者の 35 パーセントは自分の子が校内暴力を受けた際に学校は充分な対応をしてくれていないと答えています。

Another report says all the teachers say they did something about aggression problems, but 35 % of the parents say the school didn't react quickly enough when their kids were physically abused.

文部科学省の発表では 2004 年で全国公立小学校での校内暴力が 1980 件にのぼり、過去最高になりました。小中高校での合計校内暴力の件数は前年より 4 パーセント減っていて、小学校での校内暴力が際立つことになっています。

The Ministry of Education reported in 2004 that in all public primary schools there were 1980 cases of physical aggression, a record high. In all primary, junior high and high schools, the cases of physical aggression fell 4% from the previous year, which made the primary school figure stand out.

その理由として感情のコントロールができない子の増加、忍耐力や自己表現力、人間関係を築く力の低下が原因と指摘されています。

The reasons are that there is an increase in the number of kids who can't control their emotions, who are less patient and have a poor ability to express themselves or form relationships.

最近の小学生の食生活が原因だとの指摘もあります。スナック菓子や炭酸飲料の取りすぎが子どもたちに低血糖症を起こし、それで子どもたちが興奮状態になりやすいのです。	Some people point out that the diets of elementary school children are the cause. Consuming too much snack food and carbonated drinks induces low blood sugar, which could upset their emotions.
解決のためには教師と子供との触れ合いの機会の充実と日ごろからの啓発・指導、学校と家庭との緊密な連携・協力などが挙げられています。	Among solutions proposed are sufficient mingling between the teachers and kids, educating kids daily, constant communication between the families and the schools.

▶ 暴力の原因と解決について意見を述べる　　　　　　　　　CD 2 ➡ 17

家庭で暴力を受けた者は、第三者に、その鬱憤（うっぷん）を晴らそうとするでしょう。持って行き場のない自分の感情を、教師や生徒にぶつけます。 注：「鬱憤を晴らす」は、satisfy one's resentment/grudge; work off one's pent-up anger; wreak one's wrath on a person; [口] let off the steam 。	The victims of violence at home tend to give vent to their anger and use violence on a third party. Students' uncontrolled feelings could explode with a violent attack on teachers or other students.
学校と、家庭と、地域が一丸となって、共に解決していく姿勢が、早急に求められています。	School, home and local communities are urgently required to try to solve problems as a group.
家庭が孤立しないよう、昔の長屋の暮らしのように、隣近所の事情が分かり、互いに助け合うことが実現すれば、問題は減少するでしょう。	I think problems would decrease if old style neighborhoods that were once represented by the row houses of the past where people understood and helped each other were revived again.
最近は地域ぐるみの子育て支援が各地で活発化されようとしています。	Now mutual support in childrearing in the local community is being promoted at various places in Japan.

▶ 怒ることについて考える　　　　　　　　　　　　　　　CD 2 ➡ 18

| 校内暴力の原因は子どもを甘やかす親が増えたということではないでしょうか。その結果、子どもの忍耐が減ったのでしょう。 | I think a big reason we have school violence is more parents indulge their kids. As a result, their children are apt to lose their patience. |

また、学校の先生が生徒を怒らなくなったのも生徒の暴力などを助長することになっていると思います。

And the fact that teachers rarely reprimand students contributes to the rise in school violence.

怒らなくなった先生が一方的に悪いのではなく、自分の子に何かあればすぐに学校に苦情をいう保護者にも責任はあると思います。

Not only are teachers, who seldom scold, to blame but parents who complain to the school every time something petty happens to their kids are as well.

またそれにとどまらず、世間のおとなも子どもを怒らなくなりました。悪いことをした子には毅然とした態度で怒るべきです。もちろん少し自分の子どもが怒られただけで苦情を言う親が一番悪いのですが。

Besides, there are fewer adults who scold children. We should take a stern stance and scold kids who did something wrong. Of course, the worst of all are parents who easily lose their tempers just by their kids being scolded by someone.

▶ 家庭でのしつけの重要性について意見を述べる　　　　　CD 2 ➡ 19

社会的な取り組みも重要ですが、やはり家庭でのしつけが不可欠です。

We need a social remedy but more important is the need for more discipline at home.

子どもがお父さんを恐く思わなくなっています。お母さんが子どもの前でお父さんを立てるどころか馬鹿にする家庭まであるようです。これでは話になりません。

Children are no longer afraid of fathers. There are families where the mother doesn't show respect for the father and even makes fun of him in the kid's presence. It's out of the question.

子どもは親の保護下にあるのですが、同時に社会の構成員でもあります。親も社会に対して責任を持って、人を舐めずに、敬意を表する子に育てなければなりません。

Kids are in parents' custody, but they are members of the society as well. Parents should be responsible to the society and raise children who are respectful, not disdainful.

表現のコツ　「舐める」の表現

彼は世の中の辛酸を舐めてきた。
→ He went through hardships of life. [=He passes through many trials.]
彼女は自分の子供には自分がしてきた苦労を舐めさせたくなかった。
→ She didn't want to let her children see the hardships she did.
彼は人を舐めてかかる癖がある。
→ He has a propensity to hold people cheap in contempt.
火は瞬く間に数棟のビルを舐め尽くした。
→ The flames wiped out a row of buildings in a minute.
若いからといって舐めるなよ。
→ Though I am young, I am not a man to be made a fool of.

5 ゆとり教育と学校5日制

▶ 情報を述べる　　　　　　　　　　　　　　CD 2 ➡ 20

ゆとり教育が取り入れられるようになって20年ほどになります。
参考：「ゆとり教育」は cram-free education とも訳せる。

It's been some 20 years since "Yutori" education, in which latitude is emphasized than cramming, was first adopted.

1970年代には日本では受験戦争が過熱し、知識詰め込みの教育に懸念がもたれていました。当時の文部省の中央教育審議会の答申で学習内容の削減を主としたゆとり教育を提案していました。

In the 1970's, there was an exam war heating up, and many people were concerned about the cramming-oriented education. Chuo Kyoiku Shinngikai (Central Council for Education) of the then Ministry of Education in its report suggested "Yutori" education which emphasized reduced class load.

2002年に新学習指導要領が導入され、小中学校の学習内容が約3割削減され、完全週5日制が実施されました。

In 2002, a New Education Guideline was introduced, which cut the class load by 30% and put a 5-day-a-week schedule into practice.

一方、大学の入学条件や、企業の求める人材の用件などは変わっていません。

In the meantime, the conditions for the university entrance exams and those the corporate world wants from its workers haven't changed.

この条件を満たすために、小中学生の親は減った授業内容分を補おうと、子どもたちに追加の授業を受けさせなければなりません。

To meet the conditions, the parents of primary and secondary schools kids want to make up for the reduced work load and have their kids take extra lessons.

現内閣は教育改革を大きな目標のひとつにかかげています。下がった生徒の学力の回復はいうまでもなく、モラルの回復や家族を愛する気持ちなどを大切にする教育をかかげています。	The current Cabinet presents education reform as one of its targets: Education to restore not only students' academic level but moral values and an attitude to respect and love your family are its slogans.

▶ ゆとり教育の問題点を述べる　　　CD 2 ➡ 21

ゆとり教育は児童の学力の低下を引き起こしてしまいました。	"Yutori" education has brought about the decline in scholastic attainments.
20年前と比較して日本人の平均学力は落ちています。	The average academic achievement of the Japanese was lower than 20 years ago.
一方受験戦争は表立ってはいませんが今なお続いています。それが今でも問題になっています。	The situation of the so-called examination hell is not as conspicuous as before, but it still remains to a certain extent.
学校で教えなくなった分の内容を学習塾で補っている状況で、それらの生徒たちは決してゆとりがあるわけではありません。 注：have leeway（活動の余裕がある）	What is left unlearned due to the government's lax policy is to be learned at a cramming school; therefore, students do not feel they have leeway.
さらに、最近に起こった問題ではいくつかの進学校では受験用の勉強をさせるために、本来卒業までに、世界史などの必要な科目をとばして授業を行っていました。それゆえ多くの生徒が、正式には卒業できない事態になっています。	Moreover, the current problem which occurred in some college-oriented high schools is that students have not learned required subjects like world history, which resulted in a lack of credits necessary for proper graduation.

▶ 学校五日制に対する意見　　　　　　　　　CD 2 ➡ 22

ただ、学校を休ませるだけでなく、空いた時間を有効に使い、授業でできないことを体験させるプログラムがあれば、本当の意味で、ゆとりある教育に繋がると思います。

Instead of just letting students be absent from school for two days a week, we need to create programs now impossible for schools to offer by utilizing free time effectively. These kinds of efforts will lead to the 'Yutori' education in its true sense.

▶ さらに一歩進んで考える　　　　　　　　　CD 2 ➡ 23

子どもたちの教育問題は単に学力の低下だけの問題ではありません。道徳観念の欠如は切実な問題で、この国自体を破壊しかねない問題です。

The education problem is not only about lower academic levels. Lack of moral values is a serious problem, too, which could make or break Japan.

ゆとり教育はかつての受験戦争への反省からでてきたのでしょうが、実際には、受験戦争問題は解決していません。教育の場はすべてが国などの公的機関がまかなっているわけではありません。

"Yutori" education should be a product of reflection on the exam war once dominant. But in fact the exam war is still going on. Education is not all handled by state-run public institutes.

業者にとっても受験戦争を刺激してこそ利益の上がる（＝儲けるために需要を刺激するような）競争の社会です。そこを何とかしなくてはいけないと思います。

It's a competitive field where private companies want to stimulate demand to make gains. Something must be done about it.

仕事に対する偏見があります。例えば、弁護士や医者、大手企業に働く人は尊敬を受けて、職業を聞くとみんなが「ほー」と感心するのが事実です。

There are prejudices against some jobs. For example, lawyers, doctors and employees of large companies are looked up to, and wow people who come to know their jobs.

学校の成績を上げていい大学に行って給料がよくて尊敬を受ける職に、親が付けさせたがるのも無理はないのではないでしょうか。社会全体が姿勢を改めるべきだと思います。	It can't be helped that the parents want their children to get good grades at school, go to a good university and get a job which is high-paying and admired. I believe the whole society should change its attitude.
現内閣の教育改革方針には手法、人選など細部で批判もあるようですが、大掛かりな変革をもたらしてほしいとの期待感もあります。このままでは日本人は日本人としてのよき精神を失ってしまうのではないかと思うほど乱れています。	The present Cabinet's guideline gets criticisms about its method, personnel and the like. But one cannot help counting on it for a fundamental change. Japan is so screwed up that something must be done urgently, or Japanese will lose the beautiful aspect of their mentality.
賛成、反対のバランスをとりながら、大筋内閣の方向で行くのがよいと思います。	I hope the Cabinet is pursuing its current goal, keeping a good balance between the pro and con.
その名のとおり本当の意味での「ゆとり教育」を行ってもらいたいものです。おとなも含めた日本人全体が生活にゆとりを持つ方向で行かないと学校だけにゆとりをもたらすことは不可能と思いますが。	I hope the government realizes the true "Yutori" education as the word suggests. I think it's impossible to introduce yutori into school alone unless the whole population including adults try to have leeway.

表現のコツ 「姿勢」の表現

この日本語は、文字通り「体位」を指すこともあれば、「(物事に対する) 考え方」の場合もあります。英語でも posture、stance などは両方を意味します。また、attitude は後者のことです。

彼の姿勢が悪い。少し左によって、背筋を伸ばしてほしいんだ。
→ His posture is bad. I want him to move a little to left and straighten his back.
老人がひとり私たちの企画にこのようにガンと反対の姿勢だ。
→ An old man has had this firm stance against our project.

6 　教師の役割

▶ 情報を伝える　　　　　　　　　　　　　　CD 2 ➡ 24

教師の「教」という字のつくりの部分の意味は、「交」に似ていますね。実は、語源的に「交」の意味を持っているようです。

The right half of the Chinese character meaning teaching is similar in shape to another Chinese character meaning interaction. In fact, this part seems to have the meaning of interaction.

教師は、一方通行の教え方ではなく、まさに学生との交流を通して教えることが大切であると、この漢字1つから分かります。

This very Chinese character of teaching suggests that it is important for a teacher to teach through interaction with his or her students.

学校の教師は「先生」と呼ばれます。また、教職は「聖職」とも言われています。それは教師が学業のみでなく人間的に優れた人であるという意味だと思います。しかし、教員テストには人格テストはありません。このあたりのことが問題ではないでしょうか。

School teachers are called "Sensei" and their job is considered a "sacred profession." I think it presupposes that teachers are not only good scholars but superlative persons. But despite this fact, to be a teacher, one doesn't have to take a personality test. Don't you think this is something important we have to bear in mind?

▶ コミュニケーションの重要性　　　　　　　　CD 2 ➡ 25

先生は、生徒一人ひとりを尊重すべきです。できの悪い生徒は敬遠しがちですが、わけ隔てなく指導することが基本です。

Teachers should hold every student of his or her class in high esteem. The teachers tend to ignore slow learners but it is very important to give guidance to the pupils without any discrimination.

教師と生徒のコミュニケーションが大切です。コミュニケーションを密にとる先生は、尊敬されます。

Communication between teachers and their students is of utmost importance. Those teachers who communicate well with their students are respected by their students.

先生が尊敬されると、生徒は勉強するようになります。	If the teacher is respected by his or her students, they come to study harder.
生徒の態度が悪かったり、勉強の出来がよくないからといって、先生が文句を言うのはよくありません。	It is not advisable for a teacher to complain of his or her students' bad attitude or bad academic performance.
同じ生徒でも、先生によって態度が異なるものです。生徒を常に信頼し、激励する先生は、最終的には尊敬されます。 注:「最終的には尊敬されます」の部分で、視点を1つにすべき。「表現のコツ」を参照。	The same students may change attitudes according to their teacher. The teacher who always trusts and encourages his or her students finally comes to be respected by the students.

表現のコツ　1つの視点で述べることの重要性

○ His or her students finally come to think highly of him or her.（教師の視点）
○ Students finally come to think highly of their teacher.（学生の視点）
× His or her students finally come to think highly of their teacher.（視点が2つ）

▶ **教師にとって重要なことと教師自身が生徒にとって重要であること**　　CD 2 ➡ 26

教師は、生徒の中に潜む可能性を引き出し、伸ばしてやることを常に念頭に置くべきです。	What the teacher should bear in mind is that he or she has to bring out the students' potential and enhance their ability.
教師との出会いによって、生徒は自分の生き方の方向性、希望を見出すことができます。教師の存在が、時々学生の成長に対して、非常に重要な役割を演じるのです。 注:「非常に重要な役割を演じる」はplay a vital part in... も可。	A chance encounter with a wonderful teacher may change a student completely for the better and give him or her a hope in later life. The existence of such a teacher sometimes plays a very significant role in the growth of his or her student.

教師は子どもの教育を預かる、重要な職業です。それゆえ社会も教師に対して過度の期待をするようになっているとの印象はあるのですが。	The teacher is an important professional, taking care of children's education. Therefore the general public seem to expect too much of the teacher.
例えば彼らは就業時間など考えずに生徒のために働かなくてはだめだ、と思われがちです。	For example, some people might even think he should not mind working overtime for his students.
しかし教師とて普通の人間であり、自分の生活もあります。それをすべて犠牲にすることはできないでしょう。やはり、生活をささえるための職業としての一面も広く理解を示すべきです。	But the teacher is just another human having his own life. He can't compromise everything. We should tolerate teaching as a life supporting instrument.
ひとつには教師の数を増やし、教師一人当たりの生徒数を適切にするのが大切です。二人以上の教師が一クラスを担当し、ある週は一人は授業担当で、もうひとりは私生活を見る、などです。または授業を担当する教師以外に専門的に私生活の面倒を見る専門家を置くなど。	One way is to increase the number of teachers so a teacher has a proper number of students. Have two teachers for one class and for one week one of them teaches class and the other looks after students' private lives. Or besides teachers, prepare a specialist who takes care of students' private lives.

▶ **教師のあり方に対する国家の介入**　　　　　　　　　　　CD 2 ➡ 27

教師という職業は仕事内容に明確な線が引かれておらず、個々人に任されている面が大きいです。	The school teacher's job doesn't have a clear description; what he does and how he does it are up to each teacher.
国家や行政が教育に介入しない方が好ましいという考えのもとでしょう。しかしそれゆえに熱心な教師とそうでない教師の間の働きぶりに海と山ほどの差があるという印象を私は持っています。	It may be because it's desirable for the state not to intervene in education. But for this we have the impression that the difference of the work performance between the diligent teachers and the lazy ones is huge.

熱心で苦悩し、一線を越えて、自殺までしてしまう教師がいることはまことにお気の毒です。	It's a pity some teachers are so devoted that a single problem can throw them off balance so completely and can sometimes even push them over the edge or even end their lives.
しかし、現状のままで教師の負担を減らす措置をとることは不熱心な教師にさらに余計な利益を与えるだけです。	However, it would only unnecessarily benefit the lazy teachers to reduce the teachers' workload.
現に夏休み中の教師の研修でズルをして給料泥棒まがいのことをしている教師も多数いるとのニュースも流れています。	In fact, it was reported that many teachers cheated on their summer vacation assignments.
充分な対策をたててから導入してもらいたいです。	I hope the authorities will implement reform after enough discussion.
内閣が挙げている、教師の免許の更新制度は教師の質の改善に役立つでしょう。また、採用の際には人格テストも行うべきだと思います。	Renewal of the teacher's license advocated by the Cabinet would help improve the teachers' quality. And then at employment, they should conduct personality checks, too.
現状最低限の国家の介入は仕方がないでしょう。	At least a minimal amount of state intervention is indispensable under the circumstances.

▶ **人格テストの問題点**　　　　　　　　　　　　　　　　CD 2 ➡ 28

人格のテストはいろんな問題をはらんでいます。これは教師に限らずいろんな職業についていえると思うのですが、人格のテストを強調するのは雇用の際の差別につながるし、個人の思想への介入になるのでどうかと思います。	Personality check is controversial. It would apply to other professions too. To place much emphasis on personality check could lead to employment discrimination and intervention into individual thoughts.

また、いったい正当な人格の基準は誰が作るのかが問題になります。	It's also questionable who establishes the standards of the acceptable personality.
結局、教師本人の自覚に任せるしかないのでしょうか。	After all, the only way is to hope for each teacher to know what he or she is doing.

▶ 褒めることについて   CD 2 ➡ 29

教師ができない学生を教えていて、実際あまりできていなくても、「できたね」と褒めると、「できる」ようになるものです。	When a teacher praises his students even if they are rather poor at achievements in class, they may come to make a good showing.
褒められたことが嬉しくて、がんばって勉強する結果、本当にできるようになるものです。	The fact that they have been praised will encourage their study, which will actually result in fostering real capacity.
褒める人間は、褒められる人間よりも賢いものです。褒めることによって、喜ばれ、結局は、褒めた人が褒められることになります。	Those who praise others are generally wiser than those who are praised. They will make others happy by praising them; consequently, those who praise others will be praised.
100回怒るよりも、1回褒めるほうが、効果的です。	It is more effective to praise someone just one time than to scold him or her 100 times.

第8章

環境問題に関する意見を述べる

1 地球温暖化

▶ 情報を伝える　　　　　　　　　　　　　　　　　　　　　CD 2 ➡ 30

地球温暖化の原因はひと言でいうと、二酸化炭素などの温室効果ガスの増加と逆に二酸化炭素などを吸収する森林などの減少です。	To put it simply, global warming is caused by an increase of greenhouse gases like carbon dioxide and a decrease of forests, which absorb carbon dioxide.
温暖化による気温上昇そのものが即座に私たちの生活をおびやかすものではありませんが、その結果起こる海面上昇、異常気象、生態系破壊などが私たちをおびやかすものになります。	Rising temperatures from global warming itself can't be an imminent threat to our lives, but the resultant rising sea level, abnormal climates, and destruction of the ecosystem are.
地球温暖化による気温変化は何十年もの観測でわかることで、一般生活の中では気づきません。	One can never feel temperature change from global warming, which could only be detected by decades-long observation.
しかし徐々に砂漠化や海面上昇は進行しています。	But desertification and sea level rise are gradually advancing.
実際に太平洋上の一部の島国は温暖化の結果海水レベルが上がり水没し始めています。将来には土地がなくなることが予想され、人民引き受けなどの助けを近隣諸国に求めています。	In fact, some island countries in the Pacific are sinking in the water because of global warming. They expect to lose all of their land in the future and are looking to neighboring countries to help accept their people.

▶ 地球環境に対する警告　　　　　　　　　　CD 2 ➡ 31

地球はあと 80 年しか持たない！川も海も魚も植物も悲鳴をあげていると、多くの学識者が警告しています。人間の文明が原因である地球温暖化が、主として地球に悪影響を与えています。

The earth will last only for 80 years. Many scientists warn that rivers, seas, fishes and plants are all giving a cry of pain. This means that global warming caused by humans' civilization has had a bad influence on the earth.

「地球を 50 年前に戻そう！」という運動をしている人が増えてきました。

There has been an increasing number of people carrying on a campaign for the revival of the same earth as it was 50 years ago.

その運動の目的は、合成化学物質による自然の破壊をくい止めることです。

The purpose of this campaign is to stop nature from destruction by refraining from using synthetic chemical substances.

有害物質は、身の回りの洗剤、シャンプーや歯磨き粉にも多く含まれています。また、食品添加物等を見直すことも重要です。

Harmful substances are contained in everyday products including synthetic detergents, shampoos and toothpaste. Moreover, food additives are also something we have to reconsider.

ほんのちょっとした努力であっても、全世界の人が、次々にそういった行動をとることによって、自然だけでなく、人間自身も救われるのです。

If more and more people in the world try to undertake the above campaign, even a little bit of effort can be a great benefit that may lead to saving not only nature but also humans themselves.

▶ 解決方法の提案　　　　　　　　　　　　　CD 2 ➡ 32

地球温暖化の原因は二酸化炭素などの温室効果ガスが太陽熱を大気圏外に閉じ込めることです。

The cause of global warming is that greenhouse gases like carbon dioxide trap solar heat within the atmosphere.

温暖化を阻止するには二酸化炭素を増加させない、削減することをやっていかなければなりません。

To check global warming, we have to stop carbon dioxide from increasing and reduce the existing level.

それを増加させないためにはいわゆる石油燃料の使用を控えていかなければなりません。そのための代替燃料の開発が必要です。

To stop its increase, we need to make do with as little oil as we can, which is the reason we need to develop alternative energy sources.

二酸化炭素を吸収する森林を増加させることも急務です。

It's also urgent to augment forests, which pick up carbon dioxide.

▶ 温暖化を防ぐのに何ができるか　　　　　CD 2 ➡ 33

自動車や工場の機械を二酸化炭素などの排出量の少ない物に改良したり、森林を増やしたりすることは政府や大手の企業がイニシアティブをとらなければ進みません。

It's impossible to create cars and factories that emit less carbon dioxide, or augment forests without initiatives of the government or large corporations.

政府は風力、太陽熱などのクリーンなエネルギー源の開発にもっと尽力するべきです。

The government should be more committed to the development of clean energy sources such as wind power and solar power.

同時に私たち個々人も努力するべきです。

We, individuals, are also expected to make efforts.

自家用車に乗るのを減らし、できるだけ公共の交通機関を使う。無駄に電気製品をつけておかない。物を大切にして余計なゴミは出さないなどです。

Use your car less and use more public transportation. Never leave electric appliances on when not needed. Use things longer so that we can minimize the amount of extra garbage.

地球に人間は60億人いると言われています。

The world population is said to be 6 billion.

一人では少しの無駄なエネルギーも、みんなが意識すれば地球規模ではたいへんな変化を生みます。	If one person wastes a little energy, it would be translated into a vast waste of energy on a global level if everyone did the same.

▶ **大きな視野で見る**　　　　　　　　　　　　　　　　　CD 2 ➡ 34

地球温暖化は今生きている人類に即多大な被害をもたらすものではありません。百年、二百年先の私たちの子孫に大きな被害をもたらす可能性のあるものです。	Global warming is not an imminent threat to people living now. It could bring a tremendous harm to our descendents one hundred or two hundred years from now.
21 〜 22 世紀の時代が地球破壊のさきがけとなったと歴史に残らぬようにしたいものです。	We should behave wisely enough not to go down in history as the perpetrators who set off the earth's destruction in the 21st and 22nd centuries.

表現のコツ　「被害」の表現

そのビルは被害を免れた。
→ The building came out undamaged. [=The building was intact.]
その市の地震による被害は少なかった。
→ The city suffered lightly from the earthquake.
今年は稲に大きな被害が出るだろう。
→ A great deal of damage will be done to the rice crop this year.
彼女は被害妄想狂といううわさだ。
→ Rumor has it that she is a persecution maniac.
　　cf. persecution mania　（[病気] 被害妄想狂）
　　　　a delusion of persecution（被害妄想）

2　ゴミ問題

▶ 情報を伝える　　　　　　　　　　　　　　　　　　CD 2 ➡ 35

日本では家庭からのゴミだけでも年間約1千万トン出るといわれています。その他のゴミを含めるとたいへんな量です。	In Japan about 10 million tons of domestic garbage is produced annually. With other kinds of garbage combined, it'd be a huge amount.
充分に処理できれば問題はないのですが、それができないのでゴミの問題になっています。	There wouldn't be a problem if it's all disposed of, but it's not and this is part of the garbage problem.
ひとつにはゴミの埋め立て場所や焼却炉が充分ではないのです。	For one thing, we don't have enough garbage reclaimed land or incinerators.
これは「悪臭」「ダイオキシンなどの有害物」「メタンガス」「有害な煙」また「土壌への有害物質の浸透」などが懸念され、設置場所が制限されているのもひとつの理由です。	This is partly because there are only a few places where they can build them thanks to the "bad odor", "toxic substances like dioxin" "methane gas" "toxic smoke" and the "seepage of toxic substances into soil".
実際に東京などではゴミの収集場所からの有害物質が住民に健康被害を及ぼしたこともあります。 注：ゴミ捨て場も dumpsite という。	There once was an accident when toxic substances escaping from a dumpsite impaired the health of the neighbors.
また、ゴミ処理にかかる費用も問題です。ある調べでは平成16年には2兆円近い費用がかかっています。	Another problem is the cost of garbage disposal. One study shows it cost nearly 2 trillion yen in Heisei 16.
ゴミ焼却炉建設にも多大の費用がかかっています。	It also costs a great deal to build an incinerator.

ゴミの不法投棄が問題になっています。産業廃棄物などの処理に費用がかかるためにゴミ処理場ではないところにゴミを捨てる業者があとをたちません。また、最近はリサイクル法などの導入で、テレビや冷蔵庫など廃棄に費用のかかるものを不法に投棄する人もいるようです。	Illegal dumping is another aspect of the problem. Business people keep dumping garbage where they should not because of the high cost. And since the introduction of the recycle law that makes it costly to get rid of some domestic appliances, there have been people who throw appliances away illegally.

▶ 提案を述べる　　　　　　　　　　　　　　　　　　　CD 2 ➡ 36

ゴミを増やさない努力が必要です。例えば買い物ではスーパーなどで支給されるビニール袋を使わないで、買い物かごを持っていく、レストランではストローや紙のお手拭は使わない、ペットボトルは回収に出す、シャンプー類は詰め替え用を購入する、ビニールのラップはできるだけ使わない、などです。	We need to try not to produce more garbage. Examples are as follows: not using plastic bags provided by supermarkets and carrying your own basket instead; not using straws or paper napkins at restaurants; recycling pet bottles; buying refill bottles of shampoo, and trying not to use plastic wrappers.
また、買い物をするときは買う前に本当に必要かどうかを考えることが大事です。最近は百円ショップなどでは安いので何気なく買ってしまう人もいるようですが要注意です。	When shopping, consider well whether you need it or not before you buy something. We have a lot of one-hundred-yen shops, where you find yourself buying without much thought. Be careful!
ひとことで言えばものを大切にすることです。	In one word, deal with things with utmost care.
これらの行為は私が子どもの頃は当たり前だったのですが、今は生活を便利にすることばかりを考えすぎ、環境が犠牲になってしまっています。	This attitude of not wasting was taken for granted when I was a child. But nowadays people seek convenience at the expense of the environment.

家電製品のリサイクル法などは廃棄される物をリサイクルなどに回して無駄をなくそうという行政的な立場からのゴミ対策です。しかし、それにかかる費用を惜しむがゆえに不法投棄を犯す人がいるというのも残念なことです。事態を悪くしています。

The recycle law's objective is to lessen waste by reusing abandoned items, which is a measure from the administration. It's disappointing that nonetheless, some people do illegal dumping since they stint on the cost. It could only worsen the situation.

▶ 現代のゴミ問題に対するひとこと感想　　　　　　　CD 2 ➡ 37

先進国は物を持ち過ぎました。そして使い捨て時代のツケ！が私たちに帰ってきます。

There are too many consumer items in industrial nations. Now is the time when we are beginning to pay the price for the way in which we have managed economic development.

現代はもう捨てる場所がありません。その結果不法投棄の犯罪が横行しています。

There are few places to dispose of the trash that we create each day. As a result, items are being abandoned illegally on city streets and country roads.

モラルも低下したということです。

It is a clear indication that there is a marked decline in people's morals.

▶ ゴミを出さない対策　　　　　　　　　　　　　　CD 2 ➡ 38

個々人がモラルを高く持ってゴミを出さない努力をすることは言うまでもありません。

Needless to say, everyone should be ashamed of their moral void and try not to create garbage.

しかし、その努力が目に見えて利益としてはね返ってくる地域ぐるみの対策も重要です。

However, it's imperative for the whole community to introduce a measure in which people serious about reducing waste should be visibly awarded.

例えば古紙をリサイクルに出せばいくばくかのお金になるなどは以前から業者が行なっています。リサイクルショップもいいと思います。	One example is that if you recycle old papers, you can get some money, which has been done by private recyclists. Recycle shops are good too.
私の知っているスーパーではビニール袋にはお金がかかります。一枚10円です。しかしそこの店員は客が買い物カゴを持ってくるのが当たり前のようにふるまっているので、みな自分の買い物カゴを持ってきます。	At one supermarket I know, plastic bags cost 10 yen each. And besides, the cashier acts like it's the customer's job to bring his bag, which really compels customers to bring one.
このように企業側の毅然とした態度が人の姿勢を変えている例もあるのです。	This is a good example where a company's firm stance changes the customer's attitude to the better.

表現のコツ 「言うまでもない」の表現

> 本文では needles to say を使っています。これは It is needless to say that 〜 . のように通常の文の一部としても使えます。他には文では It goes without saying that 〜 や句では to say nothing of 〜、not to mention 〜 があります。
>
> 日本が世界有数の経済大国なのは言うまでもないことだ。
> → It goes without saying that Japan is one of the biggest economies in the world.
>
> 日本以外にも野球が盛んな国はたくさんあります。言うまでもなく米国もです。
> → There are many countries besides Japan where baseball is popular, not to mention America.

3 エネルギー問題と原発

▶ 情報を伝える　　　　　　　　　　　　　　CD 2 ➡ 39

日本はエネルギーのほとんどを輸入に頼っている国なので、輸入エネルギーの価格変動の国内経済への影響が大きいです。

As Japan is dependant on imports for most of its energy, the price of imported energy has a big impact on its economy.

1970年代の石油ショックにより産業部門での省エネルギー化、省エネルギー商品の開発も進みエネルギー需要は抑えられていました。しかし1980年代からの石油価格の低下と生活需要の高まりでエネルギー需要は増加しています。

The oil crisis in the 1970's helped promote industrial energy-saving and development of energy-efficient products, and energy demand has been low since. But the low oil price of the 80's and a high demand of commodities raised the demand of oil.

石油ショック以来日本はエネルギーの石油依存度を下げようと、原子力や天然ガスの導入を促進しました。

After the oil crisis, Japan prompted itself to use nuclear power and natural gas to reduce its dependency on oil.

2004年時点では全エネルギーの石油依存度は48%（1973年77%）、原子力11%、天然ガス14%になっています。

As of 2004, use of oil compared to the total use of energy is 48% (77% in 1973), that of nuclear power 11%, and that of natural gas 14%.

日本には2003年時点で53基の原子炉があります。米国、フランスに次いで世界第3位です。

As of 2003, Japan had 53 nuclear reactors, ranking third in the world after the US and France.

電気を供給するに充分な量の核物質は放射線が致死量にいたるだけでなく、発電の際に出る熱量も膨大で、熱死、焼死する場合もあるといいます。

Nuclear material enough to provide power can give off a lethal level of radioactivity. Besides, the heat produced at the power generating plants is also at high enough levels to kill a person by the heat itself or being burned.

燃料のウランの濃縮によって生じる劣化ウランやプルトニウムは核兵器の原料としても使用可能だし、逆に攻撃目標とされることも考えられます。

Uranium enrichment produces depleted uranium and plutonium, which can be transformed into nuclear weapons. And they can also make good targets in battle.

環境への悪影響が懸念される二酸化炭素の排出量は、原子力の場合はほぼありません。

Nuclear power creates nearly zero carbon dioxide, which has, we are afraid, a bad effect on the environment.

原子力発電は安くつきます。原子力は石油火力の約6割の費用で同等の電力を産出できます。

Nuclear power is economical, producing the same amount of electricity as oil at 60% of the cost of oil.

▶ 原子力発電の賛成論　　　　　　　　　　　　　　　　　　　　CD 2 ➡ 40

原子力発電は時代の必然です。環境への汚染が少なく、低コストでおおきなエネルギーが得られる。原子力発電なくして私たちの生活は成り立っていきません。すでに日本も2004年時点でエネルギーの原子力依存率が11％あります。

Nuclear power is the natural course of action. It doesn't contaminate the surrounding area much and provides much energy. We could not live without it. Japan, in 2004, got 11% of its energy from nuclear power.

その使用増は現在の日本の繁栄を維持し、中東など産油国への依存度を下げることにもなります。

Increasing its use will help Japan maintain its current prosperity and reduce its dependency on oil producing countries in the Middle East.

原子力発電反対論　　CD 2 ➡ 41

環境への心配がないというのは詭弁です。	It's a fallacy to say there's no damage to the environment.
運営がきっちりとされていれば、被害が最小限に抑えられるというのが正しいのではないでしょうか。一度事故が起こるとその被害は甚大です。取り返しがつきません。	It should be fair to say that when operations are done properly, damage is kept to a minimum. Once something happens, its damage can be far-reaching and irrevocable.
そして事故は原発があるかぎり人災として起こりうるものです。起こらない保証はどこにもありません。	Humans have accidents and they can occur as long as we have nuclear power plants. There's no guarantee it will not happen.
旧ソ連時代のチェルノブイリやアメリカのスリーマイル島での原発事故は有名です。	Well known nuclear accidents are Chernobyl of the old USSR and Three Mile Island in the U.S.
とりわけチェルノブイリでは4万人もの人が亡くなったという報告もあります。いまだに放射能の影響は続いていて、現在は原子炉をコンクリートの石棺で覆ってはいますが、恒久的な対策とはなっていません。	Some 40 thousand people died in the Chernobyl accident according to one report. Still radioactive, the nuclear reactor is covered with stone coffins, but it's not a permanent remedy.

代替エネルギーの提案　　CD 2 ➡ 42

今はエネルギー需要も高い上に、大気に対してはクリーンだということで原子力は不可欠だと言われますが、いずれ人類を滅亡に追いやる可能性のある物を建設するのは反対です。	Given a current high demand for energy and the assumption that it is clean, some people say nuclear energy is indispensable, but I'm still against construction of anything that could annihilate man.

スウェーデンやオランダなど欧州の一部の国では原子力発電を放棄し、かつ公害のないクリーンなエネルギーを促進することが実際に国家規模で行なわれています。日本人も同じ選択をするべきと思います。	In some European countries like Sweden and Holland, nuclear power generation has been abandoned and pollution-free, clean energy was pursued on a state level. I suggest Japan follow their example.
環境や人類の将来を犠牲にしてまで生活の快適さを追い求めていくことはやめるべきです。同時にクリーンでかつ安全なエネルギー開発にまい進するべきでしょう。	Stop pursuing comfortable lifestyles at the expense of the environment and the future of human beings. Engage whole-heartedly in the development of clean and safe energy.

▶ 環境保護の視点からの意見を伝える　　　　CD 2 ➡ 43

最近日本でも、風力発電所を建設したり、太陽熱の利用なども普及してきました。	In recent years, wind power plants have been established and solar power has come into wide use in Japan.
しかし、エネルギーをむやみに使うことを考えるのはどうかと思います。エネルギーを使うことによって、生産活動は増えますが、資源が枯渇することになり、同時にゴミも発生します。	However, I doubt that it is a good idea for us to use much energy. The use of energy will increase production, but on the other hand, it will deplete natural resources and generate a great amount of rubbish.
結局環境によくありません。人間が理想的な社会を望む限り、50年前の不便さに戻る必要があります。そうでないと、破滅へと向かうのではないかと私は思います。	In the long run, even the clean alternative energy generation is also harmful to the environment. If we hope for an ideal society, we should go back to the inconvenient world 50 years ago; otherwise, we will go to rack and ruin.
なぜなら、資源は限られているし、地球も汚れてくるからです。	The reason is because natural resources are limited and the earth will be polluted.

4 生態系と動物愛護

▶ 生態系について考える　　　　　　　　　　　　　CD 2 ➡ 44

生物間の相互関係およびそれらを取り巻く無機的環境との相互関係を総合的にとらえた社会のまとまりが生態系です。

A unit that comprehensively embraces the relations between living things and those between living things and inorganic surroundings is an ecosystem.

地球全体をひとつの生態系ととらえることもできるし、ある山をひとつの生態系ととらえることもできます。この考え方は 19 世紀末ごろからあります。

The Earth is one example of an ecosystem, and so is one mountain. The idea was first conceived in the late 19th century.

生態系は内部のもの同士が相互作用しながら安定していくという性質がありますが、外部からの働きで変化します。現在では人間活動が多くの生態系に急速な変化、破壊をもたらしています。

The ecosystem moves towards stability as elements within interact with each other. But it can be changed by an outside factor. Today human activities bring about radical changes and damage many ecosystems.

生態系に変化をもたらすのは人間の活動だけではありません。いわゆる外来種があります。外来種の問題は 1990 年代に世界的に注目されるようになりました。同時期に日本でもにわかに注目を浴びました。2004 年には外来生物法が施行されています。

Not only human actions but introduced species can also transform an ecosystem. The problem of introduced species caught attention worldwide in 1990. It was spotlighted in Japan around the same time. In 2004 the law concerning introduced species was enacted.

動物愛護に関しては法律があり、動物の虐待防止や適切な取り扱い方などに関して定められています。

As for animal protection there's a law, which stipulates prohibition of animal mistreatment, etc.

また、動物の人に対する危害や迷惑の防止についても定められています。	It also stipulates protections for people from animals.

▶ 動物の大量繁殖の問題について考える　　CD 2 ➡ 45

琵琶湖ではブラックバスの繁殖が問題になっています。固有の生物を食い荒らし生態系を壊しています。確認されてから、漁業者は駆除にかかっていますが、バス釣ファンからは反対があります。	At Lake Biwa, the introduction of black bass has been a serious problem. They break the ecosystem by eating up indigenous creatures. Since they were identified, fishermen have worked to remove them. But there's opposition from bass anglers.
沖縄ではハブの駆除を目的にマングースが放たれ定着しました。しかしハブ以外の小動物を襲い、生態系に被害を与えています。しかも実際にはハブの駆除にはほとんど役立っていないようです。	In Okinawa, to get rid of habu snakes, they released mongooses, which have settled there. But they attack small animals other than habu snakes and damaged the ecosystem. In fact they are nearly useless in extermination of habu snakes.

▶ 動物を飼うことから話を発展させる　　CD 2 ➡ 46

私は以前から社会の変化でひとつ懸念していることがあります。街を自由に徘徊する犬の姿を見かけなくなったことです。	One thing had me unsettled for some time. It's the fact that we no longer see dogs roaming on the street.
私が子どもの頃には街にはけっこう犬が歩き回っていました。それらの犬はどこへ行ってしまったのでしょうか。おそらくみんな人間に殺されてしまったのだろうと思っています。	In my childhood dogs used to walk around on the street. I wonder where they have gone. Perhaps they have been killed by humans, I suppose.
過保護な親が増えると街に徘徊する犬は子どもに危険なので取り除こうということになるでしょう。	As parents have become more overprotective, the idea that wandering dogs, which are dangerous to kids, should be driven away is overwhelming, isn't it?

現在では犬はすべて部屋の中で飼う愛玩用か、せいぜい狭い庭に縛られて飼われています。散歩もせいぜい日に1回か2回でしょう。	Today a dog means the toy dog kept inside a house or at best the one on a leash in a narrow yard. They get out for a walk only once or twice a day, don't they?
散歩に毎日2回はちゃんと連れて行っているからOKというのは人間の勝手な見方です。怠慢で散歩を忘れる飼い主もいることは想像に難くありません。	The idea that walking them twice a day is enough is only our one-sided view. I can even imagine some people forgetting to walk their dogs.
見せかけはともかく、動物愛護からはほど遠いものに見えます。	I think this is far from the right treatment of animals no matter what they may think.
かつて地上には恐竜が栄えていたと言われています。その恐竜は後に哺乳類や鳥類に取って代わられることになります。これは地球規模で見た生態系の変化だと思います。自然の成り行きで、それそのものに問題はないと思います。	Studies say once the earth was full of dinosaurs, which later gave way to mammals and birds. I think this was an ecosystem change on a global level. It was a natural occurrence and no problem in itself.
現在起こっている生態系の変化もある意味自然の成り行きではないでしょうか。人間による自然破壊も深刻な問題には違いありませんが、ながい目で見ればこれが自然の淘汰だという考えもできるかもしれません。	Ecosystem transformations currently happening are in one way natural occurrences. The destruction of nature by humans is a serious problem, but give it a wide scope and you could find it just an example of natural selection.

▶ 動物実験について考える　　　　　　　　　　　　　　　　CD 2 ➡ 47

生態系を少しでも知ることによって、動物や植物がお互いに共生していることや、人間の生活も生物のお世話になっていることが分かります。その意味で、生態系は、現代人には有益な面が多いです。	Even a little knowledge of ecology will make us understand how dependent animals and plants are on each other and how closely related human life is to other living things. In this regard, ecology is beneficial to people today in many ways.

動物愛護の視点から、「動物実験はナンセンス！」と訴えている人が増えています。	From the viewpoint of protection of animals, there has been an increasing number of people who are strongly against experiments on animals.
厚生労働省は、危険な添加物でも、動物実験を盾に安全性を認めています。しかし、その物質をどれくらい与えたら、動物が死ぬのかをチェックするのが動物実験です。	The Ministry of Health, Labor and Welfare use experiments on animals as an excuse for approving of the safety of even more dangerous additives. However, the purpose of the experiments on animals is to determine the additional amount of an additive that will cause the animals to die.
小動物にとって危険なものでも、それよりはずっと体重の大きい人間には危険でないと判断されるのですが、この発想そのものが危険です。	Experimenters believe that although the drugs are dangerous for small animals, humans, because of their greater size, will not be negatively affected. This way of thinking itself is dangerous.
本当に安全なものは、動物実験する必要がありません。	Something truly safe does not need any animal experiments.
また、動物実験は、多くの動物を犠牲にしているので、動物愛護の視点からも、できるだけなくすことが必要だと思います。	And as a result of such experiments, many animals will die. Therefore, we should give up conducting tests on animals from the point of view of animal protection.

実践編 第8章 環境問題に関する意見を述べる

5 交通渋滞と交通事故

▶ 情報を伝える　　　　　　　　　　　　　　　CD 2 ➡ 48

日本は車大国です。ある調べでは平成16年で乗用車だけで4千万台を越えています。東京や大阪の中心部はいつも車の渋滞でなかなか前に進みません。

Japan is a big automobile society. One study says the number of private cars exceeded 40 million in Heisei 16. Central parts of Tokyo and Osaka are chronically congested, making it difficult to move.

これは単に車が多いだけでなく、違法駐車が大きな原因です。2006年には駐車違反を取り締まるために法律が改正され、駐車違反では運転者だけでなく車の所有者にも責任を問えるようになりました。また、駐車違反の取締りを民間に委託できるようにもなりました。その他の改正も含め、駐車違反車はかなり減りました。

It can be attributed not only to the number of cars but illegal parking. In 2006, the law was modified to crack down on illegal parking more severely. Now the police can hold responsible the car's owner no matter who actually parks it. It also contracted with private companies to issue tickets thus further cracking down on illegal parking. Together with other measures, it has contributed to a reduction of illegal parking.

交通事故の原因の飲酒運転に関しても2002年には罰金などの刑が厳しくなり、飲酒運転も減っています。
注：DUI = driving under the influence
　　（飲酒運転）

As for DUI, the penalties including the fine were increased in 2002, resulting in reduced DUI.

さらに2001年に施行された危険運転致死傷罪が2004年に改正され、自動車事故で人を死に至らしめた場合には最高20年の懲役または禁固の罰を受ける可能性があります。	In addition, "the charge of reckless driving causing death" enacted in 2001 and revised in 2004 has made it possible for a person who is under the influence and involved in a car accident which results in someone getting killed to get up to 20 years in prison with or without hard labor.
危険運転致死傷罪は自動二輪車には適応されないなど、まだ問題は残っています。	Problems still remain since the law doesn't apply to motorcycles.
ある統計では平成18年の交通事故での死者数は平成8〜17年の平均よりも減っています。しかしなお月間500人ほどの人が犠牲になっています。	According to some statistics, the death toll by car accidents is smaller than the average between the 8th and 17th years of Heisei. But we still see about 500 victims every month.

▶ 交通事故の現状と原因について　　　　　　　　　　　　　　　　　　CD 2 ➡ 49

トヨタ自動車は今や世界ナンバーワンの自動車メーカーにならんばかりの勢いで車の売上を上げています。	Toyota Auto is making a large profit, and is on its way to being the biggest car maker in the world.
携帯電話などをはじめとして自動車を運転しながら扱える製品がたくさんあります。運転をしながら使用すると運転者の注意がそがれ、事故の原因になると言われています。	There are devices you can use while driving like a cellular phone. It's said that the use of such devices can distract the driver, which could lead to an accident.
もちろんいくつかのものは規制ができ、取り締まられているのですが。	Of course, use of some of them is regulated and clamped down on.
自動車事故による死者がいまだに多い中自動車事故を誘発するようなものがなぜ氾濫するのかがわかりません。	I don't understand why our society is full of accident-inducing things while having high casualty rates from traffic accidents.

177

倫理観も多大に関わっていると思います。	I think ethics has much to do with this.
交通渋滞のもうひとつの原因は都市への人口の集中があると思います。政府は政府機能のみならず、いろんな機能を地方に分散する対策を考えるべきです。	I think another cause of traffic jams is population concentration in urban areas. The government should consider scattering not only the governmental functions but other facilities across the country as well.
2016年のオリンピック予定地は国内では東京と福岡が争いましたが、人口などの分散を考えるなら福岡にするべきでしょう。東京になるのは金が絡んでいる以外私には想像できません。	Tokyo and Fukuoka vied as the candidate site for the 2016 Olympic Games. You'd select Fukuoka if you are thinking of ways of dispersing the population. I can only think of money being involved as the reason they'd chose Tokyo.

▶ 歩くことを奨励する   CD 2 ➡ 50

歩いてできること、行けるところは歩くようにしましょう。自家用車にできるだけ乗らないようにしましょう。都市部では地下鉄、バスなどの交通網も発達しているので歩いてどこへでも行けます。	Walk whenever possible: Do what you can do by walking, and walk to the place where you can walk. Try not to drive your car so often: Urban areas have public transportation such as subways and buses, so you can get anywhere on foot.
歩くようにしましょう。その方が健康にもいいです。現代人は健康面からも歩く量が少なすぎます。	Walking is better for your health too. Today people don't walk enough from the health viewpoint.
自動車がどうしても必要なことは否めませんが、最近は社会的ステータスか何かわかりませんが、やたら大きな車を買う人が多いです。	It's undeniable that the car is a must. Recently many have been buying large cars as a status symbol and for other reasons.

自動車を購入する場合には不必要に大きな車を買わずに、軽自動車などコンパクト車を選びましょう。	Choose a compact-sized car, not an unnecessarily big car when you purchase one.
また行政も税金や、車検の値段だけでなく、コンパクト車にはもっと得するような制度を導入して激励すべきです。	The government should introduce systems that would favor more those who buy a compact car, such as low taxes and low overhaul prices, which would encourage people to buy compact cars.
他にも駐車場業者にもコンパクトな自動車用の駐車はかなり安くすることなどを指導していくのも有効ではないでしょうか。	Plus, why don't they have parking lot owners lower the parking charges for compact cars? Which, I guess, would be effective.

表現のコツ　「得する」の表現

> 彼は恐らくそのプロジェクトで一番得するであろう。
> → He will probably profit the most from that project.
> 彼女の意見に賛成して何の得があるの。
> → What's the use of agreeing with her opinion?
> そんな口の聞き方をして得なことでもあるの。
> → What earthly good is that sort of talk?
> 私は近道をして20分得しました。
> → I saved twenty minutes by taking a short cut.

6 環境はどのように守るか？

▶ 情報を伝える　　　　　　　　　　　　　　　　　　　CD 2 ➡ 51

現在自然環境は際限なく破壊され続けています。このままでは遠からず人類はおろか地球上の生命すべてが存亡の危機にさらされます。

Now our natural environment has been destroyed endlessly. Keep it that way, and all living things on earth will be in danger of extinction before long.

環境破壊には砂漠化、オゾン層の破壊、温暖化、森林の減少、河川や大気の汚染などがあります。これらはすべて地球の将来に暗い影を投げかけるものです。また、生物の絶滅危機は破壊の結果ですが、新たなる環境破壊の原因ともなります。

Environmental destruction includes desertification, depletion of the ozone layer, global warming, deforestation, polluted rivers and air, which all foreshadow the future of the earth. Endangered species are a result of environmental destruction, but can also cause damage to the environment.

破壊の原因には石油やガスの使用、森林の伐採、動物の狩猟、また身近な所ではゴミのポイ捨てや自動車の運転などがあります。

Among the causes are the use of oil and gas, logging and hunting. Habits such as littering and driving automobiles also add to the problem.

▶ 発展の結果がもたらしたもの　　　　　　　　　　　　CD 2 ➡ 52

多くの環境破壊は人間がよりよい生活を求めて発展してきた結果とも言えます。

One could say human development in pursuit of a better life results in environmental destruction.

例えば私たちが使っている物の多くは工場で大量生産されていますが、工場からの煙や廃棄物が周辺地域を汚染しています。自動車の排気ガスは言うまでもありません。

One example is many things we use are mass-produced at factories and that their wastes contaminate the environs, not to mention the automobile emission.

環境を守るための努力から話を発展させる　　　CD 2 ➡ 53

環境を守るための努力は世界の各地で行なわれています。国家レベルでの取り組みは環境回復のためには必要不可欠です。	Efforts are being made the world over to preserve the environment. Effort on the national level is essential to preventing further environmental disruption.
ブラジルをはじめとするサトウキビの量産国ではガソリンに代わる自動車の燃料がサトウキビを使って開発されています。	Brazil and other countries, which are large producers of sugar cane are working on a new energy source using sugar cane, which could replace gasoline.
二酸化炭素を排出せず、大気を汚さないということです。当面コスト面では問題がありますが、普及すれば問題ではなくなるでしょう。	It doesn't pollute the air because it doesn't produce carbon dioxide. It is not economical yet, but costs could become competitive when production increases.
原子力発電、火力発電に代わる発電方法もヨーロッパのいくつかの国で始められています。風力による発電などです。もともとオランダでは風車によって動力を得ているという長い歴史がありますね。	Some European countries are engaged in developing alternative energy sources to nuclear and thermal power generation, one of which is wind power generation. Holland has a long history of getting power from the windmills.
原子力発電は大気を汚染しないと言いますが、見方によれば究極の環境破壊装置です。アメリカのスリーマイル島やウクライナのチェルノブイリで証明されています。日本で同規模の事故が起これば国全体を破壊することになるでしょう。	They say nuclear power generation doesn't pollute the atmosphere, but it could be an ultimate destroyer of environments. It's been proven at Three Mile Island in the U.S. and Chernobyl in the Ukraine. If an accident of the same scale ever happens in Japan, it could ruin the whole nation.

日本政府は企業の利益だけを考えるのではなく、国民全体の利益を考えるなら、クリーンなエネルギー源に一刻も早く切り換えていくべきです。	The government should consider the interest of not only corporations but people, and introduce clean energy sources as soon as possible.
企業が出す公害は色々あります。例えば、水質汚染や大気汚染だけでなく、最近ではかなり深刻なアスベストの問題もあります。	There are various kinds of environmental pollutions. For example, there has recently been a rather serious problem of asbestos in addition to water pollution or air pollution.
経皮毒と言われる原因をつくる日用品の成分が、人と環境を害していると、最近、本や論文などで発表されるようになりました。	Recently, some books and academic papers have come to insist that the chemical substances causing dermal toxicity have been doing more and more harm to humans and the environment.
環境は一人では守れず、一社の努力でも守れません。	The environment cannot be protected by one person or one company's efforts.
賢い消費者が徐々に増えれば、大企業を守ろうとする国や意識の低い企業が変わることにつながるでしょう。すると、結果的に環境を変える事ができるのではないかと私は思います。	If flexible-minded consumers aware of the above facts increase in number, our country, which protects big businesses, and careless profit-seeking companies may have a policy change some time in the future. Consequently, I think we can change our environment for the better.

▶ 環境を改善するために個人ができること　　　　　CD 2 ➡ 54

企業と同様、個人レベルでの努力も大切です。	Of course, efforts on an individual level are as important.

買い物ではビニール袋を使わずに買い物カゴを持っていく、本屋では不要なカバーは断わる、自動車の駐車中はエンジンを止める、会社の電気は、休暇中は消しておく、紙くずは再利用に回すなどなど。いろいろとできることはあります。 注：英文は、just 以下が主語である倒置構文。	Take your shopping bag and don't use a plastic bag, refuse unnecessary book covers at bookstores, stop the engine when the car is parked, turn off all lights at the office when it's closed, and recycle used paper are just a few things you can practice.
一人ひとりが、身近なところから細心の注意を払うべきでしょう。	Each one of us has to pay careful attention to things closest to us.
身近な取り組みとしては、ごみの分別、エネルギーの節約、有害な生活排水の制限や石油系日用品使用の見直しなど、色々あります。	Efforts we can make in our daily lives range from separating trash, saving energy, decreasing harmful household effluents to the giving up of using petroleum-related household goods.
あと80年足らずで、地球は自浄作用をなくす！と、今叫ばれている現状を深く受け止め行動すべきだと思います。	It has been pointed out that our Earth will lose its own self-cleansing action in 80 years. We have to lead our eco-friendly life with this fact in mind.

▶ 「もったいない」を考える　　　　　　　　　　　　　　　　　　CD 2 ➡ 55

日本人は環境に対する意識が低すぎると思います。低燃費の自動車を開発する反面大型車に人気があります。日本の道路、駐車場状況を考えると、小型低燃費車を多用するのが理想と思われます。趣味で不必要に大型車に乗る人が多いのには驚かされます。	I think Japanese have poor awareness of the environment. While energy-efficient cars are developed, big cars have been popular. Given Japan's road and parking lots conditions, it is best to use small, energy-efficient cars. It's surprising that many drive large cars for fun.
私が子どもの頃はものを大切にする、例えばお茶碗のお米を一粒も残さずに食べるのが美徳でした。	It was advisable to handle things with much care, for instance, eating rice to the last piece, in my childhood.

近年ではケニア出身のマータイさんが日本の「もったいない」という精神が環境の保護に不可欠だとして、普及に尽力しています。

Ms Maathai from Kenya advocates Japan's "Mottainai" spirit as needed for environment preservation and tries to promote it in the world.

環境保護、回復のためにはこの日本人の古い価値が不可欠です。

This traditional value of Japan is indispensable for preservation and restoration of the environment.

第9章

社会問題に関する意見を述べる

1 少子高齢化社会

▶ 少子化に関する情報とその理由を考える　　　　　　　　　　CD 2 ➡ 56

日本の出生率は、2006年現在で、1.25人です。	Japan's birthrate is 1.25 per woman as of 2006.
日本の少子化も深刻ですが、世界1位ではありません。実は韓国が、現在1位で、出生率は1.08人です。	The dwindling birthrate in Japan is serious of course, but Japan's birthrate is not the smallest in the world. In reality, Korea comes on top in terms of the declining birthrate. Korea's rate is 1.08 children per woman.
少子化の原因としては、4つの理由が考えられます。	There are four main reasons for this trend.
1つ目に、女性の社会進出が進み、経済的に独立した女性が増えているため、結婚をしないか晩婚になっているということがあげられます。	In the first place, partly because they have made inroads into society, more women are choosing to remain single or get married later in life.
2つ目に、結婚しても、共働きで子どもを作らない夫婦が増えている。このような夫婦はDINKSと呼ばれます。	Secondly, two-income married couples who choose not to have children are on the increase. These couples are called DINKS, which stands for double income no kids.
共働きだから子どもを育てる余裕がないという消極的な子ども軽視の面と、夫婦だけで人生を楽しむという積極的な子ども軽視の考え方があります。	Some two-income families regret that they are unable to afford to have and raise children; others are quite satisfied with their lives and have no desire to have and raise children.

3つ目に、就職難や失業率の高さがあります。子育てのためのお金に余裕がなくなっているという現状があります。	Thirdly, the reason is a job shortage or the high unemployment rate. For some couples, having children is not an option because of the expenses associated with raising children.
最後になりましたが、見逃せないのが、子どもがほしくてもなかなかできない夫婦もたくさんいるということです。現代生活における公害や添加物、経皮毒が、体の機能に影響を与えている可能性があるので、子どもができにくくなっているということもあるでしょう。	Last but not least, there are many couples who want children but cannot have them. I suspect that this infertility may be attributable to the negative effects of environmental pollution, food additives or dermal toxicity on human bodily functions, which makes it hard for them to physically have babies.

▶ 高齢化を生物学の視点から考える　　CD 2 ➡ 57

動物の世界では生殖活動ができなくなれば、さっさといなくなるのが動物としての正しい振る舞いです。	With respect to animals, it is quite natural and even desirable for them to die as soon as possible if they lose their reproductive function.
つまり、人間のように老化の状態を長く保つことはありません。	In short, unlike humans, they will not live long when they are no longer functioning at a high level.
蟷螂（かまきり）のオスなどは、交尾が終われば、メスに頭からかじられるそうです。子育てするメスに栄養を提供するためです。	I hear that the head of a male mantis may be bitten off and then eaten by a female mantis after mating. He is said to give nutrition to his partner so that she can easily take care of her eggs.
参考：蟷螂のメスがオスを食べる行為は、オスの香りをえさと勘違いしてしまった結果であるという説もあります。	cf. There is a theory that the act of a female mantis eating the male mantis occurs due to the fact that the females just mistake males for food.

象の寿命は50年から70年、ねずみの寿命は1年から2年ですが、どちらも心臓は一生に15億回打ちます。ねずみは象に比べて心臓の鼓動は速いということになります。	The life span of elephants is 50 to 70 years, while that of mice is only one to two years. However, the heart of both animals beats 1.5 billion times during their life times. This means that the beating of a mouse's heart is quite fast.
人間は生物学の視点から、超長生きであるということになります。	From the viewpoint of biology, we can conclude that human beings are considered to live extremely long.
参考：一生に心臓が15億回打つことから、人間の一生を計算すると、なんと約26.3年になります。 ※東京工業大学教授本川達雄氏による。	cf. If we calculate the life span of a human being based on the theory that the average heart beats 1.5 billion times and then dies, our life span would be only about 26.3 years.
近年では、医学の進歩により、昔に比べ、さらに長生きになっています。	In recent years, people have been able to live even longer than in the past, thanks in a large part to developments in medical care.
日本の65歳以上の高齢者の人口は、2006年9月現在で、2640万人で、総人口の20.7％を占めています。	In Japan, as of September, 2006, 26.4 million people or 20.7% of the total population is over 65 years of age.

参考：　世界の高齢者率
　　アメリカ　→　12.4%
　　イギリス　→　16.0%
　　フランス　→　16.2%
　　ドイツ　　→　18.6%
　　韓国　　　→　 9.1%

cf. the percentage of people in the world who are over 65 years of age
　　the U.S.A.　　　　　12.4%
　　the United Kingdom　16.0%
　　France　　　　　　 16.2%
　　Germany　　　　　 18.6%
　　Korea　　　　　　 9.1%

2 国際化と情報化

▶ 情報を伝える　　　　　　　　　　　　　　　CD 2 ➡ 58

国際化は大きくわけると国や企業レベルと個人のレベルになります。	Internationalization is roughly on two levels: One is the national and corporate level and the other, the individual level.
日本はずっと以前から工業製品が世界のいろんな所でよく知られています。	Japan has long been known worldwide for its industrial products.
トヨタやホンダを知らない人は世界的にあまりいないでしょう。今ではニンテンドーやプレイステーションは海外でもみんなが知っています。その意味で日本は昔から国際的な国と言えます。	I guess there are few people who don't know Toyota or Honda. Now Nintendo and PlayStation are household names abroad. In that sense, one can say Japan has been an international country for a long time.
また、イラクやその他の国へ軍事的な支援をする活動も盛んに行なわれるようになり、国際化は進んでいると言えます。	Plus, Japan's military contribution as seen in Iraq is getting larger, and Japan's internationalization is expanding in that respect too.
個人個人のレベルではどうでしょうか。日本は江戸時代に鎖国をしていましたが、ある意味今でも鎖国をしている国と言えるかもしれません。世界には経済的にゆとりがあれば移民や外国労働者を受け入れている国がありますが、日本は例外です。	How about on the individual level? Japan closed its door to the outside world in the Edo period, and one could say Japan still does in a sense. Wealthy countries in the world accept immigrants and foreign laborers but Japan is an exception.
しかし現在、各種規制緩和によりいろんな意味で日本も外国企業や外国人に門戸を開くようになってきています。	However, Japan too is opening up to foreign companies and foreign laborers in various respects by deregulation.

コンピュータとインターネットの発達は情報の流通を活発にさせています。	The development of computers and the Internet helps promote the active flow of information.
さらに情報流通の媒体としての携帯電話の普及はそれに拍車をかけています。	In addition, the spread of cellular phones helps do so further.
いずれ、もっと通信網が拡大すれば世界のどこにいても誰とでも情報交換できるときが来るでしょう。	In time, with further development of the telephone network, the time will come when anyone can communicate with anyone else anywhere on the surface of the earth.

▶ 国際化における日本のあり方を議論する　　CD 2 ➡ 59

国際化と言っても日本が戦争などの行為に参加することには反対です。	I oppose Japan's participation in military acts in the name of internationalization.
平和を長年かかげてきた日本はその主張を通すべきです。それが真の国際事業への参加だと思います。	Japan, which has long advocated peace, should stick to its slogan. I believe such an attitude is actual participation in an international cause.
特定の国に押されて考えを変えるのは国際社会への貢献というよりも、迎合に過ぎません。	Changing its stance pushed by a certain country can never contribute to the international community but is only like sucking up to it.
日本人が国際化する上での大きな障壁は言葉です。国際語としての英語その他の語をもっと話すことが必要と思います。	One big barrier standing in the way of Japan's internationalization is language. We need to speak English or other languages as international languages.

外国人労働者の日本への受け入れは基本的には賛成ではありません。日本は犯罪率が低く安全に暮らせています。	I basically oppose acceptance of foreign workers in Japan. With a low crime rate, we live in peace.
外国人の犯罪は悪質なものが多いと聞いています。外国人労働者らが犯罪行為を行なうことはよくあることです。悪質な犯罪が増えることを心配します。	I hear crimes by foreigners are very vicious, and foreign workers often commit crimes. I'm afraid there may be an increasing number of felonies.
国際化は今まで単一民族国家だった日本にいろんな言語、文化の人が入るということです。英語も話せない日本人は自国内で阻害される民族グループという立場になるでしょう。当面はたいへんな苦難を迎えるでしょう。	Internationalization means people of different languages and cultures will come into Japan, which has been homogeneous. Japanese, who can't speak English, will be an ethnic group isolated by others inside their own land. We would have to face a difficult time for the moment.

▶ **インターネットと情報の氾濫について意見を述べる**　　CD 2 ➡ 60

インターネットなどによる情報流通の活発化は私たちの生活を便利に豊かにします。それにより多くの機会が生まれ、いろんな可能性を広げてくれています。	Active info flow on the Internet can make our lives convenient and rich. It gives us more opportunities and possibilities.
しかし野放しの情報の流通は教育、モラルなどの観点からは必ずしも手放しで喜べるものではありません。	But uncontrolled flow of info is not necessarily welcome in terms of education and morals.
性欲をいたずらに掻き立てる情報は氾濫しているし、犯罪行為を呼びかけるような情報が流されたことも幾度かあります。情報収集の選択は本質的には個人にゆだねられるものと考えますが、当局による規制もある程度必要かと思います。	The Internet is flooded with info stimulating sexual lust, and info was sometimes posted inviting viewers to crimes. I think basically it's up to each individual whether to take certain info or not. Now I feel a need for some regulation by the authorities.

3 結婚と離婚

▶ 情報を伝える　　　　　　　　　　　　　　　　　　　CD 2 ➡ 61

厚生労働省調査では1970年と2000年を比較すると年間の婚姻数は減っています。初婚、再婚の総数では20万件強の差があります。	According to one research project by the Ministry of Health, Labor and Welfare (MHLW), the total number of first marriages and remarriages fell from 1970 to 2000 by a little more than 200,000 per year.
また初婚年齢は上がってきています。同調査で1970年と2002年を比べると男が2.2歳、女では3.2歳上がりました。	The age when people first get married has risen. The above research shows that the age of the average groom rose by 2.2 years from 1970 to 2000. The age of the average bride rose by 3.2 years during the same time period.
結婚の需要が減ってきているのでしょうか。	Is there a drop in demand for marriage?
離婚件数は増えています。厚生労働省によると平成14年の離婚件数は29万2000組です。これは届出のあった離婚であり、別居しているなど事実上破綻している夫婦を入れるともっと多いと考えられます。	Divorces have increased. MHLW reports that there were 292,000 divorces in Heisei 14. The figure concerns only registered divorces. The figure is probably larger when including all couples who have already broken up or separated.
ある調査によると結婚の相手に満足できなければ離婚すればよいと考えている人が男女ともに5割を超えています。	One study points out that more than half of the men and women think they wouldn't mind divorcing if they are not satisfied with their marriages.
結婚形態の変化や女性の社会進出が離婚増加の原因と言われています。	It's said that changes of married life and women's advances in society are responsible for the rise in divorces.

形態の変化というのは結婚が家と家の結びつきという考え方から本人同士の結びつきというようになってきたということです。	By changes of married life I mean that the view that marriage is about families has been replaced with the one that marriage is about a man and a woman.
しかし、他に離婚をマイナスイメージにとらえない風潮、相手の欠点に対する忍耐の減少、性の不一致などをあげる専門家もいます。	Specialists also suggest that other reasons are the trend of not seeing divorce as negative, lack of patience toward a spouse's defects, and different views on sex.
熟年者の離婚が近年取りざたされています。テレビドラマ「熟年離婚」は話題を呼びました。	There is much talk about divorces among mature couples. The TV drama "Jukunen Rikon (Mature Age Divorce)" attracted a large audience.

▶ 結婚に対する見方　　　　　　　　　　　　　　　　　　　　　　　CD 2 ➡ 62

ある調査では未婚者で結婚をしたいと思っている人は9割ほど、既婚者で結婚生活に満足している人も9割ほどです。	One survey shows about 9 out of 10 single people wish to get married. And 9 out of 10 married people are satisfied with their marriages.
結婚に対する見方はそんなに否定的ではないのです。	General views on marriage are not so negative.
法律婚か事実婚か。結婚のとらえ方は多様にあると思います。法律に従い婚姻届を提出することを結婚と考える人もいれば、本人同士が同居し夫婦だと思えば結婚しているという考えもあります。	Marriage by law or marriage by fact? There are a variety of views on marriage. Some think marriage is about getting a license and registering the marriage. Others think marriage is about living together as husband and wife without registering it.

現実にアメリカでは婚姻届を出さずに夫婦生活をしている男女は増えているそうです。	In fact, in America the number of couples who are living together as a married couple without a license is increasing.

▶ **熟年離婚の原因に関する意見** CD 2 ➡ 63

熟年層の離婚が増加しているのは今の20代30代の人だけが結婚に対して不満を持っているのではないという表れと思います。	The rise in the number of divorces of matured couples is an indication that couples in their 20's and 30's aren't the only ones unsatisfied with their marriages.
熟年離婚は女性側からの申し出がほとんどだそうですが、結婚に対する社会の見方の柔軟化や女性のさらなる解放を示唆していると思います。	In most divorces of matured couples, the wife makes the first offer, which I think suggests a more flexible way of looking at the institution by the public and the further liberation of women.
世代を超えて人間普遍の問題であることは間違いありません。	There is no doubt that this is a universal matter concerning all generations.
とにかく相手のいることなので、お互いを傷つけないように物事を進めていくのが最低限のマナーと思います。	I believe the least you have to do is take care not to hurt the other while proceeding with divorce.

表現のコツ 「示唆する」の表現

> suggest、indicate、imply などの語があります。形容詞にして suggestive や indicative も使用できます。名詞 sign や時には harbinger（前兆）も「示唆する」のニュアンスに使えます。
>
> ある新聞記事では、企業買収時代はすぐに終わると示唆していた。
> → A newspaper article suggested that M&A age will come to an end soon.
> 一連の台風は夏の終わりを示唆している。
> → The series of typhoons is a harbinger of the end of summer.

4 性の問題 ── 夫婦別姓やセクハラ

▶ 夫婦別姓の賛成論に関する情報を伝える　　　　　　CD 2 ➡ 64

賛成論は、次のような論点からなっています。	Supporters of having a different surname from one's spouse may mention the following points.
主なものを挙げてみましょう。	Let me show you some of the main points.
職業上、旧姓で業績を上げてきた女性は、その姓を、結婚後も継続したいと思う。	Those women who have important achievements to their credit in their professions want to use their surnames even after marriage.
配偶者の父母と同じ姓になることにより、配偶者の実家に縛られた感じになる。	The fact that wives are supposed to have their spouse's surname makes them feel that they are being controlled under their husband's parents' family.
法律上、どちらの姓を名乗っても良いとされていても、現在では、妻が夫の姓を名乗る率が97％と言われているので、現状は男女平等ではない。	The present situation goes against the equality of men and women, because it is said that 97% of the women who get married will change their surnames.
名前を変えることができない何らかの理由から事実婚を選択した人たちにも、平等に法律婚ができるようにさせるべきである。	Those who get married outside of the legal process just because they cannot use their spouse's name for some reason should be also given a chance to marry legally.

▶ 夫婦別姓の反対論に関する情報を述べる　　　　　　　　　　CD 2 ➡ 65

反対論は概ね、次のような論点からなっています。	The opponents of this proposal emphasize the following points.
絶対に夫婦別姓にしなければならない、切実な根拠が存在しない。	There is no urgent reason for this idea to be put into practice.
職業上の不便などは、旧姓の通称使用という方法で間に合う。	You can use your maiden name as a popular name.
子供にも、どちらの親の姓を名乗るのかを選択させるのは適切なことではない。	It is not appropriate to make children choose only one of their parents' names.
夫婦別姓に対する調査では、賛成者の割合が極めて低い。	There is a very small percentage of supporters of this idea.
参考：2001年の世論調査では、支持者は7.7％であった。	cf. According to the opinion poll conducted in 2001, only 7.7% of the people surveyed are supporters.
個人を過度に優先することが、家庭崩壊につながる。	Excessive emphasis on individuals may lead to the destruction of the family.

▶ セクハラに関する情報　　　　　　　　　　　　　　　　　　CD 2 ➡ 66

セクハラとは、主として女性に対する性的嫌がらせのことですが、広義には、相手の望まない性的な言動の全てを指します。 参考：「広義には」は in a broad sense 以外に in a wide sense ともいえる。一方、「狭義には」は in a narrow sense。	Sexual harassment refers to saying or doing sex-related things mainly towards women, but in a broader sense, it may refer to any unwelcome speech or deeds that other people find offensive.

もう少し正確に言うと、「職場などで、相手の意思に反して、女性を不快や不安な状態に追い込む性的な言葉や行為」を指します。	To be more exact, it refers to "sexual speech or deeds which drive women at working places into an uncomfortable or uneasy situation against their will."
参考:「正確に言うと」は to be more exact、exactly speaking であるが、to be more specific（具体的には）もよく用いられる。	
女性が不快と感じるかどうかが基準です。	The defining point is whether it makes women feel uncomfortable or not.
だから、同じ行為でも、その行為を行う男性によってセクハラかどうかが決まります。	Therefore, whether the same act is sexual harassment or not depends on the man who is actually involved.
ある人は、「セクハラとは好きな男性にされたい行為が、好きでない男性にされること」と定義づけしました。	Someone says that it is sexual harassment if something a woman may want done by a particular man that she likes is actually done by a man that she doesn't like.
男女雇用機会均等法では、男性に対するセクハラ、「逆セクハラ」と、職場以外のセクハラについては規定がありません。	The Equal Employment Opportunity Law doesn't stipulate sexual harassment towards men or towards anyone outside of the work environment.
セクハラは、2つのタイプに分けられます。	Sexual harassment can be classified into two types.
1つは、上下関係を利用して、卑猥な言葉や話を含む性的な言葉を吐いたり、性的行為を強要したりすることです。	One is to say something related to sex including obscene words or stories or to demand sexual acts by exercising status-related power over someone in the office.

軽いものは、酒の席での酌の強要から、ひどいものでは、昇進を人質にした性行為の強要まで、色々あります。	This type ranges from a lighter one such as making a woman serve her boss at a drinking party to a much more serious situation like demanding a sexual act, which will lead to her promotion.
もう一つは、個人または複数の人に不快感を抱かせるような性的な嫌がらせです。例えば、ヌードの写真などを職場などに貼ったり、性的な冗談や容姿についての言動などです。	The other is just playing a nasty sexually-related trick on a person or persons. For example, posting a picture of a nude woman in the working place or somewhere inappropriate, or telling a dirty joke, or speaking about the body or figure of a woman.

▶ セクハラに関する意見　　　　　　　　　　　　　　　CD 2 ➡ 67

セクハラ行為は許されるものではありません。	Sexual harassment itself is something that should not be allowed.
しかし、女子に嫌われている男性は、女性に対する全ての言動がセクハラ行為になってしまう可能性があるのが問題ではないかと思います。	However, everything that a man disliked by a woman may say or do could be viewed as sexual harassment. This is a problem, I think.
「その服似合っているね」も不快感を与えたらセクハラになる可能性があるからです。	A compliment like "You look nice in your dress" may be sexual harassment if this remark makes the woman feel uncomfortable.
つまり、否定的な響きのしない言動も、セクハラになる可能性があるのです。男性の意図に関係なく、セクハラ行為が成立するのもおかしくはないでしょうか。	In short, something which does not have a negative ring can be sexual harassment. Sexual harassment may occur regardless of the intent on the part of a male. This is a little strange, isn't it?

悪気がないのに、いいことをした人間が、セクハラで訴えられたら悪い人間とされてしまうような点が問題だと思います。	The problem is that the reputation of a person who intends to do something good may be damaged if he is accused of sexual harassment through no fault of his own.
大げさに言えば、存在自体がセクハラになる男性が存在するということになります。	Emphatically speaking, the existence of such a man itself can be sexual harassment.

表現のコツ　「上下関係を訳す」

「上下関係」をそれほど重視しない西洋文化圏では、これに相当するピッタリの英語表現はありませんが、概ね、次のような用例があります。

我々の社長は、上下関係に関係なく、スタッフを同等に扱う。
→ Our president treats his staff irrespective of social standing.
我々の会社には厳しい上下関係がある。
→ Our company has a strict pecking order.
その組織は、しっかりとした上下関係が守られていた。
→ The organization observed a hierarchy of superior-inferior relationships

5 職の問題 ――― 就職難やリストラ

▶ 情報を伝える　　　　　　　　　　　　　　　CD 2 ➡ 68

大企業が人件費の安い海外に、生産拠点を移してしまった事も就職難の一因です。それによって国内に空洞化が起こります。
注：マイナスイメージのことでも、「貢献する」の訳ができる contribute to を用いることができる。

The difficulty of finding employment results partly from the relocation of production footholds of big businesses to foreign countries where labor costs are cheap. This may contribute to the hollowing out of Japanese industry.

日本では終身雇用と年功序列という伝統がありますが、この制度のため、高齢者の採用や中途採用はなかなか難しいのが現状です。

Japan has a longstanding tradition of lifetime employment and the seniority system. Because of these customs, it is harder for older people to get jobs or for people to be hired midway through the year.

新卒を雇うのが基本です。ずっと雇うことを考えると、給料が高くなる年齢の高い求職者は雇いにくいということです。

It is a basic rule for companies to hire people fresh from school. Considering lifelong employment, older people are unlikely to be employed due to their age which requires a higher salary.

新卒だからといって簡単に採用されるわけではありません。それなりの実力と技術力、資格などが必要です。

The mere fact that one has just graduated from college does not make it easier for him or her to get a job. A certain level of ability and skills, plus licenses, are needed.

実力不足で、正規の就職ができない人は、フリーターになっています。

Those who cannot find full-time positions due to lack of ability usually become part-timers called freeters.

また、会社組織に縛られたくないということが理由で、フリーターを積極的に考える若者も増えています。

Also, more and more young people choose to be freeters because they are not subject to the company's strict rules that apply to fulltimers.

▶ 関連分野の雑学的情報　　　　　　　　　　　　CD 2 ➡ 69

厚生労働省の調査によれば、2004年度の一世帯あたりの平均所得は年間580万4千円であった。同調査によれば、56.2%の人が、生活が苦しいと答えている。

According to the survey conducted by the Ministry of Health, Labor and Welfare, the average annual income of a Japanese household was 5.804 million yen. According to the same survey, 56.2% of the people surveyed say they are in poverty.

一方、メリルリンチ日本証券の調査によれば、2005年の段階で、日本には、居住目的の不動産を除く資産が100万ドル以上ある富裕層は、141万人いる。

On the other hand, according to the survey conducted by Merrill Lynch Japan Securities, the number of the people in the "rich" bracket, those that have assets worth more than 1 million dollars excluding their homes, is 1.41 million.

この数字は、世界の富裕層の16%を占めている。

Those in the "rich" bracket here in Japan make up 16% of those classified as "rich" in the world.

世界では富裕層は、870万人いて、富裕層の割合では、アメリカが290万人でトップに位置する。

There are 8.7 million people classified as the rich bracket in the world, and in terms of percentage, the U.S.A. comes on top with 2.9 million rich people.

▶ リストラの問題を考える　　　　　　　　　　　CD 2 ➡ 70

リストラというのは、元来、経営状態をよい方向に再構築することから派生した言葉です。

The Japanese word "Risutora" comes from restructuring carried out for the betterment of management.

しかし、日本では、再構築のための合理化や規模縮小が強調されています。	However, in Japan, streamlining or downsizing aiming at restructuring are emphasized.
俗に言うクビのことを直接指すことのほうがずっと多いです。 注:「首になる」は get the ax(e)、get the boot、get the sack、be sacked などがある。	This word often directly refers to firing workers, or getting the axe.
リストラされると、多くの場合再就職ができず生活が困窮します。一方、リストラされなくても、まさに人員が減ったことが原因で、極度に忙しくなります。	If you are fired, you will be poor and needy, since jobs are scarce in many cases. On the other side of the coin, even if you are not fired, you will be extremely busy, just because of the lack of staff.
リストラされて困窮の余り、自殺したり、逆に、リストラされなかったが忙しすぎて、過労死という結末になったりすることは、仕事に関する、深刻な2大社会問題です。	Suicide cases resulting from poverty after losing a job and sudden death from overwork ironically due to attempts to escape dismissal are two of the most serious social problems regarding jobs.
景気が上向きなのは、リストラなどを断行した結果で、大企業にとってのみ景気が良いように思えてなりません。	The fact that business is picking up is just because of the resolute practice of "restructuring in its negative sense." The current economic boom is just for big companies. This is how I feel.
一般庶民はまだまだ不景気です。経済的に良くなったとはまったく思えません。	For ordinary people, business is still not good. We don't see any upturn in the economy.

6　宗教とカルト

▶ 情報を伝える　　　　　　　　　　　　　　CD 2 ➡ 71

日本には伝統的な宗教団体があります。仏教、神道系の団体、キリスト教団体が主なものです。	In Japan we have traditional religious organizations, among which Buddhist, Shinto and Christian ones are considered mainstream.
社会に根付いた生活習慣としての宗教、すなわち冠婚葬祭での宗教儀式は形式的なものです。	Religious practices rooted in our lives, such as wedding ceremonies, funerals and other rites, are just the ceremonious side of the religions.
例えば誕生は神社で祝い、結婚式はキリスト教会、葬式はお寺で行なうということも起こっています。 注：「例えば…」が ... are all examples という言い方がある。	For instance, celebrating a birth at a Shinto shrine, getting married at a Christian church and having a funeral at a Buddhist temple are all examples.
カルトとは宗教的崇拝のことですが、現状ではその崇拝が社会通念を超えて激しい集団のことをさします。	A cult is religious worship. But it refers to a group whose worshipping is so intense and goes beyond normal social customs.
これらの集団は周辺の人々に不安を与えたり、時には不法と思われる行為にでることもあります。	These groups sometimes cause their neighbors to be concerned, and take actions which can be considered illegal.

▶ 現代の若者と新宗教について考える　　　　CD 2 ➡ 72

現代の若者の多くは愛に飢えています。 注：「…に飢えている」は be thisty for ... も使える。	Many young people today hanker for love.

実践編　第 9 章　社会問題に関する意見を述べる

203

だからたとえ特殊な考えを持つ人であっても、その人に優しく迫られると、批判なしにその人を受け入れる傾向があります。	Such people have a propensity to accept without criticism strange ideas of a person who is kind to them.
こういうわけだから、愛に飢えていて、非常に素直な人は、カルトにはまる可能性があります。 参考:「素直な」を表す語は、mild、meek、obedient、submissive、compliant、docile など。	This is the reason why there is a possibility that any gentle person thirsty for love may become taken in by a cult.
宗教を選ぶなら、正しく指導してくれるものを選ぶべきでしょう。	If you want to choose a religion, it is better to select one which leads you correctly.
その際、伝統のある宗教団体を選ぶべきではないでしょうか。急に降って沸いたような新興宗教については気をつけましょう。	In that case, you should choose among traditional religions. We should be careful not to soon accept a suddenly mushrooming, newly-developed religion.

▶ カルトと信教の自由　　　　　　　　　　　CD 2 ➡ 73

カルトは宗教団体の信仰が現行の社会の規則や習慣と相容れないときにその行動が一般人には奇異に映るだけで、決してそのものの存在が犯罪というわけではないと思います。	A cult is a religious group whose belief doesn't come to terms with on-going rules or customs of the society and therefore appear to be odd. Its existence itself never constitutes a crime.
例えばアメリカにはアーミッシュという信仰団体があります。	For instance in America, there is a religious group called Amish.

この宗教は、いわゆるカルト団体と呼べるかもしれません。しかし決して犯罪を犯す集団でも周囲に脅威を与える集団でもありません。	You can call it a cult, but it doesn't mean they commit crimes or intimidate others.
ただ現行法を破る行為はたとえ宗教的信仰の上とはいえ禁止されるべきです。	Any religious group should be prohibited from doing anything which breaks an existing law even if it is conducted for religious purposes.
例えばかつてのオーム真理教は言うまでもなく、その他の信仰宗教団体が殺人などの反社会的な活動を行った例はあります。無法者に対しては、社会は毅然とした態度をとるべきと思います。	For instance, some religious groups have committed homicides and other anti-social activities like Aum Shinrikyo. I think that the society should take a strong stance against groups who violate the law.
しかし、ある団体が、カルトすなわち少々奇抜だからといって否定して社会的に断ち切ろうとするのは信仰の自由を犯すことになるとも言えます。	However, it is said that our negative attitude to deny the existence of a cult and completely drive it away socially just because it is a little radical may violate freedom of faith.

第 10 章

医療問題に関する意見を述べる

1 臓 器 移 植

▶ 情報を伝える　　　　　　　　　　　　　　　　CD 2 ➡ 74

日本では人間の死は心臓の停止であり、基本的には必要な臓器の摘出、維持が時間的に難しく、臓器移植は難しかった。

In Japan, death is established when the heart stops beating. Because of this, it's been difficult to remove and maintain organs in a timely manner. Thus, organ transplants are difficult to perform.

1997年に「臓器の移植に関する法律」が施行され臓器によっては脳死段階での摘出が認められ移植の可能性がひろがりました。

The "law concerning organ tranplantation" enacted in 1997 allows removal of an organ after brain death, which makes organ transplantation more possible.

臓器の提供者は医師が脳死と認め、本人が意思表示カードを持っていることが最低の条件になっています。

The minimal requirements to be an organ donor are to be recognized to be brain dead by a doctor and to carry a donor's card.

▶ 臓器移植の問題点　　　　　　　　　　　　　　CD 2 ➡ 75

臓器提供を勧める国がある一方では、臓器の売買の成否などのいろいろな問題がおこるでしょう。実際に臓器売買が認められている国もあります。生きた人も臓器を売ることができ、ほとんどが低所得者だということです。

On one hand some countries promote organ donation, and on the other hand, they raise issues about trading and selling organs. Some countries legitimize it. There are even people who sell their organs while they are still alive, and most of these people are in a low-income bracket.

最近日本では当人の意見などをはっきりせずに臓器を移植した例が発覚しました。悪いことには健常でない臓器が移植に使われたそうです。

Recently, in Japan, cases came to light in which some organ transplants were conducted without clear consent of the involved parties. Even worse, it's reported that some defective organs were used.

その結果健康に生活している人も報告されていますし、逆に亡くなった方もいるそうです。これを行った病院や医者の成否は別として、これは臓器移植の必要性がひっ迫している現状の表れではないかと思います。	It's been known that some recipients live in good health but that some others have died. Apart from whether the hospital and the doctor were wrong or not, I guess the case reflects the fact that there is a great need for organ transplants.

▶ 臓器移植の微妙な問題について考える　　　　　　　　　　　CD 2 ➡ 76

議論にあたり、移植ができなければ死んでしまう患者の気持ちになれることが大切だと思います。	Prior to discussing the issue, it's important to put yourself in the shoes of the patient that might die if he can't get a transplant.
また、臓器ドナーとなっている人の身内の気持ちになれるかどうかも大事な要素です。例えば自分の二十歳の子どもが事故にあって脳死を宣告されたとします。生前承諾の意思を示した息子の内臓の摘出を親として承諾できるのかは非常に難しい選択だと思います。	It's as important to sympathize with the close relatives of the organ donor. Suppose that you have a 20-year-old son who was just pronounced brain-dead after an accident and that he gave consent to donate his organs while living. Could you agree to the transplant? It is a very difficult decision, isn't it?
貧しくてお金のために自分の臓器を売る人がいます。法律で禁じても禁じ切れるものかどうかはわかりません。が、法律で許しているというのは問題だと思います。	There are people so poor that they sell their own organs for money. We cannot be sure if it should be forbidden by law. But if the law supports it, it would be a serious problem.
はっきりと臓器移植の意味の判断ができる大人で、本人の承諾がはっきりなければ臓器は摘出できないという法律は最低必要でしょう。	The bottom line is that the law must not allow it, unless the donor is an adult who clearly understands what organ transplant is and freely gives his consent.

でないと親が子どもの内臓を金のために売るようなことまで起こってきかねません。	Otherwise, such a terrible thing as a parent selling his own kid's organ for money might happen.
これは社会の根本的な問題です。貧困をなくすなど、医療倫理とは別の観点から見ていかなければなりません。	This is a fundamental social problem, which should be tackled from the angle of the eradication of poverty as well as medical ethics.

▶ 臓器移植の問題点の解決法を提案する　　　　　　　　　　　　CD 2 ➡ 77

科学、医学が進歩して交換用の内臓が人工的に作り出せる時代が早く来ればよいと思います。	I hope the day will come soon when science and medicine are so advanced that organ replacements are made artificially.
そうすればこの問題の大半はけりがつくのではないかと思います。	Then a good part of the issue will be resolved, I presume.
また、暴飲暴食などを避け、健康を維持することが何よりです。	The first and foremost is to avoid overeating and overdrinking, and to stay healthy.

表現のコツ　「けり」の表現

> その問題は何とかけりがつきました。
> → The issue finally came to peaceful settlement.
> 彼にその件のけりをつけてもらうのがいいでしょう。
> → It is better for him to bring the matter to an end.
> なんとかしてその問題のけりをつけてもらいたい。
> → I want you to fix the matter in some way or other.
> あなたのご主人のところに行き、はっきりけりをつけましょう。
> → I'll go to your husband and call for a showdown.
> 　　注：showdown は「(論争・喧嘩などに決着をつけるための) 対決」

2 安楽死

▶ 情報を伝える CD 2 ➡ 78

安楽死は治療不可能な疾患でなお強い苦痛をともなう場合に、医師などが患者を社会的に認知できうる方法で死に至らしめることです。	Euthanasia is for a doctor to let a patient of an incurable ailment with terrible pain die by a socially acceptable means.
方法などにより積極的な安楽死と消極的な安楽死とに分けられています。	Depending on the means, there are active and passive methods of euthanasia.
前者は薬などの投与により患者の死期を早めることです。	The former is to bring around an early death of the patient with a lethal injection or the like.
後者は単に無意味な延命をするための医療行為をせずに患者を死に至らしめることです。	The latter is to withhold treatment that prolongs the patient's life and let him die.
安楽死を法律で認めている国もあります。アメリカのいくつかの州やオランダ、ベルギーその他です。	There are countries that allow euthanasia by law. The Netherlands, Belgium and some states in the United States have all passed laws allowing euthanasia.
日本では法律で認められているわけではありませんが、消極的な安楽死は実際に医療の場で行なわれています。	In Japan, there's no law permitting euthanasia but passive euthanasia is performed in many clinical situations.
そのための指針が裁判所から示されたことがあります。	Some guidelines were once given by a court of law for euthanasia.

延命技術の進歩により、回復しないものの生かされただけの状態の患者も多くなりました。そういう人たちが苦しまずに、人としての尊厳をもって死を迎えさせてやろうとするのが尊厳死です。	Thanks to the development of life-extending technology, there are many patients who can't expect to recover but stay alive. The idea of letting such people meet a painless death with human dignity is "death with dignity."

▶ 安楽死反対論　　　　　　　　　　　CD 2 ➡ 79

安楽死を望む本人の苦痛、苦悩は想像に絶するものがあると思いますが、しかし、人の命を、人の手で絶つことは許されません！	Though a person who may want euthanasia suffers from an unbearable pain, it is impermissible for one person to kill another.
目に見えないお方からいただいた生命を全うし尽くす事が、この世に生を受けた物としての使命ではないかと思います。	Living life to its fullest until the very end should be the goal of every person who was given life by an invisible supernatural being.
苦しんでいる自分の親兄弟を見て、もう死なせてやりたいと思うことはあるかと思います。	It could be imagined that one would like to let his parent or sibling in terrible pain die.
しかし、後でそのことを後悔することになる場合もあるのではないかとも思います。そうすると残った者が一生苦しむことになりかねません。私は安楽死の容認には反対です。	But it is possible that one might regret that decision. Then it is also possible that the bereaved might suffer from the decision for the rest of their lives. I oppose the public accepting euthanasia.
また、これを簡単に容認すれば、場合によっては本人を苦痛から救うため以外の理由で安楽死を選択するケースが出てくるかもしれません。例えば家族の経済状態とか、遺産の問題とか。それは怖いことです。	In addition, if it's accepted publicly, there might be cases where they choose euthanasia for reasons other than freeing the patient from pain, such as the family's financial conditions, or succession problems. It's scary.

裁判所の指針では最低でも本人の意思が推定されることが条件になっています。ゆえにそれを犯せば犯罪となり、家族の利害のための安楽死への抑止力にはなっていると思います。	The legal guidelines say that the minimal requirement is that the patient's intention has to be presumed. Thus, a violation of the patient's intent could be a crime, hampering euthanasia for the sake of the patient's family.
特別な場合を除き、医者の職業意識と、家族の意思が対立する場合なども考えられます。これは本人の意思がはっきりしていないときはとりわけ問題です。	With a few exceptions, the doctor's professionalism and the family's will conflict with each other, particularly when there is no way to confirm the patient's intention.
つまり、医者は基本的に患者の病気を取り除くことを目的としていて、精神的なケアが目的ではありません。ゆえに苦痛のともなう治療でも医者は進めます。だから患者の利益が最優先ということはないかもしれません。	It means the doctor's final objective is to rid the patient of his physical illness, not to give him psychological care. So the doctor proceeds with the treatment even if it's painful and may not be in the best interest of the patient.
それで患者の安らかな休息を望む家族と対立してしまいます。	The patient's family who hope to minimize their loved one's suffering could confront the doctor.
現在では患者の苦痛の緩和治療や精神的ケアを目的として治療する病院もあるそうです。	Nowadays, I hear that there are hospitals where they also engage in pain relief and mental care.
ホスピスはその代表例でしょう。安楽死に対しても広い理解を持っているようです。そして、現代医学ではもはや助からない人たちに必要なケアを提供しています。	A hospice is one such hospital, having a deep understanding of euthanasia, and offering the care needed for those who can no longer be helped by modern medicine.

3 中絶

▶ 情報を伝える　　　　　　　　　　　　　　　　　CD 2 ➡ 80

刑法に堕胎罪が規定されており、医師などでも中絶させたときは罰せられます。 注：堕胎罪は、feticide、illegal abortion または、criminal operation とも言う。	There's an aborticide stipulated in the criminal law, and even a doctor can be punished if he does abortion under certain circumstances.
母体保護法に中絶が許される規定があります。	The Mother Health Law allows abortion in some cases.
平たく言うと中絶しないと母体に著しい害を及ぼすときと、脅迫などされ自分の意思に反し妊娠したときです。	To put it simply, it is allowed when delivery could be very harmful to the mother or when the mother gets pregnant under coercion.
中絶は通常妊娠 22 週以内とされています。	Usually abortion is permissible within 22 weeks of pregnancy.
上記以外の場合でも、経済的に養育が無理と思われる場合に中絶を認める見解もあります。	Another viewpoint is that when the mother is economically incapable of raising the baby, an abortion should be permitted even if it doesn't meet the above-mentioned conditions.
伝統的にはカトリックなどを中心に中絶は非人道的で、不道徳と反対する声は大きいです。	Traditionally, the Catholic Church and some others have voiced loud opposition to abortion, calling it inhumane and immoral.
中絶とは女性のプライバシー権とする見解もあり、現在では中絶を許容する姿勢が広がっています。	There's another view which considers abortion a privacy right of women, and the pro-choice attitude is gaining popularity.

胎児の先天的な異常の発見による中絶は法的には認められていません。一方出生前診断が多く行なわれるようになり、先天的な異常を理由にした中絶が議論されています。	The law doesn't allow abortion in cases when the fetus has been found to be abnormal. Meanwhile, many pre-birth checks are done, and abortion due to the fetus's abnormality is much talked about.

▶ 中絶消極的賛成論　　　　　　CD 2 ➡ 81

中絶は不慮の妊娠の場合求められることがあります。例えば最近では若年齢層の性交渉が増えており生活能力のない少女が妊娠してしまい中絶する場合などです。	Abortion is sought in cases of an accidental pregnancy. One such case is when a girl incapable of making a living gets pregnant by accident and has an abortion. This is just one of the results of the growing number of minors who are engaging in sexual intercourse.
ひとつには避妊知識の問題もありますが、自由の風潮、あるいは自由の取り違え（権利と責任の関係の誤解）の問題でもあります。	For one thing, lack of sexual knowledge is responsible. So is the spread of the spirit of freedom and the misunderstanding of the relationship between rights and responsibŠities.
性だけでなく社会倫理の進んだ教育が必要と思います。	Advanced educatÚn on sex and social ethics is called for.
基本的には出産して苦労してでも育てるのが妊娠した者の責任と思います。	Basically it's the responsibŠity of the one who is pregnant to give birth and raise the child no matter how hard it may be.
生まれてくる子どもの幸せを最優先に考えるべきだと思います。経済的な問題はかなり慎重に考えるべきです。親が豊かでなくとも子が苦労するとは限りません。	The first prÚrity should go to the well being of the coming baby. Economical hurdles are subtle ones because if the parents are poor, it doesn't always mean the baby wŠl have a hard life.

心身に明らかに、生まれてくればたいへんな苦労するであろう様な異常が発見された場合は、中絶も視野に入れてもよいのではないかと思います。	In cases when an abnormality which could give the baby tremendous disadvantage is detected pre-birth, abortion can be considered, I guess.
出産を選ぶ権利は母親にあるという考えは大きな声で主張するものではないと思います。そこに至るまでの段階で注意すれば不要の妊娠は避けることが可能なのだから、もっと注意するべきと思います。	I don't think one can be proud to claim that the mother has the right to choose between birth or abortion (pro-choice). Pregnancy could have been avoided, had she been more cautious in the first place.
性行為は人間の基本的な行動のひとつであり、常に計画に基づき行なわれるとは限りません。その場の衝動で行なわれ、その結果妊娠してしまうことは起こりうることです。	Sexual intercourse is one of the basic human acts, and one can't expect to always have it exactly as one intends. It can happen that one does it on impulse and gets pregnant.
それをすべからく安全に行なうことは本来の性行為の意味を失わせるものです。	If one always does it safely, it would detract from the intrinsic value of sex.
そしてそのたびに女性のみが傷つきます。ある程度の中絶は女性の権利と見るべきです。	And each time, it is the woman who must endure the pregnancy. We should see abortion as the women's right to a point.

▶ 中絶に伴う問題を考える　　　　　　　　　　　　　　　　　CD 2 ➡ 82

いろんな事情で中絶をすることになるのでしょう。	They get to abort for a variety of reasons.
中絶をした多くの女性がそのことについて精神的に苦しむそうです。	I'm told that many women who aborted suffer from mental torment because of it.

そういう人たちへの心のケアも必要だと思います。	I suggest mental health care be provided for them.
人に魂が宿るのはどの段階でなのだろうかと考えることがあります。胎児のとき、出産の瞬間、初めて赤ちゃんの目が見えたとき。	I sometimes wonder when a soul begins to reside in a person. When still a fetus? At birth? When he first sees something?
人に魂が宿るのは肉体がこの世に出てきて後のことではないかと思っています。そして命は魂なんだと考えると中絶は命を奪うことにはなりません。	I presume a soul enters the human body after the birth. And if the human life is the soul, then abortion is not identical with taking a human life.
答えは見つからないかもしれません。	I'm not sure if we can find the answer.

▶ 中絶積極的反対論　　　　　　　　　　　　CD 2 ➡ 83

中絶はよほどの理由のない限り絶対にいけません！殺人同様です！人間が人間の命を絶つことは許されません。	I am absolutely against abortion unless there is some exceptional reason. Abortion is as good as murder! We mustn't kill another human being.
命を受けた胎児も人間です。 注：「胎児」は、妊娠3ヶ月目前半までは an embryo、3ヶ月後半以降は a fetus、一般には an unborn baby/child。 参考：inborn は「生まれつきの」。	An unborn child is also a human.
中絶は母体を痛め、時には子供を産むのが難しい、あるいは不可能な身体になることもあります。	Abortion will weaken a mother's body and sometimes make it difficult or impossible to give birth again.
正しい知識で、実現性のある計画性のもとに、生命を生み出すことが極めて大切です。	It is of vital importance for parents to have a baby through correct knowledge and with a feasible plan.

4 生活習慣病とダイエット

▶ 情報を伝える CD 2 ➡ 84

生活習慣病は日頃のよくない習慣の積み重ねで起こってきます。日本人の約3人に2人が生活習慣病で亡くなっています。	Lifestyle-related diseases result from bad habits formed and continued in our lifetimes. About two-thirds of the Japanese die of these diseases.
生活習慣病には糖尿病、脳卒中、高脂血症、心臓病、肥満、高血圧などがあります。	Lifestyle-related diseases include diabetes, apoplexy, hyperlipemia, cardiac diseases, obesity, and hypertension.
日本人の6割以上の死の原因がいわゆる3大成人病です。すなわち、ガン、脳卒中、心筋梗塞です。	The so-called top three lifestyle-related diseases, cancer, apoplexy and cardiac infarction, account for more than 60% of deaths in Japan.
かつては成人病と呼ばれていました。現在では大人に限らず、貧弱な食事などの習慣が蓄積されたりすることも発症する原因となりうるということで生活習慣病と言われるようになりました。	Once called geriatric diseases, they have come to be called lifestyle-related diseases because it's been identified that one can contract them as a result of poor lifestyle choices such as a poor diet.
生活習慣病の予防や軽度の場合はダイエットや運動も効果があります。	A healthy diet or exercise can help prevent or cure lifestyle-related diseases in cases when they are not severe or when they have been detected early.
特に忙しい現代人は運動する時間もあまりないので、予防のためにダイエットに気をつけましょう。	People today, who are too busy even to find time to work out, should watch their diets.

ダイエットは病気の予防、養生だけでなくスタイルを良くし保つための手段として、特に女性に用いられています。	Dieting is popular among women as a means to improve their figures and to stay healthy.

生活習慣病予防についての意見

CD 2 ➡ 85

ライフスタイル、ストレス、経皮毒等が原因で、生活習慣病にかかると言われています。特に太り過ぎは危険であることを常に銘記することが大切です。	It is said that we may fall into a lifestyle-related disease because of our lifestyle, stress, or dermal toxicity. It is important to bear in mind the fact that being too fat is dangerous.
へそ周りが男 85cm 以上、女 90 センチ以上である場合は注意すべきだということを示しています。	The measurement of over 85 cm around the waist for men and that of over 90 cm for women indicate you should consider losing some weight.
太らないよう自己管理することが大切です。生活の習慣をすぐに変えられるものではありません。しかし朝夕に少しの時間を見つけてジョギングしたり、たばこ、酒を控えたり、肉食を減らして野菜を食べるくらいの努力は行うべきですね。	Through proper self-control, we should try to avoid gaining too much weight. It's really hard to change lifestyles. But one should make small efforts to spare some time to jog in the morning or evening, or refrain from smoking or drinking, or eat less meat and more vegetables.
子どもにあまい親もこの頃多いようです。好きな物を何でも食べさせるから、子どもの肥満や、糖尿病予備軍を作ってしまう。	These days parents seem to indulge their children and give them whatever they want to eat, thus increasing the potential for obesity and diabetes.
昔は出された物を食べないと「もう食べないでよろしい」と言われて食事を片付けられたものです。本当に冗談ではありません。糖尿病は恐い病気です。	Mothers used to clear the table saying "Don't eat." when you grumbled about the food. I'm serious. Diabetes is a horrifying disease.

テレビでは糖尿病のせいで両足を切断した人を何人か見ましたし、知り合いにも両足と目が不自由な人がいます。	I saw some people have their legs amputated due to diabetes. I have an acquaintance that has trouble walking and seeing.
ダイエットでは食事の量と中身は大事ですが、取り方もけっこう大切です。つまり時間と回数です。	What's important about diet is not only what to eat but how to eat it, meaning at what time and how many times.
できるだけ1日3回決まった時間に食べるようにしましょう。	Try to eat 3 meals a day at fixed times as much as possible.

▶ ダイエットの危険性　　　　　　　　　　　　CD 2 ➡ 86

痩身のためのダイエットは健康を害する可能性があるので注意しなければなりません。無理をして充分な栄養も取れないようでは困ります。	One has to be careful about dieting to lose weight because it could impair one's health. You shouldn't go so far as to get undernourished.
場合により将来骨粗しょう症になってしまう可能性があるという話も聞いたことがあります。	I once heard that one could even catch osteoporosis in some cases.
ダイエットでやせた人がリバウンドしてまた太ったという話は時々耳にします。	I sometimes hear that a person who attains a slim body after dieting may become fat again.
また、ダイエットしてやせてまた太って、という感じです。これも体にあまりよくないそうです。	Sometimes they even enter into an endless cycle of losing weight and gaining it back again. They say this is also bad for your health.

世の中の商業主義にのって、やせているのが美しく、自分は太っていると思っている女性はけっこう多いようです。	Affected by commercialism, many women seem to believe that they are fat and that they will be more beautiful if they are thin.
そういう女性のほとんどを男の人は太っているとは思っていないようです。	However, most men generally do not think that these women are overweight.

▶ 適切なダイエットをアドバイスする CD 2 ➡ 87

自分の好みだけでなく、健康上最適な状態も確認しながらダイエットしましょう。	When dieting, don't forget to watch your health while pursuing what you desire.
一般的には男の人にとってもあまりにやせた人よりも適度にふくよかな人がいいと思われます。うまくダイエットしてください。	Generally speaking, men like women of certain voluptuousness better than skinny ones. Have a successful diet.

▶ 心がけの重要性を述べる CD 2 ➡ 88

痩身のダイエットも療養のダイエットも常日頃の心がけといえます。	The name of the game is that daily care counts either when the purpose of the diet is to be slim or to cure diseases.
何事もなまけることなく、きっちりとした生活をすることが大切と言うことです。	Don't be lazy and stay in control of your life.

表現のコツ 「name of the game」の表現

> 「肝心要のこと」という意味の句です。他には bottom line や nitty-gritty、part and parcel があります。普通あたまに the をつけて使います。
>
> 今日の話し合いの要点はシステムの機能の仕方をどう変えられるかだ。
> → The nitty-gritty of today's talk is how we can change the way the system works.

5 癌とエイズ

▶ 情報と現在の見解を述べる　　　　　　　　　　　　　　CD 2 ➡ 89

癌（がん）は心疾患、脳卒中と並んで生活習慣病としてとらえられ、日本人の死亡原因では一番です。今でもなお、癌での死亡率は増えています。

Cancer, together with cardiac diseases and apoplexy, is seen as a lifestyle-related disease and is responsible for the most deaths in Japan. The ratio of deaths from cancer is still on the rise.

癌は現在もその原因がはっきりと解明されているわけではありません。ゆえに有効な治療法が確立されていません。

Its causes haven't been clearly detected yet. Therefore, there is no established effective cure.

癌の治療法には基本的に次の４つがあります。外科療法、化学療法、放射線療法、免疫療法です。

Basically, there are four ways to treat cancer: surgery, chemotherapy, radiotherapy and immunotherapy.

それぞれに特長を持ち、また欠陥もあります。単独の治療法でなく、複数をまぜて治療を行うのがより良い効果を期待できるようです。

Each of them has its advantages and defects. Better results can be expected when some of them are combined than when not.

癌は遺伝ではなく、生活における悪癖に起因する後天的な病気、すなわち、生活習慣病だと発表されています。

Cancer is considered to be not a hereditary but an acquired form of disease due to bad habits in our daily lives, that is to say, a lifestyle-related disease.

また、日用品（シャンプー、リンス、化粧品、洗剤）等に入っている有害物質が示す経皮毒によっても発症すると、最近マスコミや出版物からも注意を促しています。

Moreover, some recent articles and publications warn that dermal toxicity found in harmful chemicals contained in household goods including shampoos, conditioners, cosmetics, detergents may lead to cancer.

エイズは日本でも年々増え続けていて、都市によっては、エイズ撲滅運動の一環として、シンポジウムやパレードも開催され深刻さを意識するよう呼びかけています。 注：○○撲滅運動は、a crusade against ... とも表現できる。	The number of HIV carriers has been steadily rising in Japan; therefore, in some cities, organizations have been holding symposiums and parades in HIV awareness programs to remind people of the seriousness of the matter.
輸血によって感染する場合もありますが、不特定多数の性交渉が大きな原因と言われています。 注：HIV=human immunodeficiency virus	Though people may be infected by blood transfusions, having sexual intercourse with a variety of partners is one of the major causes of the spread of HIV infections.
血友病患者の方に感染したという事例は大問題です。国家は責任をとるべきです。	The fact that hemophiliacs caught HIV is a serious problem. Our country should take responsibility for the problem.

▶ 一歩進んで考える　　　　　　　　　　　　　　　　　　　CD 2 ➡ 90

癌は長い間不治の病と考えられています。現在もなおその印象が世間では強いし、事実ともいえます。一方では癌は治せる病気だということも耳にします。	Cancer has long been thought of as incurable. Even today most have that impression and it's true in a sense. On the other hand, I hear that cancer is curable.
なぜ相反する見解があるのでしょうか。	How come there are conflicting views?
癌治療の問題点は医療に対する姿勢にあると思います。	I think the problem with cancer treatment lies with the general attitude toward medical treatment.

現在の多くの病院では癌治療は癌そのものを取り去ることに主眼が置かれていて、癌患者本人の生命、健康が置き去りにされるという本末転倒が起こっています。	Now in many hospitals the first priority of cancer treatment is the removal of cancer. But the life and health of the patient himself tend to be put on the back burner, which mistakes the means for the end.
例えば抗癌剤は人体には非常に悪い影響を与えます。往々にして癌への効果よりも患者の生命への危険の方が大きい場合があるのです。	For example, anticancer medicine is quite harmful to the body. Often its bad effect on the patient's health outdoes its killing effect on the cancer.
癌患者は抗癌剤で死ぬと言われるぐらいです。	The medicine is so toxic that some even say patients die from taking anticancer drugs.
しかし、癌縮小に力を発揮するということで使われます。	But it's used because it's effective in diminishing cancer.
他の極端な例では癌はそのままでなくならないけれど、けっこう元気に生活している人もいます。	In another extreme example, I know a person whose cancer never dissipates, but who continues to lead a relatively healthy life.
癌の除去にこだわらずに、いかに健康を取り戻すかに重点を置いて治療に当たった結果だと思います。	It's an example of how the doctors focused on doing something to improve the general health of the patient, not just on removing the cancer.
エイズは避けられる病気です。現在治療法はなく、かかれば死の病気です。	AIDS can be avoided. With no particular cure in sight now, once one gets it, one is destined to die.

しかし、訳が分からないほど恐いものではありません。	However, there is no reason to have an unjustifiable fear of it.
HIV 保菌者とスキンシップをもったりキスをしただけではうつりません。しかし、保菌者と性交渉を持つとうつる可能性があります。	One doesn't get it just because one has skin contact with or kisses an HIV carrier, but one can get it if one has sexual relations with someone who has the virus.

▶ 心がけが大切　　　　　　　　　　　CD 2 ➡ 91

エイズは自分の心がけ次第で避けられるのです。	AIDS can be avoided as long as you take proper precautions.
癌は生活態度によりかかる可能性を下げられるようです。	Living a healthy life makes it less likely that a person will get cancer.
何事も節度をもって生活することです。	The thing is you better live a decent life.

表現のコツ　「make it + X」は有効な表現

> もう 3 人が来るぞ。これで 22 人ってことだね。
> → I see another three persons coming. That makes it 22, doesn't it?
> 君が彼の親だとはわかる。だからと言って彼の顔を殴るのはよくない。
> → I know you are his parent. But it doesn't make it right to hit him in the face.
> 7 時に会うって約束したけど 8 時にできませんか。
> → We promised to meet at seven, but can't you make it at eight?

6　健康法のいろいろ

▶ 情報を伝える　　　　　　　　　　　　　CD 2 ➡ 92

健康は大まかに言って肉体的健康と、精神的健康があります。	Generally speaking, we should be concerned about physical health and mental health.
肉体的健康の維持、増強法には食物の点、生活様式の点、医学的な点からのアプローチなどがあります。	There are some ways to maintain and improve physical health; these include diet, lifestyle and medical science.
世間にはいろんな健康法が出回っています。いくつかをあげますと、ビタミン健康法、足の裏健康法、一日二食法、書く健康法などです。	A variety of methods are out there, such as the vitamin method, the sole method, the two-meals-a-day method, and the writing method, just to name a few.
断食も正しくすれば健康増進になり、各地に断食をする保養所などがあります。体内に蓄積した老廃物や毒素をさっぱりと取り除こうという考えからです。	Fasting can be a good way to better health, and there are facŠities offering fasting programs here and there. The idea is to rid the body of accumulated waste matter and toxins.
もちろん方法を間違えれば逆に体に害ですので、専門家の指導のもとにしなければなりません。	Needless to say, if anything goes wrong, it would bring harm to the body. One should follow a specialist's instructÚns when fasting.

▶ 精神面の健康について　　　　　　　　　CD 2 ➡ 93

最近は学校のいじめ、その果ての自殺をよくテレビで見ます。これはある種、心の病の結果［＝心の変化に基づく病］ではないでしょうか。	Recently we often see on TV stories about bullying at school and suicides as a result. This could come from a change of heart that people have had, couldn't it?

心の健康の維持、増進は場合により体のそれより大事なこともあるのではないでしょうか。	Maintenance and improvement of mental health are sometimes more important than that of the body.
アメリカなどでは戦争から帰宅した人が戦争の精神的な後遺症におちいる例が多くあるようです。そういう精神的な病に対する施設や専門家はアメリカにはたくさんいます。	In the U.S., there seem to be many cases where veterans of wars suffer from a mental aftereffect of war. And there also are many such facilities and specialists that deal with mental illnesses.
また日常的にもカウンセラーやサイコセラピストと呼ばれる専門家その他が人々の精神面でのケアに携わっています。	Plus, in daily life in the U.S., they have professionals called counselors or psychotherapists and others who engage in mental health care.
日本でも最近でこそカウンセラーなどにかかる人もいるようですが、まだまだアメリカなどに比べると遅れています。	In Japan too, there are people who see counselors these days, but Japan is still far behind the U.S. in this field.

▶ 食品添加物から身を守る　　　　　　　　CD 2 ➡ 94

健康の維持には誰もが関心はあるでしょう。身近な者が健康を阻害され病気になったり、死亡した場合にはとりわけ健康を意識するようになります。	Everybody is interested in keeping healthy. When someone close to us falls sick or dies after his or her health is impaired, we usually start watching our health closely.
暴飲暴食をしないなどは当然のこと、普段からジョギングやウォーキングをしたり、体操をしたりと何かとできることはあります。	There are things one can do on a daily basis such as jogging, walking, and exercising. Overdrinking and overeating are out of the question.

ただ現代社会において大きな問題のひとつは食料品に含まれる食品添加物です。これが健康を害する大きな原因にもなっています。そこで添加物の入っていない食料をとることが効果のある健康法ということになってきます。	One of the very serious problems in modern society is that additives contained in foods are causing impaired health. Then you could say that a food additive-free diet should be an effective way to maintain health.

▶ 健康を考えたちょっとした行動　　　　CD 2 ➡ 95

私は仕事柄あまり動きません。じっとして時間を過ごすことが多いです。そこでせめて動く時間をとろうと家から職場まで月に何度かは歩くようにしています。	I don't move much because of my work. I spend much time staying put. So I try to walk from home to work a few times a month in an effort to move.
私は、以前はよくのどが渇くとコーラやジュース、砂糖入りのコーヒーや紅茶など糖分のけっこう入った物を飲んでいました。	I used to drink cola, soft drinks, coffee and tea with sugar in it when I was thirsty. They all contain a considerable amount of sugar.
今は健康を考えてできるだけお茶を飲むようにしています。	Now I try to drink green tea as much as possible for my health.
毎日の生活で悩みごとができることがありますね。夜寝られないことがあります。	Now and again you face a problem or two so disturbing that you have trouble sleeping at night, don't you?
そんなときは一杯お酒をひっかけるようにしています。その間はいやなことを忘れられてよく眠れます。	I'd take an alcoholic drink in that case, and I could forget my problem and sleep well.
もちろん飲みすぎは禁物ですが、「酒は百薬の長」というような言葉もありますので。	Of course, don't drink too much. We have a saying in Japan "Sake is the best medicine."

第 3 部
発展編

第 11 章

民族と宗教と国際問題に関する意見を述べる

1 キリスト教とイスラム教とユダヤ教

▶ 情報を伝える

キリスト教とイスラム教は、世界宗教で現代社会に大きな影響力を持っています。	Christianity and Islamism, which are categorized as world religions, have a great influence on the modern world.
キリスト教は西洋諸国を中心にロシア、アメリカ大陸やオセアニアに広がり、アジア・アフリカの諸国にも多くの信者がいます。	Christianity spread mainly over Western countries and reached to the American continent and Oceania, also covering some Asian and African countries where there are many Christians.
イスラム教は、アラブ諸国を中心に中国・インド・アフリカ・アジア（特にパキスタンやインドネシア）に広がっています。	Islam is centered in Arabic nations, and extends to China, India, Africa and Asia, especially Pakistan and Indonesia.
キリスト教もイスラム教も一神教で、神様は唯一全知全能であるとしています。	Christianity and Islam are both monotheistic, in which the divine being is almighty, omniscient and omnipotent.
キリスト教とイスラム教の違いは、いくつかあります。	Christianity and Islam differ in several respects.
キリスト教では、神と人間の中間者としてキリストという救世主が存在しているのに対し、イスラム教ではそのような救世主がいません。	In Christianity, a Messiah called Christ exists as the mediator between God and humans; however, Islam does not have such a savior.
預言者マホメットは神であるアラーの声が聞ける人間の代表者であって、救世主ではありません。	Prophet Muhammad is a representative who can hear the sacred voice of Allah, but is not the Messiah.

▶ キリスト教と仏教の違いに関する意見

キリスト教では、どんな極悪人でも悔い改めて神を信仰すれば、死後は天国に行き、どんなに善良な人間でも神を信仰しなければ、死後は天国には行けないとのことですが、これは少し変だと思います。	In Christianity, even accomplished villains can go to the heaven after death if they repent of their sins, whereas even very good persons cannot go to the Kingdom of God after death unless they believe in Him. I think this is a bit strange.
善良な人であれば、救われる可能性のない地獄ではなく、煉獄という地獄よりは厳しくない試練の場が提供されるとも聞きますが、生前多くの人を救った素晴らしい人であれば、キリスト教徒かどうかに関係なく天国に無条件で行けるようにするのが神の愛ではないかと思います。	I hear those good-natured people go to purgatory, which provides a less strict divine test than hell, but I think it is God's love that allows you to enter Paradise unconditionally if you have saved many people in this world, regardless of your religion.
私はキリスト教を批判しているのではなく、神はそういう優しさがあるのではないかと思っているのです。つまり、形式上キリスト教徒ではなくても、精神がキリスト的である人は皆天国に受け入れられると考えています。	I am not criticizing Christianity, but I am sure God has compassion. In short, even if you are not Christian in status, you are welcomed to the Celestial City in those cases when you have the spirit of Christianity.
キリスト教は、極悪人にも救いがあるという点で、仏教の浄土真宗に似ている側面があります。	In the sense that scoundrels of the blackest dye can be saved in Christianity, this religion is similar to the Jodo-shin Sect of Buddhism.
浄土真宗の阿弥陀仏は、ただすがるだけで極楽に往生することを約束するという優しさがあります。この宗派は、他の仏も認めますが、信仰するのは阿弥陀仏のみという一神崇拝という形も、キリスト教に似ています。	Amida Buddha in Jodo-shin Sect shows such gentility as to promise you to save you if you totally depend on the Buddha. This sect resembles Christianity in that you must worship Amida Buddha exclusively though other Buddhas are not rejected.

ところで、一神崇拝と一神教の違いは、一神教は他の神を一切認めないという点です。
注：一神崇拝＝ monolatry

Incidentally, monotheism is different from monolatry in that monotheism does not accept any other deity.

キリスト教は、掛け算の発想で人間を判断し、仏教は、足し算の発想で人間を判断していると思います。

Christianity judges humans by the principle of multiplication, while Buddhism assesses humans by that of addition.

たとえば、キリスト教では、極悪人が死ぬ直前に、心から悔い改めて神を信仰すれば、天国に行き、熱心な善良な信者が死ぬ直前に、たとえば通り魔に刺されて、「なぜこんな目に遭うんだ？」と神を疑えば、地獄に行くと考えられます。

For example, in Christianity if those who committed heinous crimes suddenly become entirely repentant right before death, they will be promised to go to the blessed land. But those pious Christians go down to hell if they question and doubt God when they are stabbed by a phantom killer.

神を疑った時点で、これまで蓄積された善の値に０が掛けられ、その人間は悪人に大変身するというわけです。

At the moment when you feel doubt about God, your points accumulated in your entire life will be multiplied by zero, leading to the same status as that of a villain.

そのような厳しい側面がキリスト教にあります。

There is this strict aspect about Christianity.

仏教では、死後の旅の途中で、閻魔（えんま）さんに会って、死者の閻魔帳に記載されたさまざまな行いを見るのです。

In Buddhism, people meet Emma on their way to rebirth after death, and he checks through the black book in which all of the good or bad things they have done during their lives are written.

よい行いならプラス、悪い行いならマイナスというように得点をつけていき、最終的にその人の価値が決まり、転生先が決まるとされています。	Good deeds will make you gain some points, and bad, lose some, and finally based on the balance between good points and bad points, it will be decided where a person will be born next.
キリスト教と仏教では、そもそも死生観に大きな違いがあります。キリスト教では、再度人間として生まれることはないとされていますが、仏教では生まれ変わりを説いています。	There is a world of difference in the outlook on life and death between Christianity and Buddhism. In Christianity, you are not reborn as humans, but in Buddhism reincarnation is expounded.
どちらが正しいのかは、死んでみないと分かりません。臨死体験者の体験は、あくまで真の死の体験を語っているわけではなく、その直前の体験なので、本当のことは分からないです。	We will not know which is correct until we die. The so-called near death experience does not tell us what the after life is all about, because those with such experience have not been 100% dead, and they have just returned without experiencing a true death.

▶ ユダヤ教そしてパレスチナ問題を語る

ユダヤ教は、ユダヤ人のみが信仰する民族宗教です。ちなみに、神道は日本の民族宗教です。	Judaism is a religion only for Jews, classified as an ethnic religion. Just for reference, Shinto is Japan's ethnic religion.
ユダヤ教は旧約聖書を聖典とします。 注：the Scripture、Holy Scripture というと「聖書」(the Bible=the Book)。	Judaism regards the Old Testament as holy scriptures.
ユダヤ教は世界宗教であるキリスト教とイスラム教の2つの宗教と兄弟の関係の宗教とも考えることができます。	We can safely say that Judaism is related to two world religions: Christianity and Islam.

というのは、旧約聖書はこの3つの宗教で共通しているからです。大雑把に言って、旧約聖書と新約聖書を聖典とするのがキリスト教で、旧約聖書とコーランを聖典とするのがイスラム教です。	This is because the above-mentioned three religions have the Old Testament in common. Roughly speaking, the Old Testament and the New Testament are considered to be the sacred books in Christianity, while the Old Testament and the Koran are looked on as holy in Islam.
エルサレムは、これら3つの宗教の共通する聖地です。 注: the Holy Land というとパレスチナのこと。	Jerusalem is a sacred place for these three religions.
ユダヤ人とパレスチナ人が長く対立しているのはよく知られた事実です。	It is a well-known fact that Jews and Palestinians have long been in conflict.
パレスチナの地において、パレスチナ定住者とユダヤ人入植者の間の紛争を総称してパレスチナ問題と呼んでいます。	The generic term for all the conflicts between Palestinians as permanent residents and Jews as settlers is the Palestinian Problem.
1948年5月14日にイスラエルが独立国となってからは、色々な抗争や戦争が続いています。	Since Israel became an independent nation on May 14, 1948, various kinds of conflicts or wars have continued.
さらに、パレスチナ人の自爆テロも深刻です。ユダヤ人だけが乗った満員のバスに爆弾を背負ったパレスチナ人が乗り込み、自爆することが多いようです。	Moreover, suicide bomb attacks by Palestinians are posing a serious problem. In many cases, a Palestinian with a bomb in his backpack gets on a bus filled only with Jews and lets the bomb go off.
私の友人でイスラエルの日本人研究者は、平気でバスに乗り込みます。	My friend, a Japanese scholar who studies Israeli culture, gets on the bus without any worries.

外国人がいるとパレスチナ人は自爆しないからということです。彼らはユダヤ人のみを狙うようです。	If there is a foreigner in the bus, the Palestinian will not carry out a suicide attack. They seem to aim only at Jews.
イスラエルもパレスチナ人を無差別に攻撃することもあり、パレスチナ側からは強い抗議をしています。	Israel sometimes attacks Palestinians indiscriminately; therefore, Palestinians usually make a strong protest against the attack.
イスラエルには、パレスチナ人を全て追放抹殺すべきだと言う強硬派があり、一方、パレスチナ側にも、イスラエル人の存在を認めないハマスのような強硬派があります。	In Israel, there are some hard-liners who insist on banishing or eliminating all the Palestinians, whereas on the Palestinian side, well-known hawks like Hamas will not accept the very existence of Jews.
ハマスは最近軟化しているようです。 注：「軟化する」は soften ともいえる。	It seems that Hamas' attitudes recently have become less aggressive.

▶ 問題の解決の方向性はあるか？

問題の解決は、宗教的には答えが出ていると私は思います。お互いに相手をこれまでのことを許せば、問題は一気に解決します。	As for the solution to this problem, I think the clue to the solution is religiously clear. The problem will instantly disappear if both sides forgive each other.
ところが、身内の者を殺されている現状があれば、なかなか許すことはできないでしょう。	However, the situation where some family members on either side were killed makes it very difficult for either side to forgive.
そこで報復合戦が起こってしまうのです。報復に対して報復するという悪循環が起こります。	It is the very reason why retaliations occur and recur. The vicious cycle of retaliations against retaliations takes place.

報復をストップさせるには、全てを許すしかないのです。これがなかなか難しいのかもしれません。

To stop this chain reaction, everything should be accepted and forgiven. This kind of attitude may be hard to take.

ユダヤ教の兄弟の宗教であるキリスト教は「汝の敵を愛せ」と言うし、イスラム教では「困った人を見ればすぐに助けよ」と教えるのに、うまくいかないのは残念です。

Christianity, which is closely related to Judaism, teaches us to love our enemy, and Islam preaches that if we find someone in trouble, it is imperative to help him or her. In spite of this wonderful teaching, it is a pity that it is so hard to solve the problem.

参考 キリスト教、イスラム教、ユダヤ教の違い一覧表

	キリスト教	イスラム教	ユダヤ教
神	ゴッド　God	アラー　Allah	エホバ　Jehovah
信仰対象	ゴッド　God キリスト　Christ 聖霊　Holy Spirit	アラー　Allah	エホバ　Jehovah
聖典	旧約聖書と新約聖書 The Old Testament The New Testament	コーランと旧約聖書 The Koran The Old Testament	旧約聖書 The Old Testament
メシア Messiah	キリスト Christ	救世主はアラーのみ	終末に現れる
開祖 Founder	キリスト Christ	マホメット Muhammad	創始者はない
安息日	日曜日　Sunday	金曜日　Friday	土曜日　Saturday
偶像崇拝 Idolatry	カトリックではキリスト、マリア像はOK	絶対禁止 absolutely banned	絶対禁止 absolutely banned
聖都	エルサレム Jerusalem	エルサレム Jerusalem メッカ Mecca メディナ Medina	エルサレム Jerusalem

注1：メッカはマホメットの生誕地で、メディナにはマホメットの墓がある。
注2：キリスト教とイスラム教は世界宗教であるが、ユダヤ教は民族宗教。民族宗教には通常開祖はいない。同じく民族宗教といえる日本の神道にも開祖は存在しない。

2 天皇について一歩進んだ知識

▶ **天皇に関する情報を伝える**

天皇家の起源は、神話時代にさかのぼります。	The origin of the Imperial family dates back to mythological periods.
日本の国を生んだイザナギ・イザナミの神話にさかのぼるのです。	The Imperial family originated in the mythology of Izanagi and Izanami, who gave birth to Japan.
イザナミが死んで黄泉（よみ）の国に行ってしまったので、イザナギはこの国を訪問します。 注：「黄泉の国」は、Hades、the netherworld、the abode of the shades と訳される。	Izanagi, a male deity, visited the land of the dead because Izanami, his wife, died and had gone there.
黄泉の国訪問から戻ったイザナギが、禊（みそぎ）を行ない、顔を洗ったとき、一番最初に生まれたのが、アマテラスでした。	It was Amaterasu, or the Great Sun Goddess, that Izanagi first gave birth to when he washed his face at the time of purification just after coming back from the netherworld.
太陽の神であるアマテラスはイザナギの左目から生まれました。ちなみに、イザナギの右目からは月の神ツクヨミが生まれ、鼻をかんだらスサノオが生まれたのです。	Amaterasu, the deity of the sun, was born out of Izanagi's left eye. Incidentally, out of his right eye, Tsukuyomi, the deity of the moon, was born, and when Izanagi blew his nose, Susano was born.
アマテラスの子孫が初代神武天皇を生んだとされています。	A descendant of Amaterasu is said to have given birth to the first emperor, Emperor Jimmu.

発展編　第11章　民族と宗教と国際問題に関する意見を述べる

第25代の武烈天皇に子がなかったので、第15代応神天皇の5世の孫である継体天皇を即位させたといいます。	It is said that since the 25th emperor, Emperor Buretsu, did not have a son, he enthroned a fifth-generation grandson from the 15th emperor, Emperor Ojin, as Emperor Keitai.
なんとか「体」を「継いだ」ということが天皇の名前に表れています。	This emperor's name consists of two Chinese characters meaning "inherit the body," which is clearly suggestive of the importance of blood relations.
この継体天皇は、大阪府枚方市樟葉で即位したとされています。 ※枚方市は著者の住所	This emperor is said to have been enthroned in a place called Kuzuha, in Hirakata City, Osaka.
日本史のいろいろな場面で、仏教が天皇に影響を与えたのは、第45代聖武天皇が、国家予算を傾けてまでも、大仏を造営したことから明らかです。	There are many scenes throughout Japanese history in which Buddhism influenced the emperors. The 45th Emperor Shomu issued the imperial edict ordering the casting of the Great Buddha, which nearly brought the nation to bankruptcy.
第72代白河天皇が天台宗のお坊さんに翻弄されたという話をしましょう。	Let me tell you a story about the 72nd Emperor Shirakawa, who was completely baffled by a priest of the Tendai Sect.
白河天皇は子がなかったので、三井寺の高僧頼豪(らいごう)に子授けの祈祷をお願いしました。	Since Emperor Shirakawa did not have a child, he asked the Priest Raigo, a high-ranking priest of the Mii-dera Temple, to conduct an incantation for childbirth.

頼豪は、うまくいけば、戒壇を作ってほしいと天皇に懇願し、天皇は了承しました。	The priest implored the emperor to establish a Buddhist ordination hall if the incantation proves successful, and the emperor accepted the request.
祈祷のおかげで、無事子供ができたのですが、天皇が約束を守らなかったので、その坊さんは「息子の命もいただきます」という言葉を残し自害したとのことです。その後、まもなく王子はなくなりました。	Thanks to the priest's prayer, a baby was born, but the emperor broke the promise. The priest is said to have committed suicide, leaving the message that he would take the baby's life. Soon after the incident, the baby passed away.
悲しみに打ちひしがれた白河天皇は、(三井寺に対立する)比叡山延暦寺の高僧良真（りょうしん）に子授けを依頼しました。すると、すぐに子ができて、後の第73代堀河天皇です。 注：stricken は合成語を作る。 　→ cancer-stricken（癌にかかった）	The grief-stricken Emperor Shirakawa asked the learned and virtuous priest Ryoshin of the Enryaku-ji Temple to perform an incantation ceremony for the birth of a child this time. Then, he luckily got a child very soon thereafter. This child grew up to become the 73rd Emperor Horikawa.

発展編　第11章　民族と宗教と国際問題に関する意見を述べる

表現のコツ　「さかのぼる」の表現

その船は川をさかのぼっていきました。
→ The boat went upstream along the river.
その起源は鎌倉時代までさかのぼらなければなりません。
→ We have to trace the origin back to the Kamakura period.
　[=We must go back to the Kamakura period to trace the origin.]
この法律は3月1日にさかのぼって適用されます。
→ This law is retroactive to March 1.
　[=This law is backdated to March 1.]
この祭は中世にさかのぼります。
→ This festival dates back to the Middle Ages.
　cf. the middle age は「中年」、the Mesozoic era は「中生代」。

3 イラク問題とテロ

▶ 情報を伝える

2001年9月11日アメリカのマンハッタン世界貿易センターツインビルが飛行機による体当たり爆撃を受けました。

On September 11, 2001, the World Trading Center twin buildings in Manhattan, New York, were attacked by airplanes.

アメリカはこの首謀者をイスラム系テロ組織アルカイダと位置づけました。

The American government decided the mastermind behind the attack was Al-Qaeda, an Islamic terrorist organization.

そのリーダー、オサマビンラディンを追い、テロ支援国と思われる国を締め付け、同時に、テロに対して国内の防御を固めました。

The U.S. claims that it is pursuing the Al-Qaeda leader, Osama bin Laden, and squeezing countries presumed to be terrorist sponsors. The U.S. has also taken steps to consolidate its interior defense against terrorism.

その後オサマビンラディンとの関係と大量破壊兵器の保有を理由に、イラクがアメリカの攻撃を受け、当時の大統領フセインは犯罪者として捕らえられました。

Later the U.S. attacked Iraq, and the then president Hussein was captured as the culprit on grounds that they were linked to Osama bin Laden and that they possessed weapons of mass murder.

フセイン元大統領はイラクで裁判にかけられ、2006年11月5日に人類に対する犯罪で有罪とされました。彼は、1982年に148人のシーア派イスラム教徒殺害で絞首刑を宣告されました。

Ex-president Hussein was tried in Iraq and on November 5, 2006 found guilty of crimes against humanity. He was sentenced to hang for the 1982 killing of 148 Shiites.

2006年12月30日午前6時に、死刑が執行されました。

The death sentence was executed at 6 a.m. on December 30, 2006.

一方イラク国内では内戦が激化しておさまる様子はありません。ボランティア活動で入国した日本人も数名命を失っています。	Meanwhile, in Iraq the civil war has intensified, showing no sign of abating. Some Japanese volunteer activists staying there were killed.

▶ なぜイラク戦争を起こしたのかという問いに対する1つの考え

フセイン政権が大量破壊兵器を保有していたかどうかはアメリカ国内でも議論を呼びました。	Whether the Hussein regime had weapons of mass destruction was a controversial issue in America.
ブッシュ政権はイラクに新アメリカ政権を置くべくテロを口実にイラク侵略をしたのではないですか。	Isn't it true the Bush government used terrorism as a reason to invade Iraq with a view to establishing a new American government in Iraq?
一方オサマビンラディンもその消息は確認できていません。	In the meantime, Osama bin Laden hasn't been located.

▶ テロとは何かを考える

日本に住んでいると、テロリズムを一方的な見方でしかとらえられないと思います。すなわちテロ行為をした人即悪です。	I think living in Japan, one might only take a one-sided view on terrorism, meaning people who resort to terrorism are evil.
テロを肯定するわけではありません。	I don't mean to approve terrorism.
ところで世間はテロ行為と戦争行為を区別して考えているようですが、無実の人を殺戮するという点ではアメリカなど西側社会が行なっている戦争もテロの一形態と思います。	Incidentally, people in general seem to separate terrorist acts and act of war. But I think that wars Western countries like the U.S. carry out are also one form of terrorism in that they kill innocent people.

無実の人をもその対象としているテロ行為と西側社会が行なっている戦争とは本質的に違うと思います。例えばマンハッタン世界貿易センタービルへの攻撃は明らかに無差別殺人です。	Terrorism, whose targets include the innocent, is fundamentally different from wars waged by the Western countries. For example, the attack on World Trading Center in Manhattan was no doubt an indiscriminate murder.
一方アメリカなどのイラクへの攻撃は基本的に軍や兵器の施設を狙うものです。	On the other hand, American attacks in Iraq are basically intended to destroy military facilities and arsenals.
ある程度の犠牲を払ってでも破壊しなければならない敵が現実にいるのです。でないと逆に私たちの生命が危険にさらされます。	And in reality, there are enemies you have to destroy even if you have to pay a price. You could be put in danger unless you do so.
私はテレビなどで多くのイラク人が愛する者を失って嘆き悲しんでいる姿を見ても他人事のように思っている日本人たちが恐いです。	I'm horrified that Japanese think they don't have anything to do with it, when they see on TV some Iraqis crying over the loss of their beloved ones.

▶ テロを定義する

どこに行ってもおとなしく、慎ましやかに自分たちの生活を営んでいる人はいます。	You can see people who are living their lives quietly and decently wherever you go.
その人たちの平和や生命をおびやかす行為は、何であっても、テロだと思います。	Any act that threatens the peace or lives of such people should be classified as terrorism.

▶ 解決の糸口は何か？を考える

アルカイダをはじめとするテロ組織は恐ろしいものです。しかし彼らの行動の裏にも理由があるのではないでしょうか。

力に対して力で迎えるだけでなく、その根本的理由を掘り下げて考え、話し合い、折れるところは折れることが真の問題解決につながると信じています。

Terrorist organizations like Al-Qaeda are so scary. But aren't there reasons behind their acts?

Countering muscle with muscle is no solution to the problem. To dig deeper till you get to the bottom of it through talks and give what you can is the way to the true solution, I believe.

表現のコツ　「折れる」を訳す

「妥協する」ことです。本文では give を使いましたが、他に concede、yield、bend、compromise などがあります。

日本の代表団はフランスの代表団の要求に折れた。
→ The Japanese delegation conceded to the request of their French counterpart.

誘拐犯たちは警察からの圧力にすぐに折れるだろう。
→ The kidnappers will soon bend under the pressure from the police.

4　北朝鮮と核

▶ 情報を伝える

2006年北朝鮮は2度にわたりミサイル実験を行ないました。10月には世界各国の反対を押し切って核兵器の地下実験を行いました。

In 2006, North Korea conducted two missile tests. In October, amongst opposition from the world they pressed ahead with an underground nuclear bomb test.

その後金正日は「経済制裁などの圧力は宣戦布告と見なす」と言っています。

Later Kim Jong-Il said "we consider any pressure like economic sanctions a declaration of war on us."

同盟国である中国が以降の実験を中断し6カ国会議に戻ることを説得しましたが、かんばしくなかったようです。

Its ally, China, persuaded N. Korea to stop the test and return to the 6-party talks, but the talks were not successful.

北朝鮮はアメリカによる金融制裁を解除することをアメリカと話しあうことを望んでいましたが、アメリカ政府は、直接二国間会談は飲もうとしませんでした。

North Korea wanted to have talks with the US and asked the US to lift the financial sanction, but the US was unwilling to talk face to face with N. Korea.

日本政府は核実験後、北朝鮮の船舶の日本立ち入りを全面禁止にしました。

The Japanese government prohibited all the N. Korean ships from entering Japan after the nuclear bomb test.

日本は拉致問題という重要な問題をかかえており、日本人拉致被害者の生命を最重要事として北朝鮮問題にあたらねばなりません。

Japan has the abduction issue with N. Korea and therefore has to bear in mind the abductees' lives when handling N. Korean affairs.

北朝鮮について考える

拉致事件の発覚以来、北朝鮮政府に対しては憤りを感じています。	I've been furious at N. Korea since the abduction case came to light.
自国民が貧困と飢餓に苦しんでいるときに核実験にお金をかけるのは為政者のすることではありません。	It's unforgivable for a political leader to waste much money on nuclear tests while his people are suffering from poverty and starvation.
北朝鮮政府は犯罪集団と主張する人もいます。	Some people even say the N. Korean government leaders are a bunch of criminals.
アメリカに敵国視されている国がアメリカの侵略から身を守るために独自の軍隊、兵器を維持しようとするのは当然です。	It's natural for a country considered an enemy by the U.S. to have its own military or weapons to defend itself from the U.S.
イランやイラクと同様に北朝鮮もアメリカ現政権からは悪の枢軸国と見られています。	Together with Iran and Iraq, N. Korea is regarded as an Evil Axis country by the current U.S. government.
核開発は効果と費用の関係では北朝鮮にとって仕方ない選択とも考えられます。	Nuclear weapon development can be the only choice for N. Korea given its effectiveness and cost.
しかし隣国の日本人としては北朝鮮政府には核を捨て、前向きに隣国と協調してアジアの平和を目指してもらいたいものです。	Japan, however, as its neighbor, would certainly want N. Korea to abandon its nuclear weapon program and take a positive stance in cooperating with its neighbors and seeking peace.

ロシア・中国と北朝鮮との関係

ロシアや中国などの大国が戦略的に北朝鮮の存在を必要としているのも事実です。

しかし中・ロは北朝鮮の動きには動揺しているようです。あまりに過激な動きをするとアメリカなどに攻撃の口実を与えるからです。実際にアメリカはすでに日本の近海に潜水艦などの船舶を配備しているとのことです。

中国は北朝鮮に対して影響力を持っていても、核その他の武装の緩和を勧めません。北朝鮮で食糧がなく餓死する人が大勢出ていてもです。

これがもし中国の一部だったら中国政府が国際社会から非難を浴びることでしょう。しかし、現状では中国への非難は間接的であり、かわしえるものです。

そういう意味でも中国にとって北朝鮮のキム体制は対アメリカ戦略として便利なものなのです。

It's a fact that super states like Russia and China need N. Korea from the strategic point.

But they seem to be baffled by N. Korea's moves. Too radical a change could give the U.S. an excuse to attack. In fact, I have heard that the U.S. has already deployed vessels including submarines in the seas around Japan.

China would never push N. Korea to somewhat disarm though it has influence on N. Korea, despite the fact that many people are starving to death in N. Korea.

Had it happened in China, it would have been the target of international criticism. But actually China only gets censured indirectly, and it can usually deflect the criticism.

In this respect, N. Korea's Kim regime is very useful for China in its strategy for the U.S.

核開発の危険性

北朝鮮の核開発は核兵器また、その製造能力を保持することがいかに危険かを如実に表しています。

N. Korea's nuclear development has clearly shown us how dangerous it is to possess nuclear weapons or the capability to make them.

つまり、万が一アメリカやロシア、フランスなど核保有国にキムのような指導者が選ばれたらどうなるのか。	I mean if the U.S., Russia or France should have a leader like Kim, what would happen?
そういうことはあまり考えられませんが、まったくないという保証はありません。	Chances are very small but there's no guarantee.
核を管理する体制は確実ではありません。核を持たないことが確実に人類の将来を保証します。	Nuclear management systems aren't perfect. The only perfect way to guarantee a future for us is not to possess it.

▶ 問題解決に向けた一つの意見

世界に核を持ってよい国と持ってはいけない国があるのはおかしいと思います。 注:核保有国は nuclear powers という。	It is quite strange that the haves and have-nots exist in the world.
核保有国が他の国に核を持つなと言えるのでしょうか。	Can nuclear powers tell other nations not to have nuclear weapons?
核を持つことを賛成しているのではありません。核保有国が核を放棄する努力をすべきだと言っているのです。	I don't agree with nuclear armaments. I just say nuclear powers should make efforts to discard nuclear weapons.
北朝鮮の現状は世界に対して迷惑な面がありますが、少なくとも世界に向けて、今のところ戦争をしていません。	The present situation regarding North Korea is quite troublesome to the world, but this country is not making war on the rest of the world at the moment.
これまで多くの戦争をしてきた国は、むしろ現在繁栄している国であるのも矛盾しています。	It is ironical to see the fact that those countries which had gone to war in the past have been relatively prosperous.

このまま、北朝鮮を追い詰めて、戦争が起こらないとも限りません。核爆弾を日本に落とされると、日本は壊滅状態になります。
注：「追い詰められる」は be pushed to the wall とも表現できる。

If North Korea is driven into a corner, there may occur a war. If Japan were to be A-bombed, it would be a fatal blow.
cf. fatal の代わりに crushing も可。

アメリカが救ってくれても、ものすごい被害となります。

By the time the U.S. is able to help us, Japan will have been utterly destroyed.

日本としては、早く国交を回復して、北朝鮮の国民を救うことを考えるべきではないでしょうか。

I think it better for us to restore diplomatic relations with North Korea as early as possible to save the people living in that country.

北朝鮮を救うことを先に考えると、拉致問題も解決の糸口が見つかるのではないかと思います。

I feel that if we think of saving North Korea, we can find the clue to the solution of the abduction problem.

日本にとっては、拉致問題は非常に大切ですが、一方的に拉致問題のみを常に訴えることは、逆効果ではないかと思います。
注：unacknowledged は「無視されてしまう」の意味。

The abduction issue is of vital importance to us Japanese of course, but our constant unacknowledged requests on the problem may be counterproductive, I am afraid to say.

表現のコツ　「逆効果」の表現

犯した間違いのことで大人をきつく叱りつければきっと逆効果になる。
→ Telling off adults for their mistakes will surely be counterproductive.
相手の政治家のマイナス面を宣伝することは多くの場合逆効果である。
→ Negative political advertising backfires in many cases.
彼女の言っていることは、彼女自身の期待に反して逆効果となっている。
→ The effect of what she says is contrary to what she expects.
彼らに差し伸べた彼の優しさは逆効果となった。
→ His kindness extended to them had the contrary effect.

第 12 章

法律と憲法に関する意見を述べる

1 死刑制度の是非

▶ 情報を伝える

死刑制度については世界で多く議論されています。死刑制度のない国、ある国、あっても実際に執行されていない国があります。また、一般国民には廃止されているが、国事犯や軍事法廷で死刑を残している国もあります。

Capital punishment is much discussed the world over. Some countries have it. Others don't. Some others do but haven't carried it out. There are also countries that don't have it for the general public but maintain it for crimes threatening the nation and for court-martial.

現在では74カ国で死刑制度は維持されており、方法には絞首刑、電気刑、注射刑、斬首刑その他があります。

Today 74 countries maintain the practice. The methods range from hanging and electrocution to lethal injection and beheading.

死刑の目的として挙げられるものに、予防論や応報論などがあります。

The purposes include preventive theory and revenge theory.

予防論は犯罪を予定している者に対して、命を奪われる結果になるぞと威嚇するためと、矯正不能と思われる犯罪者を社会復帰させては犯罪の再発の恐れがあり、それを予防するためである。

The preventive theory says that the threat of the death penalty is a deterrent to crime, and it eliminates felons who cannot be rehabilitated and would otherwise commit more crimes in the future.

応報論は被害者およびその親族の無念を晴らすためだというものです。

Proponents of the revenge theory believe that executing the criminal relieves the mental stress of the victim and the victim's family of feelings of revenge or resentment.

▶ 国内での反対、賛成論のいくつかを紹介する

反対論：
明確な犯罪の抑止効果が証明されていない。人の重大な権利を奪う生命刑がその明確な抑止効果を証明しない限り、近代国家で認められてはならない。

死刑は憲法上の残虐な刑罰に当たる。殺人にも残虐なものと人道的なものがあるとすればかえって生命の尊厳を損ねることになる。すべての死刑は残虐刑である。

冤罪（えんざい）の場合取り返しがつかない。財産や自由を失う刑と比較にならないほど取り返しがつかない。

賛成論：
終身刑や無期懲役も明確な抑止効果が証明されてはいない。凶悪犯罪を犯し、他人の生命を奪った重大な権利侵害加害者が受けるべき当然の刑である。

懲役刑にも長期の独房禁固など残虐とされるものがある。死刑そのものが自由権や生命権の尊厳を損なうとは考えられない。

Cons:
It hasn't proven effective in crime prevention. Unless its preventive effect is definitely proven, it shouldn't be allowed in a modern state.

The death penalty is a brutal punishment specified in the constitution. If murder is classified as brutal or humane, it would rather mar the dignity of human life. All capital punishment is brutal.

In the case of a false charge it's irrevocable. The degree to which it's irrevocable is far beyond that of punishment for taking freedom or property.

Pros:
Life or indefinite imprisonment is not proven effective in prevention. A serious offender who's committed a serious infringement of human rights by taking another's life deserves death.

Among imprisonment penalties there are some that are considered brutal like long solitary. Capital punishment in itself doesn't lower the dignity of human freedom or life.

▶ 議論できることの重要性

最重要の課題であり、議論が途切れずに続くことは大切です。	This is the most important subject, and I hope discussion will go on.
人が組織的に人の命を絶つ（戦争ですら組織的とはいえない）ことには背筋が凍る思いですが、必要悪という言葉もあります。	I shudder to the bone at the idea that people systematically take others' lives. (Even war doesn't kill systematically.) But we have the concept, necessary evil.
真実はわかりませんが、この議論が力によって押しつぶされる社会にだけはしないようにしたいものです。	I can't tell where the truth is. We should make sure that pressure is not allowed to stop this discussion.

▶ 死刑制度に対する積極的反対論

死刑は廃止すべきだ！と、思っている人が少なくありません。人を死に追いやる権利は何人も有しないと思います。	Quite a few people agree with the abolition of the death penalty. Nobody has the right to put another person to death.
死刑の判決がくだり、それが執行される直前まで人の業では考えられない深い改心をする死刑囚の書物を読むとき、生かせてこの世で100倍の実を結ぶ新しい生命を与えるほうが、どれほどの償いとなるかと痛切に感じます。	When I read a book about a criminal on death row reflecting extraordinarily deeply up until the execution, I firmly believe that giving him or her a chance to live will serve as a much greater atonement, because he or she may contribute 100 times more to this world than we expect.

2 憲法9条改正の是非

▶ **情報を伝える**

現行の日本国憲法はその9条で戦争行為と戦力の保持を放棄し、平和憲法として知られています。	Article 9 of the current Japanese constitution rejects acts of war and weapons of war. Japan is one of the few countries whose constitution renounces war.
この憲法は第二次大戦後にアメリカを中心とした連合国軍によって作成され当時の政府が受け入れたものです。	The constitution was made by the Allied represented by the United States, and accepted by the then Japanese government.
歴代内閣は憲法9条についてそれぞれの解釈を示しています。	Our Cabinets in the past each gave an interpretation of the 9th article.
それは自衛隊の存在と9条との整合性を弁解するもので、矛盾は避けられていません。	They tried to explain the relationship between Article 9 and Self Defense Force. They all failed to disprove the contradiction.

9条解釈には4つの主説があります。
1. 自衛権を含めた一切の戦争行為、戦力を認めない。
2. 自衛権は認め、戦争行為と戦力は認めない。
3. 自衛目的では戦争も戦力も認める。
4. 個別的自衛権は認めるが、集団的自衛権は認めない。

The four major interpretations are as follows:
1. Not allow any act of war or weapons including the right to self-defense.
2. Allow the right to self-defense but not act of war or weapons.
3. Allow acts of war and weapons for self-defense.
4. Allow the right to self-defense for itself but not collective self-defense.

▶ 9条改正の背景

現政権は憲法9条を変え自衛隊の海外での活動を合法的なものにしようとしています。	The present Cabinet is trying to revise Article 9 to make the deployment of SDF overseas constitutional.
日本は戦後、憲法のもと平和を維持してきました。それができたのは日本がその間自衛隊を保持するも、海外への派兵その他戦争行為と見られる行為をしてこなかったのも理由です。	Japan has been peaceful since the end of the Second World War under the constitution. What's made it possible while maintaining the SDF is that we've kept away from anything that could be considered an act of war like sending SDF overseas .
また、アメリカの軍事力の傘の下にあったからとも考えられます。	Another reason can be that we've been under the umbrella of the U.S. military force.
現在極東地域は北朝鮮がミサイルの次に核兵器の実験を行い、きな臭い状態にあります。	Currently, the Far East is smoldering, since North Korea tested missiles and nuclear weapons.
自国を近隣からの脅威から守るのは当然のことであります。もし常軌を逸した脅威からの自衛権を憲法が妨げているとしたら、見直しは必要だと思います。	It's natural to protect your own country from a threat from a neighboring country. If the constitution prohibits us from doing so, we should reconsider it.
一方、多くの人が憲法9条を擁護しています。日本は唯一の核兵器被爆国であり、戦争の悲惨さ、平和の尊さを世界に伝えていくべきだとの主張もあります。	Meanwhile, many people support Article 9. Some people claim Japan should convey to the world how terrible war is and how precious peace is as the only country hit with a nuclear bomb.

▶ 9条改正とアメリカとの関係

政府が憲法を変えたり、自衛隊を海外派兵したりするのは、アメリカ主導の世界戦略に従っているからではないかと思います。

The government is to revise the constitution or send SDF overseas maybe because it stands by the U.S. global strategy.

今回の9条改正の動きも、アメリカとの関係を視野に入れてのことで、日本自らが独自に決断を下しているのではないと思います。

This time its bid to revise the Article 9 is in line with its relations with the US. It is never a decision Japan makes by itself.

日本が属国と揶揄（やゆ）されるゆえんです。

That's why Japan is criticized for being subjugated by the U.S.

現行の憲法議論はアメリカの軍事力の傘の下での議論で、このままでは議論自体が空虚なものになります。

The current discussion about the constitution can be unrealistic as long as we do it while Japan is under the U.S. military umbrella.

改憲派はアメリカとの関係を強化して日本を守ろうとしているわけです。

The pro-revisionists try to protect Japan by further solidifying relations with the U.S.

しかし日本はもっと自主性のある国になるべきです。

But I believe Japan should be more independent.

護憲派については、日本がアメリカの軍事力の傘から抜け真の独立を果たしたときに、現在9条を守り、軍事力を放棄しようと主張する人も、真の議論を迫られるのではないでしょうか。

As for the anti-revisionists, the argument of those who insist Article 9 be kept and the military power be abandoned should be really tested when Japan really gets its independence.

▶ 9条改正の積極的反対論

防衛の名の下に、戦争に備える準備をすることは、世界で唯一の被爆国として、その犠牲になった方の魂に申し開きできません。

As the only country in the world to be a victim of the A-bomb, we cannot explain the act of preparing for any war under the name of self-defense in the way it would be satisfactory to the souls of the war victims.

現状の憲法を厳守してきたからこそ、今日までの平和があります。

It is just because of the strict observance of our Constitution that peace has been long kept since the end of the war.

絶対に9条改正は押し留まるべきです。被爆国だからこそ、平和を世界に訴え、武器を持たないのです。戦争に向かってはいけないのです。

This is why Article 9 should not be amended under any circumstances. Just because of being the only A-bombed country in the world, we should always advocate peace to the world and not resort to arms. We should not head for any war.

表現のコツ 「空虚な」を表現する

> 文字通り empty を使うことができます。「むなしい」の意味もあります。「虚飾の」という意味では vain を使うことが多いです。「うわべだけの」は hollow, superficial が使えます。
>
> ナンシーを失ってから人生がむなしい。
> → Life has been empty for me since I lost Nancy.
> 彼女のうわべだけの親切さに私たちはうんざりしている。
> → We are tired of her superficial kindness.

3　裁判員制度

▶ 情報を伝える

平成16年に裁判員制度に関する法律が可決され、近く実施されることになっています。	In Heisei 16, a law concerning lay judges passed and is expected to take effect in the near future.
この制度は選挙権のある国民に刑事裁判に参加してもらい、被告人の罪の有無や刑の内容を裁判官とともに決めるものです。	This system allows registered voters to participate in the trial and make decisions on the guilt or innocence of the accused together with the judges.
これまでの刑事裁判は検察官、弁護士、裁判官の専門家が中心に行なってきました。丁寧、慎重な検討がなされてきましたが、ときには国民にとっては理解しがたいものであったりしました。 参考：「(芸術などが) 理解しがたい」はarcaneが用いられる。	In the past, trials have been conducted by such experts as the prosecutor, the defending attorney and the judge. Cases have been deliberated most carefully, but the process could be confusing for the public.
より国民の理解しやすい裁判を実現しようと裁判員制度が導入されることになりました。	In order to make it easier to understand, the system is being introduced.
国民が裁判に参加する制度はアメリカ、イギリス、フランス、ドイツ、イタリアなどでも行われています。	Trials in which the general population participate also exist in the U.S., the UK, France, Germany and Italy.

▶ 裁判員制度に対する反対論

刑事事件を審査する裁判官が被告人や被害者、その他の関係者に個人的、その他の偏見を持っていてはいけません。しかしながら専門家の裁判官でさえ、時にはそれは難しいのではないかと思います。	A judge trying criminal cases should not be biased about the accused, the victim or anybody else involved. But the reality is that it's sometimes very difficult even for the judge.

例えば、裁判のドラマの多いアメリカの映画などでは、ときに裁判官がもろに特定の人に偏見を持っているシーンが見られます。 注：unmistakableは「明白な、もろの」の意味。	For example in the U.S., where there are many TV dramas about trials, some movies show the judge to have an unmistakable bias against certain people.
訴訟に関する、知識や訓練のない裁判員はましていわんやでしょう。公平性の欠けた審理が予想され心配です。	Lay judges should be more prone to biased judgement, lacking expertise or training. Unfair trials can be expected, which makes me worry.

▶ 裁判員制度に対する賛成論

これまで刑事事件は3人の裁判官で行ってきました。むしろ審理の内容が偏るのは一握りの人間が判断をするときではないでしょうか。	Criminal cases have traditionally been tried by three judges. I guess the process of a trial can be more lopsided when a handful of people are judging.
また、この3人の関係なども問題です。上下関係があると他の人の意見に自分の意見が左右されたりしないのか、あるいは裁判官も上司の意見に左右されないのかなど心配の種はあります。	In addition the relations between the three can be another problem. When there is superior-subordinate relationship, one can influence the other's view. And they might have a superior who has influence over their judgements. These are further concerns.
これに裁判所という役所から直接給料をもらっていない国民が加われば、もっと自由な審理が期待できると思います。	However, by adding lay people who are not paid to the trial procedures, we can expect a free judging process, I believe.

裁判員制度慎重論

審理の際に裁判官は専門家だから、すべて（最終判断も加えて）裁判官に任せておこうという安易な考えの人が裁判員になるのではないかという懸念があります。

Another potential problem is that among the citizen judges, there may be some who rely totally on the judge's decision (including the final one) during deliberation just because he or she is considered a professional.

おそらく裁判員になる人たちは前もって簡単な研修などがあるのではないかと予想されます。しかし、本来は訴訟に対してある程度時間をかけた教育を受けた人が裁判員になるべきと思います。

I expect citizen judges would be required to take some summary lectures in advance. I'd like to suggest people who have studied the legal procedure for a certain period of time should be chosen as citizen judges.

その意味で、教育のさらなる充実、そして中等教育レベルでの司法、訴訟に関する教育の必修化などが裁判員制度の前提としてあるべきです。

In this sense, what is expected is a rich and profound education, and introductory lessons on judicial and legal procedures as compulsory study at the high school level, prior to the implementation of the new system.

表現のコツ　「任す」を訳す

本文では「頼る」ととらえて、rely on を使っています。他には depend on、lean on が同種の表現です。仕事などを誰かに「任す」と言うときには let a person handle、let a person take care of、leave ～ to a person などが役立ちます。

君が忙しいのはわかっているよ。この場は僕に任せて。
→ I know you're busy. Let me handle the situation.
今回彼らは 100％警察に任せるわけにはいかないと思うよ。
→ I don't think they can fully depend on the police this time.

第 13 章

コミュニケーションに関する意見を述べる

1 日本語と英語の違い

▶ **文法的な特徴とそれに関する意見**

日本語は敬語が発達しています。	The Japanese language has a developed system of honorific expressions.
敬語には、表現を丁寧にするという丁寧語と、相手を敬う尊敬語、自分をへりくだる謙譲語が存在しています。	Honorifics are divided into three classifications: polite expressions for making words polite, respectful expressions to respect others, and humble expressions to lower oneself.
たとえば、「食べる」に対して「食べます」といえば丁寧語で、「召し上がる」といえば尊敬語で、「いただく」といえば話し手が自分の食べる行為について使う謙譲語です。	For example, 'tabemasu' is the polite expression for 'taberu,' meaning eat. Moreover, 'meshiagaru' is the respectful expression to others and 'itadaku' is the humble expression used by the speaker for his or her own act of eating.
日本語は、英語における種々の文法事項がほとんど助動詞によって行われているという文法現象があります。	Japanese is characterized by the syntactic phenomenon that various kinds of grammatical functions can be conducted by auxiliaries.
英語では過去を表すのに動詞の過去形を、受身を表すのに be ＋過去分詞を、使役を表すのに使役動詞を用いますが、日本語ではすべて助動詞を用いるのです。	In English, the past tense of a verb is usually used for expressing the past, the constuction 'be plus past participle' for the passive, and causative verbs for the causative. However, in Japanese auxiliaries have all the above functions.

だから、「勉強させられた」は、使役の「させる」、受身の「られる」、過去の「た」という助動詞を組み合わせる必要があり、順番は使役、受身、過去にしなければなりません。	Therefore, the expression "was made to study" must be made by combining the causative helping verb 'saseru,' the passive helping verb 'rareru,' and the past helping verb 'ta,' in this order.
敬語と助動詞の存在が、外国人にとって日本語を難しいものにしていると思います。	The existence of honorifics and auxiliaries make Japanese hard for foreigners to master.

▶ 文字に関する意見

外国人にとって日本語が難しい要因は、漢字の存在です。	One of the factors which make Japanese difficult for foreigners to learn is the existence of Chinese characters.
加えて同音異義語が多いことが、その難しさに拍車をかけています。	In addition to this, the large number of homonyms makes Japanese even harder to master.
たとえば、「たいしょう」と呼ばれる日本語は、少なくとも対照と対称と対象の3つの意味を持ちます。漢字がすべて異なっています。	For example, the Japanese word pronounced as 'taisho' has at least three meanings: contrast, symmetry and object, all expressed by different Chinese characters.
また、同じ漢字でも読み方が異なって意味が異なるという例もあるので、ややこしいです。	What makes Japanese even harder is that the same Chinese characters can be read differently depending on their meaning.
たとえば、大きい家（「大家」）と書く漢字があります。この漢字を、オオヤと読むと家主の意味です。	Take Chinese characters of "big house" for example. If they are read as 'ooya,' it means a landlord, or the owner of a house.

タイカと発音すれば、権威の意味です。	If they are pronounced as 'taika,' it means an authority.
なお、タイケと読むと名家や金持ちの意味となります。	And moreover, if they are pronounced as 'taike,' it means an honorable family or rich family.
日本人にとっても、よく似た表現は使い分けが難しいです。	Even for us Japanese, the similar expressions are difficult to use properly.
「死体」と「遺体」の違いが分かりますか。殺人事件などでは、「死体」は身元不明の場合で、身元が判明したら「遺体」というのが普通です。	Do you happen to know the difference between 'shitai' and 'itai' in Japanese? In a murder case, 'shitai' is simply the dead body which is not identified, but once identified, the dead body is called the remains, or 'itai' in Japanese.
科学の分野でも、漢字の微妙な使い分けがあります。	In the field of science, we should know the proper use of Chinese characters.
たとえば、「殺菌」と「滅菌」の違いが分かりますか。「殺菌」とは病原体のみを死滅させること、「滅菌」はすべての微生物を死滅させることで、無菌状態にすることを指します。	For example, can you use the words "sakkin" and "mekkin" properly? Both are translated as sterilization but "sakkin" means destroying only germs, and "mekkin" means killing all the microorganisms, both benign and malign, to make a totally germ-free condition.

▶ 面白情報を伝える

日本語は、母音だけで文を作るのが、比較的簡単です。	In Japanese, it is comparatively easy for us to make a sentence only composed of vowel sounds.

例えば「おい、魚を追い合う鵜を追え」や「いい家、多い青いエイを覆う」などは母音の発音だけでできた文です。	For example, there are sentences like "Oi, uo-o oiau u-o oe, (meaning 'Run after cormorants competing in chasing fish')" or "Iiie, ooi aoi ei-o oou (meaning 'A good house covers many blue rays')."
英語では純粋な母音のみで文を作ることはほとんど不可能なだけでなく、母音のみの単語もほとんどありません。	It is almost impossible for us to produce a sentence consisting only of vowel sounds in English and is almost as hard to find a word pronounced only in vowel sounds.
ミツユビナマケモノという単語ぐらいしか思いつきません。	The only word I can hit upon at the moment is ai.
日本語は、いろは歌、すなわち日本語のひらがなすべてを1つずつ使った文は比較的簡単に作れます。	It is comparatively easy for us to make an Irohauta, or a sentence using each letter of the Japanese alphabet just one time respectively.
英語では、アルファベットを1つずつ使った文を作ることはきわめて難しく、次の文が知られているだけです。「テレビクイズ博士のジョックさんは、オオヤマネコをほとんど袋に入れない」	It is extraordinarily difficult for us to make a sentence using each letter of the English alphabet in the same way. The only sentence so far known is as follows: Mr. Jock, TV quiz Ph.D, bags few lynx.

▶ **意見を伝える**

若い人たちの、最近の日本語の乱れには腹が立ちます。	I am irritated at recent young people's indecent way of speaking Japanese.
日本語をもう一度見直して、美しい日本語を使用する努力をすることが大切だと思います。	I think it is important for us to reconsider the values of Japanese and to make utmost effort to use beautiful Japanese.

2 日本人と外国人の発想の違い

▶ 情報を伝える

外国人とりわけ、西洋人は、YesとNoがはっきりしていると言われています。	It is often pointed out that foreigners, especially Westerners, give clear-cut answers of yes or no.
日本人は、はっきりとYesやNoを表明しないことが多いです。ぼかすか、2つの意味に取れるような場合もあります。	Japanese often give no clear answer but have it remain vague or even ambiguous in some cases.
つまり、いい加減に思われても仕方がないでしょう。	It may be natural for foreigners to think that Japanese say things irresponsibly.
また、日本人は否定したくても「はい」と一応言ったり、また、肯定の意見であっても「いいえ」と言ったりする可能性があります。	They say sometimes yes when they have a negative opinion, while there is a possibility for them to say no even if they agree.
つまり、日本人のYesはNoで、NoがYesのこともあるのです。	In short, Japanese yes is sometimes no, and Japanese no is sometimes yes.
西洋では、結論をはっきり言ってから、その理由を付け加えるのが、コミュニケーションの基本です。	In the west, the basic communication style is to mention a conclusion and then give reasons for it.
日本人は、結論は言わずに相手に察してもらうことを期待する場合が多いです。	Japanese often expect the other party to guess what they want to say; therefore, they don't clarify their conclusion.

あるいは、結論は最後のほうにしか言わないということが起こります。	There are some cases where they don't disclose what they really want to say until the end of their story.

▶ 意見を伝える

日本語では、「明日のパーティ出席しませんか？」に対して、「明日はちょっと」と言うだけで、これが断りの表現であることが分かります。	In response to the invitation like "Why don't you attend tomorrow's party?," Japanese may say "Asu-wa chotto...," the direct translation of which is "Tomorrow is a little..." This clearly means refusal.
「明日はちょっと別の用事があるので、行けません」とはっきり言うと失礼だと考えてしまうところがあります。	Japanese tend to regard it as rude to say clearly, "I cannot attend the party because I have some other things to do tomorrow."
また、行間を読めない、すなわち察することができない人はレベルが低いと考える向きも、日本人にはありますね。	Also, they even are likely to think of those who cannot read between the lines as unsophisticated.
英語で、「明日はちょっと」は訳せませんね。(Tomorrow is a little. ではわけが分かりません)	The expresson "Asu-wa chotto" is actually untranslatable. (It makes no sense if we say that tomorrow is a little.)
少なくとも西洋人と話をするときは、言いたいことをはっきりと述べるべきだと思います。	We should say clearly what we want to say at least in cases when we speak with Westerners.
だらだらと述べて結論が分からないようにするのも避けるべきですが、一方、簡潔に述べすぎて失礼のないようにすることも大切です。	We should avoid beating around the bush and taking a lot of time, but we should be careful not to be impolite by speaking too briefly.

「明日は行けません。用事があるからです。」というのも、目上の方や初めての方には、丁寧に「すみませんが・・・」など丁寧表現を添えることも重要です。
注：目上の人に2つの言い方がある。
　→地位が上　　one's speriors
　　年が上　　　one's elders

When we speak to our superiors or elders and to those who we meet for the first time, it is important to know that we should add some polite expressions to a simple statement like "I can't join the party because I am busy." For example, we should use the phrase "I am afraid to say but..." or something like that.

西洋人ならとにかくはっきり率直に言えばよいということではありません。それぞれの場面での最小限のマナーは守るべきでしょう。

We should always be cautious about speaking directly. There is certainly a minimum requirement of good manners which are suitable for each situation.

表現のコツ　「最小限」を訳す

これは彼らが考えうる最小限の要求のようです。
→ This seems to be the lowest conceivable demand they can make.
彼女の即座に対応するという機転で被害は最小限にとどまった。
→ Her tactful and immediate actions kept the damage to a minimum.
最小限に見積もっても、大体1千万円はかかるだろう。
→ Even at the most conservative estimate, it will cost around 10 million yen.

3 言葉の使い方について考える

▶ 相手の身になって考えることの重要性

地域、職場、学校などの国中のいろいろなところで、民族、男女、年齢、容姿、職業等からくる数え切れない差別語が飛び交い、人を傷つけています。 参考：○○差別は discrimination in ... で表せる。 →雇用差別は discrimination in employment。	There are an innumerable number of discriminatory words uttered in all parts of the country including local districts, workplaces or schools. Those words result from discrimination on the basis of race, sex, age, appearance, occupation and the like. Such words almost always hurt the feelings of the people who hear them.
話し相手や話題の人を自分に置き換え、その人の痛みを味わうことが大事です。	It is important for us to put ourselves in the shoes of the person we are speaking to or about and to attempt to understand his or her feelings.
一般に、自分が言われたくない言葉を人にぶつけてはいけません。	In general, we should not use words which we don't want others to say to us.
その言葉をそっくりそのまま返したいということがよくあります。	I often come across the situation where I would like to give exactly the same words uttered toward me back to the very person who has used them.
不良っぽい高校生がコンビニの前にしゃがんで、タバコを吸いながら、「最近の中学生は分からんわ！」と言っている場面に出くわしたことがあります。	I once saw some delinquent senior high school students squatting and smoking. I heard them say something like "Recent junior high school students are hard to understand."
「あなたはどうなの？」と思います。	I would like to say to them, "How about you?"

傷つく言葉の対処法

悪気がないのに、相手を傷つける言葉を発してしまったことはないでしょうか。

Have you ever uttered words without evil intentions which resulted in hurting people's feelings?

そんな場合は、きちんと謝りましょう。そして相手が許してくれない場合でも怒ってはいけません。

If that were ever the case, it would be better for you to apologize to them. And you should not get mad even if they don't forgive you.

もう謝ったからいいじゃないか！と言ってしまっては振り出しに戻りますよ。

Forgive me because I apologize! ... That will turn everything back to the starting point.

逆の立場を考えてみましょう。

Let us see what we should do if our position and theirs are reversed?

今度は、自分が傷ついた場合です。相手は悪気がなかったとします。

This time, suppose someone has hurt our feelings and that the person who said something that hurt us did so without malice.

それが分かった時点で、優しく許してあげましょう。すると、たいてい全てが丸く収まります。

We should be kind enough to forgive him or her once we understand the situation. Then everything will go well.

いつまでも、傷ついたことを根に持っていてはいけません。

We should not harbor a grudge against him or her for a long time.

このことは、たとえ相手に悪意があって、あなたを中傷した場合でも、そのようなひどい言葉はさっさと忘れましょう。

Try to forget harsh words quickly even if the other party criticizes you scathingly in acrid language full of malice.

この言葉は一生忘れないぞ！という妙な頑固さは不要です。	We should not be so strangely stubborn to say that we will never forget the words.
私は今は、少なくともそう考えています。	This is all I can say at the moment.
言葉は単なる音波に過ぎません。ひどいことを言われたら、天が私にもっと偉大になれということだな、と考えましょう。	The words are nothing more than a sound wave. Let's believe that God wants us to be much greater than now, if we are hurt by some poignant words.
「この人の口を通して天は何を私に伝えたいのだろう？」と客観的に悪意の言葉を考えてみる余裕が欲しいものです。	You should be calm and composed enough to objectively wonder what God is teaching me through the abusive language uttered by this person.

▶ **男性に対する言葉と女性に対する言葉**

ある男性が、仕事の後で付き合っている彼女とデートすることを約束しました。	Suppose a man promised his steady girlfriend to go with her after work.
ところが、残念にも残業するように上司から命じられ、断りの連絡をしました。	But unfortunately, his boss ordered him to work overtime and he called her to cancel the date.
女性の中には「私と仕事とどっちが大事なの？」と男性に迫る人がいます。	In this situation some women present the question, "Which is more important, me or your job?"
「仕事だ」といえば彼女はショックだし、「もちろん君だよ」と言えば「すぐ来て」と言われます。	If the answer is "My job," she will be shocked, and if it is "Of course you," then the girl may ask you to come soon.

発展編　第13章　コミュニケーションに関する意見を述べる

271

こんな場合、男性が喜ぶ言葉は「お仕事大変そうね。無理しないでね。私のことは気にしないで。デートはまた今度ね。」というような感じのことです。	In this case, what the man wants her to say is "You must be busy today but don't work so hard. Don't worry about me. Ask me out next time," or something like that.
男性はプライドがあるので、そのプライドを傷つけないことです。それから、男性はおだてると、いい気分になりますよ。	Any man has his pride, so it is better not to hurt his pride. Moreover, he will feel some relief if you flatter him.
男性から女性に連絡を入れる場合、「仕事だから今日は会えない」だけでは冷たいです。	When the man declines the date, the words like "I cannot see you today because of my job." are merciless to her.
女性が喜ぶ言葉は、「今日は仕事が長引きそうだ。ごめんな。さびしい思いさせるかもしれないけど、今度は必ず会うからね。」など感情のこもった言葉です。	The words which might please her are those that show that you are considerate and thinking of her like "Today I am so busy. Very sorry. I know you are lonely and I also miss you. I won't make you sad next time."
論理的に諭すと逆効果です。そして、女性には、謝ることが有効です。	Logical persuasion often backfires. An apology often has a good effect on the mind of a woman.

第14章

日本文化に関する意見を述べる

1 日本の西洋化・近代化と日本文化

▶ **情報を伝える**

日本は、明治維新のころからヨーロッパに多くを学び、西洋化が始まりました。	Japan began to be Westernized during the Meiji Restoration and learned many things from the West.
西洋化は、近代化をも意味しています。また、産業が興り、経済が発展してきました。	Westernization also means modernization. Accordingly, the development of various industries helped Japan progress economically.
だから、日本では西洋化と近代化と産業化がほとんど同時に起こったということになります。	Therefore, in Japan, Westernization, modernization and industrialization occurred almost simultaneously.
西洋の近代化や産業化は、市民革命後に起こってくるのですが、日本では、むしろ国王が復権するという珍しい形で歴史が発展しました。	Modernization and industrialization in the West came after revolutions and the overthrow of autocracy. But in Japan, the restoration of emperors' power coincided with social progress, which is quite a rare case.
王政復古の前は、もちろん、武家政権として、将軍が力を発揮する封建制度の社会でした。 注：「王政復古」は他に主に2つの言い方がある。 → the reestablishment of the Imperial regime / the return to the Imperial regime	Before the Restoration of Royal Rule, Japan was, of course, a feudalistic country where the Shogun exercised great power in its militarist government.

▶ **日本文化の偉大さを主張する**

西洋化したとはいえ、日本的なものは残っています。	Though it was Westernized, there remain things that are Japanese.

たとえば、衣食住の側面から、いくつか例を挙げることができます。	We can mention some examples from the standpoint of food, clothing and shelter.
「衣」においては、洋服が主に着られていますが、特別の機会、たとえば初詣、成人式、卒業式、結婚式などでは伝統的な着物を着用する女性が多いです。	In clothing, Western clothes are mainly worn, but on special occasions like a visit to shrines or temples at the beginning of the year, a coming-of-age ceremony, a graduation ceremony, a wedding ceremony and the like, many women wear traditional kimonos.
また、着物の先生はもちろんのこと、華道や茶道の先生、日本式旅館の女将などは着物姿が普通です。	Also, not to mention teachers of kimono, teachers of flower arrangement or tea ceremony and female managers at Japanese style inns usually wear kimonos.
「食」においては、日本料理は無視できません。寿司やすき焼き、丼、うどんやそばなどいろいろ存在しています。豆腐や納豆などが注目に値しますが、健康によい食材も豊富です。 参考：親子丼 は a bowl of boiled rice with egg and chicken。 　　　他人丼 は a bowl of boiled rice with egg and beef。	With respect to food, Japanese cuisine is something not to be ignored. It ranges from sushi, sukiyaki, and bowls of rice with something on top called Domburi, to Japanese white noodles or buckwheat noodles. There is an abundance of food considered to be good for health, among which bean curd and fermented soybean are noteworthy.
醤油は日本語のひらがなやカタカナとともに、日本の数少ない発明の中に数えられます。	Soy sauce is counted among a small number of things invented in Japan along with the writing system of Japanese like hiragana and katakana.

日本の西洋化以前の時代は、中国からいろいろなものを学んできました。本当に純粋に日本的といえるものは少ないと考えられています。

Japan had learned a wide variety of things from China before the Westernization of Japan. It is pointed out that there are very few things which are purely Japanese.

「住」においては、都会ではビルが建ち並び、西洋化が根付いているようですが、日本の家屋にいったん入れば、たいてい和室があります。非常に重要な間として「床の間」があります。日本の家屋は、風通しがいいですが、これは湿度の高い気候に適した構造です。

In housing, Westernization seems to be deeply rooted because we see many buildings in the city, but we can find Japanese style rooms in most houses. There is a very important space called Tokonoma. Japanese houses are well ventilated, which suits a humid climate.

日本建築は柱中心といわれています。「窓」という言葉は、柱と柱の「間」に「戸」を入れたことから派生した言葉といいます。

Japanese architecture is said to place emphasis on pillars. The Japanese word "mado," which originally meant a door between pillars, derives from the combination of "ma," or intervals between pillars, and "do," or doors.

一方、西洋建築は壁中心です。だから、window という言葉は、壁に穴を開けて風を通す目的の物を指したのです。だから wind という単語が、この言葉に含まれています。

On the other hand, Western architecture centers on walls. The word "window," which contains "wind," once referred to an object made by forming a hole in the wall which was used to let air in.

日本的な精神性も残っています。たとえば、自然に対する繊細極まりない感情です。雨は単なる粒が拡大した水蒸気の落下現象に過ぎないのですが、この雨を楽しんできました。だから雨にも色々と名前があり、風情があるのです。

Japanese mentality also remains. Subtle sensitivity toward nature is an example. Raining is a simple phenomenon of the falling of drops of water that formed from the vapors, but Japanese enjoyed this rainfall. Accordingly, there are many names and special feelings for raining.

2 日本の宗教と日本人の宗教観

▶ 情報を伝える

日本古来の宗教は神道です。神道は、古来から存在していた自然崇拝、先祖崇拝、英雄崇拝が組み合わさってできた宗教といえます。

Shintoism is a religion native to Japan. It is said that Shinto is a religion which came into being through the gradual combination of nature worship, ancestor worship and hero worship that had lasted for centuries.

仏教の公伝は6世紀です。仏教は、釈迦が創始した仏になるための教えです。

参考：釈迦は正式には「釈迦牟尼ゴータマ・シッダールタ」で、「釈迦」は氏族の名前、「牟尼」は尊い人の意味、「ゴータマ」は姓、「シッダールタ」は名。

Buddhism was officially introduced into Japan in the 6th century. Buddhism is a religion founded by Sakyamuni (Gautama Buddha) which teaches how to become a Buddha.

神道と仏教の2つが、日本文化に大きな影響を与えてきたといえます。

The two religions Shinto and Buddhism are said to have exercised great influence on Japanese culture.

キリスト教はクリスマスやバレンタインデーなど日本におけるイベントで有名ですが、信者数は100万人ほどで、日本の全人口に比べると少ないです。

Christianity is noted for its Christmas and Valentine Day, popular events observed here in Japan. However, the number of adherents to Christianity, which is about a million, is rather small when compared with the total population of Japan.

しかし、日本にキリスト教系の学校や病院がたくさんあることから、キリスト教はいろいろな社会的貢献をしています。

But Christianity contributes very much to our society in many ways through its many Christian schools and hospitals in Japan.

日本社会は宗教的複数性を特徴とし、日本人は宗教的寛容性を特徴とします。	Japanese society is characterized by its religious plurality, and religious tolerance is characteristic of Japanese people.
つまり、神道の氏子と仏教徒の総数は日本の人口を超える（1億8千万ぐらい）といわれる点が、確かに宗教的複数性です。 注：宗教的複数性を文で表すと、Many people practice to some degree both Shintoism and Buddhism. といえる。	The long and short of it is that the total combined number of Shintoists and Buddhists in Japan exceeds the total population of Japan (about 180 million), which clearly shows religious plurality.
また、面白いことに、日本人は神道の神社と仏教の寺院のどちらも平気でおまいりします。この点が宗教的寛容性の意味するところです。	Another interesting point is that Japanese visit both Shinto shrines and Buddhist temples without hesitation, which shows religious tolerance.

▶ 仏教に関する面白情報を伝える

仏教の「仏」は、「佛」と書くのが正式です。佛教の「佛」という字の元の意味について述べましょう。	The ordinary Chinese character（仏）for Buddha in Buddhism is sometimes written in a more formal way（佛）. Let me tell you what the formal Chinese character meaning Buddha originally meant.
人偏のつく字は人間に関係あることを示します。一方、佛の旁（つくり）の部分は、否定を意味します。	Any character with a left-hand radical meaning 'a human' means something related to a human. On the other hand, the right-hand radical means negation.
だから、「佛」は、「人であって人でない」ということを示すことになります。	Therefore, we come to the conclusion that the formal Chinese character means "a human but not a human."

この不可解で矛盾した意味は、「本質は人だが、状態は人ではない」という意味と解釈できます。	This enigmatic inconsistent meaning can be interpreted as "human in essence but not human in state."
結局、迷いの状態の人間ではない人間が佛ということになります。	The top and tail of it is that a human who is not a human in a state of suffering is a Buddha.
これは、「沸」という字を考えると分かります。	Another Chinese character (沸) similar to this will make you understand the point.
「沸」は、本質が水だが、状態は水でないことを示しています。確かに状態は、水蒸気（水から成るけれど）ですね。	This Chinese character (沸) is indicative of water in essence but not water in state. What this Chinese character means is that it has the same composition as water but is in vapor form rather than a liquid state.

▶ 仏教の考え方に関する意見を述べる

お寺のシンボルマークは卍です。これはLを4つ集めた形に見えます。不思議なことに仏教で重要な4つのコンセプトが、英語では、Lで始まっています。 注：シンボルマークは symbol で OK。	The symbol of a temple is a swastika. This shape looks like a combination of 4 L's. Strangely enough, four basic concepts important in Buddhism all start with L in English.
何よりも、仏教では、生き物全体を大事にします。だから、Life がキーワードです。	First of all, in Buddhism all life is highly esteemed; therefore, "Life" is a keyword.
また、仏の特徴として、知恵と慈悲がありますが、これらは、Light（光）と Love（愛）で象徴されます。	Buddha features wisdom and mercy, which are symbolized by "Light" and "Love" respectively.

さらに、仏になるのに精進が必要です。精進は、Labor という単語で表すことができます。

Furthermore, we have to make efforts to become a Buddha. Buddhist efforts can be expressed by the word "Labor."

▶ 現代仏教における疑問点

仏教寺院を維持していくのに、ある程度の費用がかかります。だから、檀家の人間はある程度お金をお寺にお布施することが必要です。

To maintain a Buddhist temple, a certain amount of money is needed. Therefore, parishioners are required to make a monetary offering to the temple to some extent.

しかし、葬式や法事で高額のお金を要求されると矛盾を感じます。

However, if the temple demands we pay a huge amount of money for a funeral or memorial service, I kind of wonder why.

戒名でも、価格リストがあるのが変だと思います。中には 1000 万円かかる最高級の戒名もあるようです。

I think it strange for a temple to prepare a list of prices for posthumous Buddhist names. I hear it will cost 10 million yen to get the posthumous name of the highest degree.

仏壇でも家が一軒買えるぐらいの高級なものがあります。お坊さんの中には、ベンツを乗り回したり、美食家で美味しいものしか食べない人がいます。

There are some high-class Buddhist altars for the home which cost almost the same amount of money as it needs to buy a whole house. Some Buddhist priests enjoy driving a Benz or some of them are epicures who eat only palatable and toothsome food.

みんながそうではないのですが、仏道修行をする人は、質素でなければならないと思います。
注：live in a small way も「質素に暮らす」

Of course not every priest is like that, but I think those who claim to have the practice of Buddhistic austerities should live a simple life.

お茶に関する情報を伝える

茶は3種類に分類できます。不発酵茶である緑茶と、発酵茶である紅茶と、その中間の半発酵茶であるウーロン茶の3種類です。

Tea can be classified into three categories. They are non-fermented teas represented by green tea, fermented tea represented by black tea, and half-fermented tea as the tea between the above two. Oolong is typical of a half-fermented tea.

平安時代に唐から、固まった団茶が伝わりましたが、広がりませんでした。

Brick tea was introduced from Tang in the Heian period, but it did not spread.

鎌倉時代に宋から、粉末にした抹茶が伝わりました。抹茶を始めて伝えたのは、喫茶養生記(現代の日本語で言えば「お茶健康法」)を表した日本臨済宗の祖、栄西でした。

Powdered tea came to Japan from the Sung dynasty in China during the Kamakura period. It was Eisai, founder of the Rinzai Sect of Zen Buddhism and the author of Kissa-yojoki (a book on how to keep fit by tea), that brought powdered tea to Japan for the first time.

江戸時代には、明から煎茶が伝わりました。煎茶を伝えたのは、黄檗宗という禅宗開祖で、宇治に万福寺を創建した隠元です。そして万福寺は煎茶道の本山です。

During the Edo period, middle-class tea was introduced from Ming by Ingen, founder of Obaku Sect of Zen Buddhism, who established Mampuku-ji in Uji, headquarters of middle-class tea cult.

なお、隠元はフジマメを伝えたのであって、インゲンを伝えたのではありません。しかし、関西ではフジマメをインゲンと呼びます。

Incidentally, Ingen brought fuji-mame, or Egyptian kidney beans, not Ingen, or French beans. But this fuji-mame is called Ingen in the Kansai district.

3 日本の年中行事、お正月・お盆

▶ **日本の年中行事についての一歩進んだ情報**

日本の年中行事は、穢れ（けがれ）をはらうことに関係するものが目立ちます。

Annual events which are related to a practice of warding off evil are noted in Japan.

2月3日には節分の行事があります。節分の原型は、飛鳥時代、706年に初の儀式が行われ、豆まきが始まったのは室町時代です。

A Setsubun festival is held on February 3. The first ceremony of the prototype of Setsubun was performed in 706 during the Asuka period, but it was during the Muromachi period that a bean throwing ceremony started in Japanese history.

節分は、季節の変わり目の邪気をはらう儀式です。これは、現代的には、風邪のウイルスなどに代表される、いわば外的鬼の駆除の儀式といえます。

Setsubun is a rite whose purpose is to expel evil between the seasons. This is said to be a ceremony which drives away what we call outer demons represented by cold viruses from the modern perspective.

3月3日には、ひな祭りが行われます。人形を作ってお払いする習慣は奈良時代以前にも見られますが、流し雛が始まったのは平安時代です。段飾りは江戸時代からの風習です。

Dolls' festival is observed on March 3. The custom of exorcism by means of dolls was seen before the Nara period, but it was in the Heian period that the practice of setting dolls adrift began, and the dolls started to be arranged in tiers in the Edo period.

ひな祭りは、人形に穢れをつけて流すという機能を持っています。これは、人間の罪に代表される、いわば内的鬼の駆除といえるでしょう。

Dolls' festival has a function of floating dolls contaminated with defilement down the water. This is regarded as a rite of dispelling the so-called inner demons symbolic of human sins.

5月5日のこどもの日は、もともと端午の節句と呼ばれ、元来邪気をはらう儀式ですが、男の子の成長を祈念する催しになりました。現在は子供全体のための風習となっています。

Children's Day, which is observed on May 5, was originally called Tango-no-sekku. Fundamentally speaking, this custom was a ceremony for clearing evil away, but it became an event which aims at offering a prayer for the growth of boys. And now, it is a custom geared for all children.

こいのぼりの風習は、鯉が滝を登って竜になるという力強さを、男の子が身につけるよう願うことに端を発しています。

The practice of hoisting carp streamers originated in the wish that boys would grow up to be as strong as the carp which goes up the waterfall to become a dragon.

▶ お正月のトリビア的情報を伝える

お正月は神道的な習俗であるのに対し、お盆は仏教的な習俗です。

Shogatsu is a Shintoistic event, while Bon is a Buddhistic event.

正月の火祭りは、邪気を追い払う意味があり、お盆の火祭りは、死者の霊の迎え火と送り火の意味があります。

Fire festivals conducted during the New Year holidays have a function of expelling evil, whereas fire festivals performed during the Bon season function as a sacred method of welcoming and sending off the souls of the dead.

正月遊びも、邪気の払いと関係あります。たとえば、羽根つきは、「つき」を出す遊びで、負けたときの墨は穢れを象徴し、これを洗い流して、再生するという意味がこめられています。
参考:「再生」は、resuscitation（生き返ること）、a reincarnation（生まれ変わり）、a second birth、rebirth という。

Games played during the New Year days are related to exorcism. For example, the game of battledore and shuttlecock is a practice of having a swell run of luck, the Japanese word for which sounds like tossing up the shuttlecock. The India ink painted on the loser's face is symbolic of defilement and the washing away of the India ink means rebirth.

こま回しも、そのときの音が邪気を退散させるのだと考えられました。	The noise made by top spinning was considered to function as a charm against evŠ.
初夢では、一富士二鷹三茄子がよいとされました。それは富士は「不二」（2つとないもの）、鷹は「高い」、茄子は「成す」に通じるめでたいものの代表とされているからです。	Mt. Fuji, hawks and eggplants are regarded as auspicious when you see them in a dream on the first night of the year. Fuji, Hawks and eggplants are suggestive of 'unequaled,' 'high,' 'success' respectively.

▶ **お盆のトリビア的情報を伝える**

盆踊りの説話上の起源は、釈迦の十大弟子の1人、目連の体験にさかのぼります。	The legendary origin of Bon dancing dates back to the experience of Mokuren, one of the ten greatest disciples of Gautama Buddha.
目連は、自分の母が死後、餓鬼道に堕ちて苦しんでいるのを夢で見ました。	Mokuren dreamed about his mother suffering in the world of hungry demons after death.
どうしたら救えるのかを釈迦に聞いたら、ご馳走を人に施して、しっかり供養するように言われ、その通りにしました。	When he asked Gautama Buddha what he should do, he was advised to hold a memorial service for his mother and treat people to a gorgeous dinner, and he actually followed Gautama's advice.
すると、母親が救われたのです。それを夢で見て、目連は大喜びしましたが、この喜びの表現が盆踊りになったということです。 注：「大喜びする」は get transported with joy と表現できるが、やや硬い表現。	Then his mother was saved. On seeing her saved in his dream, Mokuren felt a great sense of joy. The expressÚn of his joy is said to have become a form of dancing.

お盆のときに、野菜で馬や牛を作るのは、先祖の霊を、速く迎えて、ゆっくり送るという意味があります。

The reason why a horse and a cow are made of vegetables is that we welcome ancestors' spirits quickly and send them back slowly.

速く迎えるには馬が、ゆっくり送るには牛が最適ということです。

A horse is an animal suitable for the quick invitation of them, and a cow, for the slow send-off.

なるほどという気がします。

That explanation satisfies me.
[=I can understand the reason naturally.]

第 15 章

自分自身の生き方を述べる

1 私の人生観と世界観

▶ 情報を伝える

日本人は「人」という漢字を用いて、お互い支え合うことの大切さを訴えますが、西洋人は、人間を表す単語の頭文字Hを用いて、独立する精神の重要性を説きます。

Japanese often insist on the importance of mutual help by showing the Chinese character meaning a human, while people in the west advocate the significance of independence by using the letter H of the alphabet, the first letter of the word "human."

この文字を用いる理由は、この文字が2人の人が自立して、握手している姿に似ているからです。

The reason why H is used is that its shape looks like two people who are independent of each other shake hands.

4Hクラブは、アメリカとカナダにある農村青年教育機関ですが、頭と心と手と健康の向上をモットーとしています。

The 4-H Club is an educational institution for young people in the farming villages of America and Canada, in which the motto of the organization is to enhance Head, Heart, Hands, and Health (4H).

▶ 人生観を伝える

世の中はそんなに甘いものではない。
注：somethingとnothingを使って、Don't try to get something from nothing. とすることもできる。

You are wrong if you think things would work as you expect.

普通の子供を見て「可愛そうに、一歩一歩死に近づいている」とコメントする人に人は集まりません。

People are not attracted to any person who, when looking at ordinary children, comments that they are unfortunately dying gradually.

実際、このような人はほとんどいませんが、マイナス思考に陥るとこれに近いことを我々も言っている場合があるので、気をつけましょう。

In reality, there are almost no such people that say this, but in some cases we may say things like this if we fall into a negative way of thinking. Be careful.

未来に対しては、期待せず、希望を持ちましょう。期待していたら期待はずれになってショックです。でも、希望は外れません。「希望はずれ」という言葉はないでしょう。
参考：unhoped-for という言葉があり、プラスイメージで使用される。
　→ unhoped-for good luck
　　（思いがけない幸運）

As for the future, we should have a hope, but not expectation. Unexpected things may happen, making us sad. Something falls short of our expectation, but not of our hope. Though we have the word "unexpectedly," there is no such word as "unhopedly."

過去に対しては、後悔せず、反省しましょう。後悔していたらキリがありません。後悔してクヨクヨ思うより、反省してヨクヨク考えるほうがよいですよ。

As for our past, do not repent but reflect. We may fall into a vicious cycle of repentance. It is better for us to reflect optimistically rather than to repent pessimistically.

補足：失敗したことに対して「ばかだった」と後悔するより、「今度はこうしよう」と反省するほうがよい。

cf. Don't repent negatively toward your failure but reflect positively by thinking about what should be done next.

いやなことがあったら、話すのではなく、書き留めておきましょう。数年後に読み返してみると、そのときの自分の小ささに驚くでしょう。

If something bad happens to you, don't say this to others, but put it down in your notebook. You will probably be surprised to know how small-minded you are if you read it several years later.

いやなことを言う人がいたら、100年後を想像しましょう。きっとその人はこの世にはいないでしょう。自分もいないけれど。

If you find someone saying something offensive to your ears, imagine the world 100 years later. Certainly, neither that person nor you would still be living.

大変な問題が起こったら、自分の最も尊敬する人物なら、この事態をどう解決するかを想像してみましょう。(たいていのことはたいしたことありませんよ)	If something quite serious happens to you, imagine how the person you respect most will deal with the problem. (Most things are not so serÚus as you feel.)
天は、その人がぎりぎり耐えられるだけの試練を与えます。苦難が大きければ大きいほど、自分は天に認められた偉大な人間であると悟りましょう。	God will give you the greatest hardship which you can manage to handle. You should know the greater the suffering is, the greater you are; i.e. God loves you.
どんな問題でも、解決できるものです。もし、解決できなければ、それは問題ではありません。	We can solve any problem. If we cannot solve it, it is not a problem at all.
何で自分だけこんな目にあうのか？と思ったときは、天に感謝すべきでしょう。この困難を乗り越えるチャンス、つまり、あとで幸せになる機会を与えられたからです。	You should thank God, if you ask yourself why this kind of bad luck comes only to you, because you are given the chance to get over it and therefore most likely become happy afterwards.

▶ ユニークな人生観を伝える

私はアルファベットの文字の中では、Hが大好きです。というのは、この文字が、独立心の重要性を暗示するだけでなく、この文字の発音が「英知」に聞こえるからです。	I like H best of all the alphabetical letters, because its pronunciation sounds like Eichi, meaning wisdom in Japanese, besides its shape which is suggestive of the importance of independence.

ユニークな世界観を伝える

代表的な使役動詞にLET、MAKEおよびHAVEがありますが、私は世界の文化がLET文化、MAKE文化、およびHAVE文化に分類できると考えています。

Representative causatives in English are LET, MAKE and HAVE. I think we can classify all the cultures of the world roughly into the three different cultures: LET culture, MAKE culture and HAVE culture.

LET文化は何でも許す「甘え」が生じる文化で、日本文化がその代表でしょう。

The LET culture is the one where people let others do anything, causing "amae," the spirit of dependence. Japanese culture falls under this culture.

MAKE文化は強い主張で相手を動かす「正義」がキーワードの文化で、西洋文化にその特徴が見られます。

The MAKE culture is characterized by the keyword of justice, which makes others do something with its strong assertion. The Western culture shows its traits.

HAVE文化は、状況に応じて、謙ってお願いしたり、命令的になったりする、ちょうどLETとMAKEの中間的な文化で、インドやイスラム社会が当てはまります。

The HAVE culture is somewhere between the above two. Depending on the situation people ask or tell others to do something. Indian or Islamic culture follow this path.

参考 LET、MAKE、HAVEのニュアンスの違い

> He let his daughter go to a graduate school.（娘が大学院に行くのを許した）
> He made his daughter go to a graduate school.（娘に大学院に行くのを強要した）
> He had his daughter go to a graduate school.（娘に大学院に行ってもらった）
> 注：letはallow、makeはforce、haveはaskのニュアンス。ただし、haveは単なる使役の意味（＝「～させる」）も出る。

2 私のユニークな発想法と考え方

▶ 意外な情報を伝える

勉強のできる小学生は、勉強部屋よりも居間で勉強しているというデータがあります。その理由には、居間で親と話す機会が多くなるということがあげられます。時事的な内容を親と議論する機会が増えるということです。このことが子供の知識だけでなく、知的好奇心を高めるのに役立っているのです。

注：「好奇心をそそる」は arouse one's curiosity, whet one's curiosity

According to a reliable source, those elementary school pupils who do very well more likely study in the living room than in their study. This is partly because they will have more chances to talk with their parents; this simply will lead to positive discussions about current topics with them. This kind of interaction will help them increase their knowledge and burn with intellectual curiosity.

▶ ユニークな意見を伝える

私は、5つの母音字が入った英単語には、重要なものが多いと感じています。例えば、「教育」は英語で education といいますが、5つの母音が入っています。

I kind of feel an English word which contains five vowel letters is important in many cases. For example, "kyoiku" is EDUCATION in English, which word contains five vowel letters.

英語教育では、コミュニケーション能力の向上の重要性が叫ばれて久しいですが、この「意思疎通をする」という動詞にも5母音が入っています。すなわち、communicate という単語がそれです。

A long time has passed since communicative ability came to be emphasized in English education. This very word meaning a person-to-person exchange of information and opinions also contain five different vowels. I mean the word COMMUNICATE!

▶ 問題に対する対処法

私は、困難に対処する方法は4つあるという意見を持っています。それは、同じ数の単語で代表できます。即ち、WITH、OVER、AGAINST と AWAY です。

I am of the opinion that there are four ways of coping with hardships, which are represented by as many words: WITH, OVER, AGAINST, and AWAY.

WITH の法というのは、問題と共に生きる、つまり、言い換えれば、その問題を受け入れるというようなやり方で、寛容性と勤勉性が要求されます。

The WITH method is the one in which you live with problems, or in other words, accept them, which requires generosity and diligence.

OVER の法は、その問題を乗り越える解決法で、知性と努力を組み合わせることが要求されます。

The OVER method is the one under which you try to overcome them, where you need to combine your intelligence and efforts.

AGAINST の法は、その状況と戦う方法です。そのためには、決断と勇気が必要です。

The AGAINST method is the one in which you fight against the situation, for which decisiveness and courage are needed.

AWAY の法は、その状況を避ける方法です。それは、節約と時間管理の知恵があれば、可能です。

The AWAY method is the one under which you will avoid the situation, which results from the wisdom of economy and time management.

参考 上記の4つの方法について、with と反対の手法は against の手法、over と反対の手法は away の手法であるといえます。つまり、with と against は「現実に対してどう対処するか」をテーマとし、現実肯定の考え方が with で、現実否定の考え方が against です。また、「困難に対する努力」をテーマとし、努力をするのが over の手法で、努力をしないのが away の手法。away の手法は、努力が徒労に終わる判断できる場合には、有効です。実際には、全ての対処法をうまく組み合わせて用いるとよいでしょう。

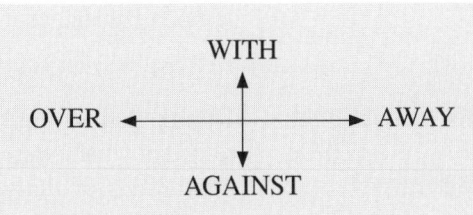

```
            WITH
             ↑
  OVER ←─────┼─────→ AWAY
             ↓
          AGAINST
```

私のユニークな文化論

西洋文化では、「個人」が重視されますが、日本文化では、人間と人間の間の関係、即ち「間」が大切なのです。

Western culture places emphasis on an individual, while in Japanese culture, the relations between the two people are important. This relationship is considered MA of humans.

個人主義が度を越すと、meism（＝「私主義」）になります。

Individualism may fall into "meism"(or selfish ways of thinking) when it goes wrong.

これに対し、私の造語である maism（＝「間イズム」）が、人生における原理として考える必要があると考えています。「間イズム」とは間という概念が重視される考え方です。

In contrast, I have coined a word, "maism," which we should regard as a principle we have to bear in mind in our life. Maism means the way of thinking in which the concept of MA is emphasized.

人間の個性を伸ばす、すなわち、プラスの自己を高めることを重視するのがキリスト教です。

The importance of displaying your originality or enhancing your positive ego is the name of the game in Christianity.

一方、仏教では、人間の我執を抑える、すなわち、マイナスの自己を弱めることを目標に修行をすることが基準となっています。

On the other hand, the severe practice of driving away your selfishness or discouraging your negative ego is the norm in Buddhism.

このように、日本に紹介された宗教は、それぞれ自己管理の側面では、きちんと棲み分けができていると思います。

I think that in this way each of the religÚns which were introduced from other parts of the world in the past now has its own particular role in the field of self control.

意外な主張その1　真のプラス思考と幸せの方程式

プラス思考をしないとだめになるよ！と脅す人は、プラス思考しかないという思いにとらわれているマイナス思考の「プラス思考唱道者」といえます。	Those who stick to positive thinking and always insist that we surely will ruin ourselves unless we think positively are advocates for positive thinking in a negative frame of mind, since they are possessed by the idea that positive thinking is the one and only thing valuable in the world.
そんなことを言ったら、マイナス思考の人は益々マイナス思考になります。	If they advise a person who tends to think negatively, he or she is more likely to think negatively.
本当のプラス思考の人は、マイナス思考すらマイナスにとりません。「マイナス思考も悪くないよ」とマイナス思考の人を励ますものです。	Truly positive people will not see even negative thinking negatively. They will encourage negative people by saying negative thinking is often not so bad.
幸せの方程式があります。	There is an equation for happiness.
それは、幸せは成果を欲望で割ったものであるということです。	The equation is as follows: Happiness is a division of accomplishment by desire.
この方程式は、欲望を減らすと、幸せ度が上がることを示しています。	This equation shows that if you can diminish your desires, the degree of your happiness will increase.
だから、幸せになるためには欲を抑える必要があるのです。	Therefore, in order to be happy, you should restrict your desires.
補足：欲を抑えると皮肉なことに不幸せな気分が高まるかもしれません。	cf. If you restrict your desires, ironically enough, your unhappy feelings may increase.

▶ 意外な主張その2　笑いと拍手

「笑うかどには福来る」という諺（ことわざ）があります。笑うと幸せになるということです。

There is a proverb like "Fortune comes to a merry home." This means laughing will make you happy.

確かに、笑っている人の周りには、人が集まります。怒っている人は避けますね。その笑っている人は、人を幸せに導き、自らもますます幸せになります。

In fact, people come to a laughing person and avoid approaching an angry person. The laughing person will make others happy and then himself or herself even happier.

神道的には、我々が笑うことが神霊を震わせて神様が喜び、そのお返しに我々は「福」というエネルギーをいただくことになるので、幸せになると考えられています。

From the Shintoistic viewpoint, laughing will vibrate the souls of deities, which makes them happy. Then deities will give us the energy of Fuku, or happiness, in return.

幸せだから笑うのではなく、笑うから幸せになるのです。

The point is not that we laugh because we are happy, but that we are happy because we laugh.

「幸せなら手をたたこう」という歌があります。素晴らしいコンサートの後は、幸せがこみ上げ、拍手喝采ということになりますね。

There is a song containing the words going, "If you are happy, clap your hands." In fact, after a wonderful concert, a storm of handclapping will arise with the audience feeling a lump of happiness rise in the throat.

神道的には、手をたたくから幸せなのです。手をたたくと、その振動が神霊を震わし、笑いの場合と同様、神様は最終的に我々を幸せにします。
注：「楽しいから笑うのではなく、笑うから楽しい」と実践心理学者の William James も唱えている。

From the Shinto standpoint, we are happy because we clap our hands. Clapping will vibrate deities' souls, which will make us happy in the same way laughing does.

不幸を感じたら、笑いながら手をたたいてみましょう。きっと本当に幸せになってくるでしょう。

If you feel unhappy, why don't you laugh and clap your hands at the same time? Happiness may come to you.

▶ 漢字を利用した主張

「育」という字の上半分の「云」は、「子」が上下逆にひっくり返っていることを示しています。これは、子供が生まれるときの姿を表しているといいます。子供は頭から出てくるので、この逆立ちが「正しい」のです。

The upper half of the Chinese character meaning "growth" indicates the state of a child being upside down. This is supposed to be the proper situation where a baby is going to be born. Since the baby comes out into this world from its head, this upside down posture is right.

だから「云」は、語ることが「正しいこと」そして性格が「正直であること」を表しているといえます。

Therefore, we can say that the upper half of the Chinese character originally means correctness in what you say and honesty in what you are like.

一方、下半分の「月」は、しっかり育って肉がついた状態を意味しています。つまり、「強く」成長したことを示しているわけです。
注：「肉付きがよくなる」は gather flesh, grow in flesh や pick up flesh ともいう。

On the other hand, the lower half of this Chinese character shows the state of the child putting on flesh. In short, this is suggestive of strength in growth.

以上のことから、子育ては、その子供が「正しく、強く」なるようにしなければならないということがいえます。

For the foregoing reasons, the childrearing which is meant by the Chinese character should be conducted in the way that the child should be honest and strong.

「忙」と「忘」は、似ています。どちらも「心」を「亡くす」と書くからです。

The Chinese character meaning "busy" and that of "forget" are similar in the sense that both contain the meaning of the absence of mind.

この場合の心は「思いやりの心」であると、私は考えています。その心がないと、物事を忘れるし、また逆に、忙しいと思いやりがなくなります。	I think the mind is considerateness in this case. Without this sort of mind, we tend to forget things, and conversely if you are busy, you tend to be lacking in thoughtfulness for others.
「食」は「人が良い」と書きます。食生活を改善すれば、人は良くなるというように、この漢字は主張していると私には思えます。	The Chinese character meaning "eating" seems to read "humans are good." It seems to me that this Chinese character insists that if you improve your eating habit, you will surely be good.
しかし、加工食品や冷凍食品など、「食品」とつくものはあまり健康によくありません。	However, those things whose names contain the two Chinese characters, directly translated as "eating item." are not so good for our health. Such things include processed food or frozen food.
そのような食品を山のように食べると病気になります。「品」の「山」にヤマイダレをつけると、「癌」という字になりますね。 参考：漢字の一部のことを radical という。 　偏（へん）→ left-hand radical 　旁（つくり）→ right-hand radical 　垂（たれ）→ upper left-hand radical 　冠（かんむり）→ upper radical	If you eat a mountain of such food, you will become ill. The Chinese character you can find when you add the upper left-hand radical meaning "disease" to the combination of Chinese characters meaning "item" and "mountain" is cancer!
「聖」は耳から書きますね。もし聖人のように立派な人になりたければ、聞くことが最も重要だとこの字が教えているように感じます。	The Chinese character meaning "saint" is to be written with the part of "ear" at the first stroke. I feel that the character teaches us that listening is of the greatest importance if you want to become a respectable person like a saint.

しっかり人の話を聞けば、情報も得ることができ、かしこくなります。	If you listen to others, you can get useful information and become intelligent.
また、人の悩みなどをじっくり聞ける人は、やさしい人です。	Moreover, those who can listen to others' worries or complaints are kind.
「聞くことによって、知恵がわき、慈悲を実践できる」というわけです。このことを目指し努力する人を聖人と呼ぶのです。	Therefore, listening makes you wise and leads you to put your kindness into practice. Those who are trying hard to be wise and kind are called saints.

▶ 英単語を利用した主張

何も考えずに eat を繰り返すと、e の部分が f になります。つまり、eat は fat の原因となるのです。	If you eat and eat without any reflection, the first letter "e" of the word "eat" will become "f." I mean "eat" is a cause of "fat."
そのまま、fat の状態を無反省に継続していると、最後に e がついてしまいます。つまり、fate ということになりかねません。	Moreover, the continuation of the state of being fat without any consideration will end up making the situation where "e" is put at the end of the word "fat." The word is fate!
eat に注意することが、健康維持の基本です。	Being careful in eating is the basis of keeping good health.

3 私の英語に対する考え方と勉強法

▶ 外国語学習に関する情報を伝える

世界の多くの国では第1外国語を小学校から学んでいます。

In many countries, people begin to learn their first foreign language in elementary school.

たとえば、フランスやイタリア、南アフリカやタイでは小学校1年から、ドイツ、ギリシャ、イスラエルでは小学校3年から、スペイン、ポルトガルおよび中国では、小学校1年から3年の間に、第1外国語教育が始まります。

For example, the first foreign language education starts in the first year of elementary school in France, Italy, South Africa and Thailand. It starts in the third year in Germany, Greece and Israel, and during the first to third years in Spain, Portugal and China.

中学生になって初めて外国語を学ぶ国は、日本以外ではアメリカ、ブラジル、インドネシア、ニュージーランドとトルコぐらいです。

The countries where foreign language education starts in junior high are the U.S.A., Brazil, Indonesia, New Zealand, and Turkey, to say nothing of Japan.

▶ 日本の英語ブームを歴史的に探る

明治維新から約40年周期で、英語ブームが起こっています。

Since the Meiji era, the boom and bust cycle in learning English has been about 40 years.

明治の初めに「英語国語化論」が叫ばれるほどのブームが起こりました。

In early Meiji, the idea that English should be our language came into being.

しかし、1889年に帝国憲法が成立してからは、日本人は自信を取り戻し、国語教育強化論が出て、英語ブームは去りました。

However, as Japan recovered its confidence after the Imperial Constitution in 1889, Japanese came to be more emphasized, driving away the boom in English.

日露戦争後、大正デモクラシーとともに、再び、英語ブームが起こりました。これが第2回英語ブームで、明治40年ごろです。	With Taisho democracy after the Russo-Japanese War, another boom in English came. This was the second boom, which started about the 40th year of Meiji.
しかし、1927年には英語教育廃止論が起こり、徐々に英語は無視され、戦争に突入し、敵国語となりました。	But the theory of abolishing English education was presented in 1927, which gradually lowered the status of English to an enemy's language during World War II.
戦後は手のひらを返したように、英語ブームが再度巻き起こりました。3回目の英語ブームです。1947年に英語が義務教育に導入されたのが象徴的です。	After the War, the third pro-English boom took place totally unexpectedly. English was incorporated into compulsory education in 1947, which was a symbolic event.
しかし、その後日本が高度経済成長するに従い、自信を取り戻し、英語軽視の傾向が見られるようになりました。	Later, as the Japanese economy progressed, Japan regained its power, resulting in the negative outlook on English.
明治維新から約120年を過ぎたころ、日米経済戦争の敗北とも言えるバブル崩壊が起こると、再び、英語教育が強調され始めました。2001年には「英語の教育言語化」論が出ています。	About 120 years after the Meiji Restoration, the bubble burst, a defeat in the economic war with US in a sense, helped emphasize English education. In 2001, the theory of using English for teaching became a norm.

▶ **日本人はなぜ英語ができないのか？**

日本人が、英語があまりできない理由は、英語教育の分野で指摘されている問題点に加え、さらに3つあると思います。	There are three main reasons why Japanese are not so good at English besides some of the problems pointed out in the field of Japanese English education.

1つは、言語学的な理由です。日本語と英語は、語彙が違うだけでなく、音声体系と文法構造がまったく違います。 参考：文法構造上、語順については「形容詞＋名詞」の語順のみが共通して、ほかの語順はすべて違います。	First of all, I can mention a linguistic reason. Japanese and English totally differ in sound systems and grammatical structures, not to mention the difference of vocabulary.
2つ目は、社会心理学的な理由です。日本社会に浸透している3つの宗教的発想が日本人の精神性と作法に、影響を与えています。	Second, I have to point out a sociopsychological reason. Three different religious thoughts deeply rooted in Japanese society have had an influence on the mentality and manners of the Japanese.
神道では、言葉には言霊があるとし、言葉を安易に発することに慎重になるべきであるという発想があります。	In Shintoism, language has its spirits and implicitly encourages us to be careful in the use of words.
また、禅仏教では、言葉では本当に言いたいことを100％表すことが不可能であるとし、言葉よりも心を重視する考え方があります。	Moreover, Zen emphasizes the fact that language cannot express perfectly what we really want to say and explains to us that mind is more important than words.
さらに、儒教では、上下関係を重視するあまり、言葉遣いに気をつけることを奨励します。	Furthermore, Confucianism suggests to us that we should be careful in words and manners because of the vertical relationship between the two people.
これらの宗教的発想により、言葉を使うことに慎重になってきたという側面があります。	Just because of these religious thoughts, Japanese have come to assume a cautious attitude in speaking.

だから、日本人の傾向として、たとえ日本語であっても、人前ではあまり堂々と意見を言いません。	Therefore, Japanese have a tendency not to speak out their opinion in public even in Japanese.
3つ目の理由は、単純です。日本の現状として、英語が日常的に使用されていないからです。	The third reason is simple. The present situation in Japan does not require us to use English in our daily life.

表現のコツ　「傾向」を用いた表現を英語にする

> 語学教育の新傾向としてコンピュータ支援システムがあります。
> → The new direction in language learning is to use computer assisted systems.
> 最近は脱税の傾向が著しくなってきている。
> → A marked tendency to evade taxes is seen these days.
> 彼女は人の言ったことを自分の意見にしてしまう傾向があります。
> → She has an inclination to make what others say into her own opinion.
> 彼の政治的傾向は左翼です。
> → He is leftist in political orientation.

終 章

意見表明の最強原則と力のつく勉強法

意見表明の達人になるために

★単語も文法も「3」の世界

　コミュニケーションを基礎から支えている「単語」は、発音と意味と綴りの3つを最低覚えなければなりません。この「単語」は、接頭辞と語幹と接尾辞の3つの要素のどれかを含んでいます。接頭辞は意味に関する付加的情報、語幹は中心的意味、接尾辞は品詞に関する情報を提供します。例えば、incomprehensible（理解不可能な）は、次のように分析できますね。

接頭辞	語　幹	接尾辞
IN （不）	COMPREHENS （理解）	IBLE （可能な）
反対語を示す	中心的意味	品詞を示す

　さて、コミュニケーションに不可欠な、単語の並べ方の法則と言える「文法」の世界も、「3」に関わっています。

　動詞に関しては、時制が「現在」「過去」「未来」と3つあり、動詞の変化形は、「現在形」「過去形」「分詞形」（分詞は現在分詞と過去分詞に分かれる）が基本で、動詞に準ずる準動詞も、「分詞」「不定詞」「動名詞」と3つあり、準動詞を形で分けても「done 形」「doing 形」「to do 形」の3種類になります。

　代名詞は、「人称代名詞」(you や he など)、「指示代名詞」(this や those など)、「不定代名詞」（all や some など）の3つが主流で、人称代名詞には、「1人称」「2人称」「3人称」の3つの人称が存在します。

　動詞の周りに存在する名詞も、「主語」「目的語」「補語」の3種類あり、文自体も「主語」「助動詞（成分）」と「述語」の3部から構成されているのが普通です。

　また、一般的な構文の視点からは、英語はＳＶＯ、即ち、ＳとＶとＯの3つからなる構造を中心としています。5つの構文のうち、ＳＶＯは真ん中に位置していますね。第3文型がＳとＶとＯの3つからなっているのです。（ここでもキーナンバー3がオンパレードです。）

参考　英語はＳＶＯが中心の言語

　　例えば、次の日本語には主語がなく、「・・・になる」や「・・・される」という表現が入っていますが、英語では、ＳＶＯで表現するのが自然です。

　→「仕事は首になるし、彼女には逃げられるし・・・」
　　I lost my job and my girlfriend left me....

★コミュニケーションに必要な３技能

　私は、コミュニケーションに必要な技能は４技能ではなく、３技能だと考えています。この３技能には２つの捉え方があります。

　　（あ）受信技能　→　思考技能　→　発信技能
　　（い）思考技能　×　音声技能　×　文字技能

　受信技能は「リスニング技能」と「リーディング技能」、発信技能は「スピーキング技能」と「ライティング技能」のことです。音声技能とは「リスニング技能」と「スピーキング技能」、文字技能とは「リーディング技能」と「ライティング技能」のことです。

　（あ）は通時的発想（＝時間の流れを意識した考え方）で、（い）は共時的発想（＝時間の流れを意識しない考え方）です。（あ）では、例えば、情報を受信して、それについて思考して、それに関する意見を発信するという＜時間的流れ＞が想定できますね。

　コミュニケーションの発信技能の中核を成すのは、スピーチです。このスピーチも、序論、本論、結論と３部構成になっています。

★意見表明も「３」がキーナンバー

　本書のテーマである「意見表明」も「3」が大きな役割を果たしています。意見表明は、コミュニケーションの３重構造の中核をなしています。

```
┌─────────────────────────────────────────────┐
│ コミュニケーション（Thinking, Reception and Production）│
│  ┌───────────────────────────────────────┐  │
│  │ 発信型コミュニケーション（Thinking and Production）│  │
│  │  ┌─────────────────────────────────┐  │  │
│  │  │ 意見表明スピーチ（Production of Opinions）│  │  │
│  │  └─────────────────────────────────┘  │  │
│  └───────────────────────────────────────┘  │
└─────────────────────────────────────────────┘
```

説得力のあるスピーチのための勉強法

スピーチを充実したものにするための予備練習として、次のようなことが必要でしょう。

★定義を考える

　自分の意見を述べて、相手を説得するためには、まず、何をしゃべっているかを理解させる必要があります。そのためには、スピーチ内で用いるキーワードの定義をする習慣をつけましょう。

　そのためには、英英辞典を読むことが、その第一歩です。まずは、基本的な単語を英英辞典で調べてみましょう。

　たとえば you はどのように説明しているでしょうか。通例、次のような説明になっています。

　　a person or a group of persons spoken or written to
　　（話や手紙の相手で、1人または複数の人たち）

　たしかに、単数の場合や複数の場合があり、また、spoken と written の両方があります。定義するのに、注意すべきことが2つあります。

　　(a) 論理的に表現する
　　(b) 表現を単純化する

　つまり、単純で論理的な定義をすべきでしょう。

★自分の意見を構築する

　どんなにぺらぺらと英語がしゃべれても、自分の意見がないと、外国人の人たちを楽しませることはできません。どんなことであっても、自分自身の意見を持つように普段から、問題意識を持ちましょう。

★あいまい性に敏感になる

　スピーチは、わかりやすく、ためになり、面白いものでないと、人は聴こうとしないものです。その最初の「わかりやすいスピーチ」をするためには、言葉のあいまい性に敏感になる必要があります。

　たとえば、「彼女の話」や「彼の批判」という表現はあいまいですが、どうあいまいでしょうか。考えてみましょう。そのあいまいさを英語で表現してみましょう。

　　(1)「彼女の話」
　　　(a) 彼女が話していること　　what she says [=what is said by her]
　　　(b) 彼女についての話　　　　what others say about her [=what is said about her]
　　(2)「彼の批判」
　　　(a) 彼が批判していること　　criticism by him
　　　(b) 彼を批判すること　　　　criticism about him

　このようなちょっとしたことのあいまい性を見抜く力を養っておきましょう。(1)と(2)をそれぞれ、her story や his criticism としてもあいまい性は残ります。あい

まいでない表現にするためには、(1)の(a)と(b)のように節にするか、(2)の(a)と(b)のように前置詞を使い分けるかのどちらかです。

ここで、応用問題です。次の英文と日本文のあいまい性を考えてください。そして、どのようにするとあいまい性が消えるかを考えましょう。

(3) She is walking toward the lake in the park.
(4) 太郎が好きな花子にキスをした。

この問題に対する答えを表にしてみましょう。

No.	どうあいまいか？	どうしたらあいまい性が消えるか？
(3)	(a) in the park が lake を修飾 → 彼女は公園内の湖に向かって歩いている。 ※彼女は公園の外を歩いている可能性がある。 (b) in the park が walking を修飾 → 彼女は公園内を湖に向かって歩いている。 ※湖が公園の外にある可能性がある。	(a)の意味のみが出る文にするには、toward 以下を文頭に出す。 → Toward the lake in the park, she is walking. (b)の意味のみが出る文にするには、in the park を文頭に出す。 → In the park, she is walking toward the lake.
(4)	(a)「私は」が省略され、「太郎」が「好きな」の主語。 → I kissed Hanako, whom Taro likes. (b)「私は」が省略され、「太郎」が「好きな」の目的語 → I kissed Hanako, who likes Taro. (c)「太郎」がこの文の主語 → Taro kissed Hanako, whom Taro likes.	(a)「私は」を入れて、「太郎が好きな」を「太郎が好意を抱いている」に変える。 → 私は、太郎が好意を抱いている花子にキスをした。 (b)「私は」を入れて、「太郎が好きな」を「太郎に好意を抱いている」に変える。 → 私は、太郎に好意を抱いている花子にキスをした。 (c)「太郎が」を「太郎は」に、「好きな」を「好意を抱いている」に変える。 → 太郎は好意を抱いている花子にキスをした。

(3)では構造を変化させ、(4)では表現を変化させています。つまり、あいまい性のない文を作るには、「構造」または「表現」を変えるということがポイントとなるのです。

この章で学んだことを念頭に置き、素晴らしい意見表明のスピーチができるよう、日々努力をしてくださいね。私は常に応援していますよ。

エピローグ

私の本を最後までお読みくださり、ありがとうございました。

ところで、「末」という漢字は、何偏であるか分かりますか。これは、木偏の漢字です。「木」の上のほうに傷をつけて、「端」を表したのが、この漢字の起こりです。これに対して、「木」の下の方に傷をつけて、「根元」を意味したのが、「本」という漢字です。だから「根本」や「本音」というような漢語に見られるように、物事の根幹にかかわる意味が「本」を用いた表現に多いわけです。

また、本と末が対照的な漢字であることは、「本末転倒」という四字熟語に現れています。重要な「本」の部分を枝葉末節である「末」の部分と混同しないことは、いつの時代も、どんな場面でも大切なことですね。

いろいろな意見を形作る根本的な部分にも着目し、単に表面的な表現を示すだけではなく、さまざまなジャンルにおいて、より深みのある＜漢字の「本」が示す根本＞にかかわる事象も取り扱ってきました。本書で扱っている例文を、じっくり読まれた皆さんは、本書の深みをしっかりと味わうことができたのではないでしょうか。

****

コミュニケーションに必要な２つの要素があります。それは、言葉と心です。言葉がなければコミュニケーションが不可能なのは当たり前ですね。本書で、最後に主張したいことは、「心」の重要性です。言葉だけのうわべのコミュニケーションではなく、心のこもった素晴らしいコミュニケーションを目指すべきだからです。

心には２つの側面があります。英語で心は mind と heart の２つに訳せますね。mind は知的な側面で、heart は情的な側面です。つまり、心をしっかり磨いていると、知的な側面（＝賢さ）と情的な側面（＝優しさ）の２つが備わってきます。

心の磨き方について、heart という言葉を眺めていると分かってきます。heart という単語の中に hear（聴く）が入っていますね。「聴く」（hear）という行為は、心を育てます。

聞くことによって情報が得られ、知的な側面が育ち、悩みなどを聞いてあげることは、相手に対する優しさがなければできないので、情的な側面を向上させることにつながります。

意見表明の場でも、hear することは、知的にも情的にも不可欠です。相手から情報や意見を得ない限り、知的な議論は不可能だし、また、相手の身になって、親身に聞いてあげない限り、相手を感動させるような話はできません。

最後に、読者の皆さんに、次の言葉を贈ります。
A good conversationalist is a good listener.
(会話上手は聴き上手)

TIPS：Heart と「聴く」の不思議な関係

heart という単語に hear（聴く）が、hear（聴く）には ear（耳）が含まれています。
　　ear ・・・耳
　　hear ・・・聴
　　heart ・・・心
ところで、hell という単語をさかさまから読むと、1134 のように見えます。(だから 1134 は hell を表す暗号になっています)
ということは、h は「四」を表すといえますね。また、t は「十」に見えます。
ここで、heart という単語は、次のようにも分解できるので、それぞれの漢字を当てはめてみましょう。
　　h ＋ ear ＋ t   ＝ heart
　　(四)　(耳)　(十)　　　(心)
上の等式の下の漢字を集めて、うまく組み合わせると、不思議なことに「聴」(hear)が出現します！

■付録1　面白雑学情報

▶ 文系的な面白情報

世界で一番短い手紙は、「レミゼラブル」を書いたフランス作家のヴィクトル・ユーゴーの売れ行きを出版社に聞いたときの手紙です。彼は本の売れ行きを聞く本文が「？」である手紙を送りました。出版社からは、「！」（上々です）の手紙が届いたと言います。

The shortest letter known in the world is the one written by the French writer Victor Hugo, who wrote Les Misérables, asking about how the book sold. He sent a letter containing '?' only as a main passage. The publisher is said to have replied to him by the letter containing '!'

江戸時代には、おならをした娘の身代わりになる役職がありました。「屁負い比丘尼」と呼ばれています。

In the Edo period, there was a professional "wind-breaker" called Heoi-bikuni, a nun whose job is to pretend to break wind, in substitute for a woman who has actually broken wind in public.

乾杯でグラスをカチンと合わせる風習は、古代ギリシャに起源があるとされています。古代ギリシャ人は、お酒の中に悪魔が宿っていると信じ、それを追い払うためにグラスをぶつけたと言われています。

The custom of clinking glasses when toasting is said to have originated in ancient Greek culture. It is said that ancient Greek people believed that there would be evil in wine and that they began to clink glasses of wine to drive it away.

▶ 理系的な面白情報

ウサギは毎朝自分のウンチを食べます。腸内で植物を発酵させてビタミンを作っているのです。ウンチに含まれるこのビタミンを食べないと、ウサギはビタミン不足で死んでしまうのです。

Rabbits eat their droppings every morning. This is because they make vitamin by fermenting plants in their intestines. They will die due to lack of vitamin unless they eat the vitamin contained in their droppings.

参考：アリジゴクは2年間ウンチをしません。

cf. Ant lions will not excrete for two years.

アメリカでは、2005年度に行われた美容整形手術の総数は、1142万件に上ります。	The total number of operations in cosmetic surgery in the U.S. as of 2005 amounts to 11.42 million.
にんにくを食べた後口臭がくさい理由は、にんにくの細胞が破壊されたときに、アリシンという物質ができ、それが匂いを発するからです。	The reason for a foul breath after eating garlic is that allicin gives out bad smell when cells of garlic are broken to pieces.

■付録2　考え方と生き方のヒント

▶ 考え方を示す面白発想

口癖は人生を変えます。「自分は成功する」という良い口癖を身につけるとよいと思います。	By having a habit of self-talk, we change our lives for good or bad. We should practice the positive self-talk: I can be successful.
生物学的には、4億分の1の確率で生まれた我々は、皆運がいいのだと思います。	We are all fortunate because the probability of our being born was on 1 in 400,000,000.
忘れっぽいと思っている人は、忘れたことを覚えているので、本当は忘れっぽくない。本当に忘れっぽい人は、忘れたことも忘れている。	Those who think of themselves as forgetful are not forgetful because they remember the fact that they forget something. Those who are really forgetful forget the fact that they forget something.
過去のことについては、後悔せずに反省すること、現在については、非難せずに批判精神を持つこと、未来については、期待せずに希望を持つことが大切だ。	As for something which happened in the past, you should not repent of it but reflect on it. Regarding what is happening now, you should not complain of it but criticize it properly. As regards what may happen in the future, you should not expect it but hope for it.

「地球的に考え、地域的に活動すること」は大切だと思いますが、コミュニケーションの分野では、その両面が重要です。だから私は、次のようなスローガンを掲げています。＜グローバルに考え、グローカルに語り、ローカルに行え＞と。

I think "Think globally and act locally" is an important attitude but in the field of communication, both aspects are needed. Therefore, I have the following catchword: Think globally, speak "glocally" and act locally.

▶ 成功する人の特徴

成功者は失敗をしない人ではなく、失敗に負けない人です。

Successful persons are not those who never fail in anything but those who are not defeated by any failures.

例えば、あなたが大学受験に失敗したとします。自分より実力が下と思うライバルの友達が、彼らの実力では不可能だとあなたが思った大学に合格したとします。

For example, suppose you failed in your college entrance exams. Your rivals that you think rank lower in ability than you succeeded in the exams that you thought were impossible to pass.

この状況で、友達の合格を心から喜べる人だけが、人生における成功者です。

If you can be happy with your rivals' success from the bottom of your heart in this situation, you will surely succeed in your life.

成功者は、失敗を成功の一部と考えます。

Successful people consider failures to be part of success.

エジソンは、成功の秘訣は何ですか？と尋ねられて、「失敗をしすぎたので、もはやする失敗がなくなったから、成功したのかもしれない」と答えたといいます。

It is said that when asked what was the secret to his success, Edison answered that he had succeeded when there would be no more failures to experience as a result of too many failures.

靴を売ろうと、アフリカへ行って、皆が靴を履いていないのを見て、「これはチャンスだ、靴を売れる」と考える人は成功します。	Suppose you go to Africa to sell shoes as a salesperson. If you think there is a good chance of selling shoes when you see Africans wear no shoes, you will be successful.
同じ状況で「だめだ、皆靴を履く習慣がないから、靴なんて売れない」と思うと、失敗するかもしれません。	In the same situation, if you think it is impossible to sell shoes because they don't have a habit of wearing them, you may fail in selling them.
あなたは今の会社を、いきなりリストラされたらどう思いますか。	What would you think if you were suddenly fired?
リストラされちゃった。これも良かったかもしれない。新しいことに挑戦できるから・・・と思った人は成功します。	If you think, "I lost a job but this may be a good chance because I can try to do something new," you will succeed in anything.
のどが非常に渇いているときに、グラスに半分水を入れて出されたとしましょう。	A glass half-filled with water was served when you were very thirsty.
この状態を半分しか入っていないと感じるか、半分も入っていると感じるかの姿勢の違いで、人生が変わります。	What kind of life you will lead depends on how you feel about the amount of water.
半分しかないと感じず、半分も入っていると発想する人は成功します。その人は、文句を言う代わりに感謝しているからです。	If you feel "I am happy I got water up to half of the glass" rather than "I am unlucky because I got only half," you will succeed. The reason is that you are thankful instead of being ungrateful and complaining about the situation.

参考：努力は実力を向上させ、感謝は運気を上昇させる。	cf. Efforts will enhance your skills and gratitude will enhance your fortune.
幸せは自分の心が作ります。つまり、心の持ち方を少し変えるだけで、幸せになるのです。	Happiness is made in your mind. Even a very small change in your way of thinking leads to your happiness.

▶ 偉大な人の言動に学ぶ

マザーテレサは、「世界平和のために、我々ができることは何ですか」と尋ねた記者に「早く家に帰って家族と一緒に過ごしてください」と言いました。	When Mother Teresa of Calcutta was asked by reporters what they could do for world peace, she said, "Go back to your home soon and stay with your family."
確かに平和への第一歩は、ごく基本的なことから始まります。まず、家族から大事にしましょう。	It is true that a step towards peace starts with something quite fundamental. First of all, take good care of your family.
マザーテレサは、死を待つしかない病人一人ひとりに「あなたもこの世で必要な存在でしたよ」と優しく声をかけました。	Mother Teresa very tenderly gave to each of the dying patients suffering from incurable diseases the following words: You are the very person who is quite valuable and necessary for this world.
1979年にマザーテレサは、ノーベル平和賞を受賞しましたが、「私は受賞に値しない、でも世界で最も貧しい人に代わって受けます」と言って、賞金を全額寄付しました。	In 1979, Mother Teresa was awarded the Nobel Peace Prize but she said something like "I do not deserve the prize, but I will get it in place of the poorest people in the world." She donated all the prize money.

インド建国の父であるガンジーは、イギリス人に差別されているインド人が、不可触民を差別している状況を憂って、自ら不可触民の人たちとともに生活をしました。	Mahatma Gandhi, father of the founding of India, began to live with the Untouchables, lamenting over the situation in which the Indians who were discriminated against by the British were in turn discriminating against the Untouchables.
誰からも差別されている不可触民の人たちに、「あなた方は神の子です」と勇気づけました。	He encouraged the Untouchables who were discriminated against by everybody by saying to them, "You are children of God."
インド人たちは、ガンジーの真意を察し、差別をする心と戦うことの重要性を悟り、不可触民を差別するのを止め、自らを差別するイギリス人に対して、非暴力主義で立ち上がりました。 注：ahimsa は「不殺生」の意味。	The Indians came to know what Gandhi wanted to say and they realized the importance of fighting against the discriminatory mind by stopping discrimination against the Untouchables and instead set themselves to go against Britains who look down on them, under the name of nonviolence, the doctrine of ahimsa.
ガンジーは、人生の最後、自らの暗殺の場面で、暗殺者に向かって手を合わせました。暗殺者の幸せさえ、祈ったようでした。	At the last moment of his life, his assassination, he joined his hands peacefully toward the assassin. He seemed to pray for the happiness of his assassin.

著者略歴

石井　隆之（いしい　たかゆき）

　近畿大学総合社会学部教授。オフィスエングライト代表、（社）高等教育国際基準協会代表理事、言語文化学会会長、TAC通訳ガイド協会会長、通訳ガイド研究会会長を務める。
　著書に『CD BOOK 国際会議・スピーチ・研究発表の英語表現』、『前置詞マスター教本』（以上、ベレ出版）、『英文法急所総攻撃』、『TOEIC テスト990 満点英単語』（以上、明日香出版社）など多数。

著者に対するメッセージ・質問は以下のアドレスまで。
オフィスエングライト
englight36@yahoo.co.jp

CDの内容
- DISC1　71分5秒　　DISC2　74分25秒
- ナレーション　Howard Colefield ／ Carolyn Miller
- 収録内容　英語表現のみ
- 本書のCD（DISC1とDISC2）はビニールケースの中に重なって入っています。

CD BOOK 意見・考えを論理的に述べる英語表現集（いけん・かんがえをろんりてきにのべるえいごひょうげんしゅう）

2007年3月25日	初版発行
2014年2月22日	第8刷発行

著者	石井　隆之（いしい　たかゆき）
カバーデザイン	赤谷　直宣

© Takayuki Ishii 2007, Printed in Japan

発行者	内田　眞吾
発行・発売	ベレ出版 〒162-0832 東京都新宿区岩戸町12　レベッカビル TEL (03)5225-4790 FAX (03)5225-4795 ホームページ http://www.beret.co.jp/ 振替 00180-7-104058
印刷	株式会社文昇堂
製本	根本製本株式会社

落丁本・乱丁本は小社編集部あてにお送りください。送料小社負担にてお取り替えします。

ISBN978-4-86064-147-4 C2082　　　　　編集担当　安達　正

英語で意見を論理的に述べる技術とトレーニング

植田一三 著

A5並製／定価1995円（5％税込） 本体1900円
ISBN978-4-86064-048-4 C2082　■ 312頁

英語圏の人たちは、自分が話している相手に対して自分の意見がより強いことを示そうとします。わかりやすくて説得力のある英語のスピーキング力は英語圏の人たちとコミュニケーションするために必須のものです。本書はさまざまな社会情勢や事情に関する知識と、それらを英語で論理的に述べる表現力を養うトレーニングブックです。

ネイティブとの会話をスムーズにする技術と表現

黒川裕一 著

四六並製／定価1575円（5％税込） 本体1500円
ISBN978-4-86064-092-7 C2082　■ 352頁

ネイティブと話しやすい雰囲気をつくるテクニックから、会話の流れをよくするテクニック、話を盛り上げるテクニック、そして相手の答えを引き出すテクニックまでを、豊富な使える表現と一緒に紹介していきます。最後に、本音を当てられる究極の聞き上手になる実践練習で、ネイティブが話をしたくなるような英語力とコミュニケーション力が身につけられます。

国際会議・スピーチ・研究発表の英語表現

石井隆之 著

A5並製／定価2835円（5％税込） 本体2700円
ISBN978-4-86064-111-5 C2082　■ 328頁

国際化と情報化の現代、英語による一歩進んだコミュニケーションをする機会が増えてきています。国内・国外を問わず、英語で会議、講演、研究発表をするという状況も珍しくなくなりました。本書は国際会議やセミナーの場で、英語で講演や研究発表をする研究者、学生、ビジネスマンのために有益な英語表現を、状況別・テーマ別にまとめた使える英語表現集です。CD2枚付き。